INTRODUCING

CHRISTIAN THEOLOGIES

Introducing Christian Theologies

Voices from Global Christian Communities

VICTOR I. EZIGBO

VOLUME ONE

CASCADE *Books* · Eugene, Oregon

INTRODUCING CHRISTIAN THEOLOGIES
Voices from Global Christian Communities, Volume 1

Cascade Books
An Imprint of Wipf and Stock Publishers
199 W. 8th Ave., Suite 3
Eugene, OR 97401

www.wipfandstock.com

ISBN 13: 978-1-4982-1391-2

Cataloguing-in-Publication data:

Ezigbo, Victor I.

Introducing Christian theologies : voices from global Christian
communities / Victor I. Ezigbo.

xvi + 288 pp. ; 23 cm. Includes bibliographical references and index.

ISBN 13: 978-1-61097-364-9

1. Theology, Doctrinal. 2. Globalization—Religious aspects—Christianity. I.
Title. II. Series.

BX1751.3 .E954 2013

Manufactured in the U.S.A.

To my parents,
Rev. Alfred Chukwuemeka Ezigbo and Mrs. Bridget Elewechi Ezigbo,
who were my first informal theology teachers.

And to my great friends
Jon Semke and Debbie Cornett,
whose love and generosity made it possible for me
to complete my PhD degree in theology
at the University of Edinburgh.

Contents

Contents

Tables

Acknowledgments

This textbook is the result of several years of conversation with my students and colleagues. I began imagining this book while working as a tutor of Christian Theology at the University of Edinburgh (UK). I moved forward with the decision to write the book after taking a teaching position at Bethel University (USA). I would like to thank my colleagues and students in the department of biblical and theological studies at Bethel University for their immense support during the writing process. I especially thank Gary Long, Christian Collins Winn, Mike Holmes, Pamela Erwin, and Samuel Zalanga for their constructive criticisms and suggestions. I am grateful to Bethel University's administration for giving me a course release in the spring of 2012 to complete the manuscript. I received a Bethel Alumni Grant, for which I am most grateful. I would like to thank my TA, Amanda Nelson, for reading the entire manuscript and providing very helpful comments and suggestions.

I am grateful to the editorial staff of Wipf and Stock Publishers, especially Charlie Collier and Jacob Martin, who patiently worked with me during the writing process. Patrick Harrison's design has given this book its polished format and layout. Thanks to my early theology professors Rev. Dr. Thompson Onyenechehie and Dr. Eunice Abogunrin. Finally, I thank my wife, Adamma Rita Ezigbo, for her patience, wisdom, criticism, and support.

Abbreviations

ANF	The Ante-Nicene Fathers
ESV	English Standard Version
IVP	InterVarsity Press
NASB	New American Standard Bible
NIV	New International Version
NIDOTE	New International Dictionary of Old Testament Exegesis
NPNF	Nicene and Post-Nicene Fathers

Introduction

Many Christians would prefer to skip the study of theology and get on with sharing their personal beliefs about God. Some of them think that the study of theology is unnecessary for the proclamation of the Christian message. Others believe that theology leads to doubts, which can destroy a person's faith or belief. Studying theology, however, has several benefits. It has an effect on every aspect of a Christian's life. For example, theology can help Christians to deepen their knowledge of Christian doctrines, which are necessary for personal edification (e.g., dealing with doubts) and the proclamation of the Christian message.

The vibrant expansion of Christianity in places outside of Europe and North America, namely in Africa, Asia, and Latin America, raises a question about the "theological face" of Christianity. Should Christianity's theological face remain largely European and North American in the twenty-first century? Like all important questions, the question about the "theological face" of Christianity cannot be ignored. For too long, African, Asian, and Latin American theologians have been left out of mainstream theological discussions. Few standard textbooks on Christian theology acknowledge the unique contributions theologians from these continents have made to global Christianity.

Introducing Christian Theologies: Voices from Global Christian Communities is a two-volume textbook that alters the predominantly European and North American "theological face" of Christianity by interacting with the voices of Christian communities from around the globe. *Introducing Christian Theologies* explores the works of key theologians from these communities, highlighting their unique contributions to global Christianity. This first volume covers the following topics: preliminary issues in Christian theology, God's revelation, Christian Scripture, Trinity, Jesus Christ, Holy Spirit, and divine providence. The second volume will cover the topics of theological anthropology, Christian hope, salvation, church, the Christian life and social problems, and theology of religions.

Intended Audience

Introducing Christian Theologies is primarily designed for undergraduates taking an introductory course in Christian theology. However, the depth of the content also makes it a useful text for seminary students and graduate theology students.

Features of the Book

Accessibility: I taught Christian theology at the undergraduate level in Nigeria and in the United Kingdom. I currently teach theology at the same level in the United States. In my experience, very few introductory textbooks on Christian theology are written in a manner that is accessible to undergraduate students who have no previous knowledge of how to interpret and integrate Christian doctrines. This is a serious problem that *Introducing Christian Theologies* addresses.

Contextualization: This is one of the unique features of this book. Every theology is contextual and ought to be so. Although many theologians, especially in the West, have ignored the contextual nature of theology in their theological discussions, theologians should *intentionally* construct their theologies to befit the contexts of the intended recipients. Theologies must reflect a rigorous and constructive engagement with the social location, religious aspiration, culture, experience, and sociopolitical condition of the communities for which they are intended. The contexts of the theologians whose works are explored here will be highlighted. This will help students to appreciate the contributions of these theologians and also to rethink how to appropriate such theologies in their own contexts.

Diversity of Viewpoints: The textbook presents and discusses several positions on the major Christian doctrines. These positions are described in a manner that highlights their differences, similarities, and unique contributions.

Global and Multidenominational: Unlike the majority of the existing introductory textbooks on Christian theology, *Introducing Christian Theologies* covers a vast range of theological positions written by theologians from Africa, Asia, Latin America, North America, and Europe. The theologians whose works are discussed in this book are Protestant, Roman Catholic, Greek Orthodox, Coptic, or Pentecostal.

Key Terms: The textbook has definitions of theological terms at the end of each chapter.

Charts and Tables: Charts and tables are used to buttress key points or to compare similarities and differences of theological positions.

Primary Sources: Excerpts from primary sources that are keyed to the discussion of the major topics are included at the end of each chapter with the exception of chapter 1.

Exercises: A few assignable exercises have been included in some chapters to help students evaluate their knowledge of the topics discussed.

Review Questions: Several questions have been included at the end of each chapter to help students review the major themes and position discussed.

Texts for Further Reading: A list of important texts on the topics covered is provided at the end of each chapter.

1

Preliminary Issues in Christian Theology

Christian theology can be a daunting subject for students because of the large volume of material to be learned. This chapter discusses the introductory issues that relate to the construction of Christian theology. The knowledge of these issues will be helpful for grasping the idea, tasks, nature, sources, and forms of Christian theology.

Defining Christian Theology

The word *theology* is a combination of two words—God (*theos* in Greek) and reason (*logos* in Greek). Theology can be defined as the "discourse about God," or the "study of God," or the "thought about God." However, defining theology in this way is too broad and fails to account for the uniqueness of the theologies of different religions of the world. For example, it does not account for the differences between Christian theology and Islamic theology. While both Christianity and Islam hold a monotheistic view of God, they understand monotheism differently. Christianity's view of monotheism allows for a plurality of divine persons (the Trinity), whereas the Islamic view of monotheism does not. In fact, the doctrine of the Trinity is appalling to many Muslims. Since this textbook focuses on Christianity, we must describe Christian theology.

FOCUS QUESTION:
What is Christian theology?

Ideas of Christian Theology

Christian theology is concerned with the imagination and interpretation of God from the perspective of the life and teaching Jesus of Christ. Christian theologians have pursued these Christ-centered acts of imagination and interpretation of God in diverse ways. This diversity of theological views within Christianity exists because theologians do theology with disparate agendas. To illustrate these agendas, I will describe the understandings of Christian theology of four theologians whose works continue to shape Christian theological discourse globally.

Anselm of Canterbury (c. 1033–1109 CE)

Anselm, the former archbishop of Canterbury (England), was a theologian and philosopher. His view of theology can be summarized as "faith seeking understanding."[1] He emphasized the priority of faith or belief in God-talk. Anselm's goal was to demonstrate to his contemporaries, especially Christians, that belief in God's existence was rational. He drew inspiration from St. Augustine of Hippo (354–430 CE), who summarized his view of the relationship between *faith* and *reason* on the basis of his reading of Isaiah 7:9: "Unless I believe, I shall not understand." Daniel Migliore's comments on

---

1. Anslem, "An Address (*Proslogion*)," 70.

Augustine's view of faith and reason are helpful for understanding Anselm's definition of theology. He writes that the "Christian faith prompts inquiry, searches for deeper understanding, dares to raise questions."[2] Again he states, "Theology arises from the freedom and responsibility of the Christian community to inquire about its faith in God." Theology is "a continuing search for the fullness of the truth of God made known in Jesus Christ."[3]

For Anselm, theology must begin with faith and confidence in the existence of God. This act of faith is the beginning point of a theological inquiry. A Christian should, however, take the next step, namely, to explore logical and coherent ways to explain the mystery of God's existence and actions in the world. Anselm sets an example by developing the *ontological argument* for the existence of God. His argument can be summarized in this way: (*a*) God is that which none greater can be conceived (that is, the greatest possible being); (*b*) since human beings can imagine God, it is possible that God exists; and (*c*) since something that exists is greater than that which does not exist, it follows that God exists. Theology is a field of study that deals with faith in the existence of God. This faith, for Anselm, does not oppose the use of reason to explain or demonstrate God's existence.

Karl Barth (1886–1968)

Karl Barth, a Swiss theologian, was arguably the most prominent twentieth-century Christian theologian. Like Anselm, Barth saw Christian theology as faith seeking understanding. For Barth, human beings come to know God when God gives them the gift of faith and enables them to encounter and experience God's self-revelation. Human beings can talk about God because God has given them God's own knowledge of God's self. Unlike Anselm, Barth was Christocentric (Christ-centered) in his theology. One of the unique contributions of Barth to Christian theology is his presentation of Jesus Christ as the *primary test* of adequate interpretations of God's self-revelation. For him, any theologies that conflict with God's revelation in and through Jesus Christ are inadequate for the Christian church. Barth's description of Christian theology emphasizes the priority of God's revelation (Jesus Christ) in the construction of theology. Barth also perceived Christian theology as "a function of the church" and the "scientific test which the Christian Church puts [itself] regarding the language about God which is peculiar to [it]."[4] He saw theology as the task of the church. Christians must

2. Migilore, *Faith Seeking Understanding*, 2.
3. Ibid., 1.
4. Barth, *CD* 1/1, 3–4.

continue to test their views of God in light of Jesus Christ, the revelation of God.

Rosemary Radford Ruether (b. 1936)

The American theologian Rosemary Radford Ruether unearths the mystified patriarchal assumption that has permeated the structures of Christian theology. Prior to the rise of feminist theology, many Christian theologians either assumed or affirmed the inferiority of women. Like the majority of feminist theologians, Ruether aims to deconstruct and expose both classical and contemporary Christian theologies that diminish and distort the full humanity of women. "Theologically speaking," writes Ruether, "whatever diminishes or denies the full humanity of women must be presumed not to reflect the divine or an authentic relation to the divine, or to reflect the authentic nature of things, or to be the message or work of an authentic redeemer or a community of redemption."[5] Christian theologies, in the minds of some feminist theologians, must be presumed guilty of patriarchy and androcentricism until proven innocent.

Theologies do not arise in a vacuum. Those theologies that ignore human experiences are in danger of being irrelevant to humanity. One of the main contributions that Ruether's writings and the works of other feminist theologians have made to Christian theology is the discovery of human experience, particularly the experience of women, as an important source of theology. In the words of Ruether, "The uniqueness of feminist theology lies not in its use of the criterion of experience but rather in its use of *women's* experience, which has been almost entirely shut out of theological reflection in the past."[6] Within the broad context of women's experience, feminist theologians have found the courage to upset the status quo by reflecting upon the diversified experiences of women in different cultures and societies. For example, the experience of a white American woman must necessarily differ from the experience of an African American woman, although they live in the same country. Feminist theologians, therefore, explore the experience of women in their theological works in ways that engage gender, class, social location, and race. Ruether places emphasis on the experience of women, which for her must be used to rethink the classical Christian doctrines of God and humanity.

5. Ruether, *Sexism and God-Talk*, 19.
6. Ibid., 13.

Gustavo Gutiérrez (b. 1928)

Gustavo Gutiérrez, a Peruvian theologian, describes theology as the reflection that "arises spontaneously and inevitably in the believer, in all those who have accepted the gift of the Word of God. Theology is intrinsic to a life of faith seeking to be authentic and complete and is, therefore, essential to the common consideration of this faith in the ecclesial community."[7] In his theology, the experience of the poor reigns supreme. Like Karl Barth, Gutiérrez construes theology as the task of the church. Gutiérrez, however, makes two noteworthy contributions. First, he argues that all Christians ought to become involved in theological reflection. He writes, "There is present in *all believers*—and more so in every Christian community—a rough outline of theology. There is present an effort to understand the faith, something like a pre-understanding of that faith which is manifested in life, action, and concrete attitude."[8] Theology should not be construed as an ivory-tower enterprise and a discrete academic field for highly trained scholars and analysts. All Christians ought to be preoccupied with the question of theology: how are we to live intellectually and practically in a way that reflects the life of Christ?

Second, he contends that theology must be imagined in a way that engages both the needs of the church and the world at large. In his own words, "Theology as critical reflection on historical praxis is a liberating theology, a theology of the liberating transformation of the history of humankind and also therefore that part of humankind—gathered into *ecclesia*—which openly confesses Christ. This is a theology which does not stop with reflecting on the world, but rather tries to be part of the process through which the world is transformed."[9]

EXERCISE 1.1

Using the box below, identify and state the implications of the preceding four definitions of Christian theology. State what is helpful and striking to you in these definitions. Highlight their similarities and differences.

7. Gutiérrez, *Theology of Liberation*, 3.
8. Ibid.
9. Ibid., 12.

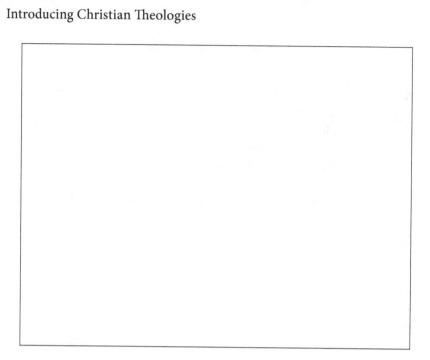

Theology and Faith

In Christian theology faith refers to the human act of trust or commitment. To have faith is to trust in or commit to something or someone. The Christian notion of faith may be described as the trust in God that arises out of people's encounter with the person and work of God in Jesus Christ of Nazareth.

Faith has two integral dimensions: intellect and volition. The volitional dimension of faith refers to the commitment of the human will to God. It is to trust God completely as the creator, savior, and provider of the world. This submission of the human will to God arises from people's encounter with God. They trust that God has their best interest in mind. Faith in this sense is antithetical to the mistrust of God. The intellectual dimension of faith deals with the role of the human intellect in attaining and articulating faith. It concerns itself with the intellectual inquiry about the nature and content of Christianity's beliefs about God. To have faith is not to trust blindly or to have beliefs that cannot be proved. The human intellect does not operate in isolation from a volitional commitment to God. On the one hand, having faith in God should not depend upon one's ability to prove God's existence with certainty. On the other hand, to say that one's faith in God is not contingent on one's ability to prove God's existence is not to suggest that the suspension of the human intellect is a precondition of faith. Faith welcomes rigorous inquiry. The theologian's task is to reflect on and express the nature and content of Christian faith commitments and beliefs. Faith (both in the intellectual and volitional dimensions) is dynamic: it grows and can be stretched and developed.

Faith is an important component of theology. This is because human beings do not have direct or immediate access to God. Our knowledge of God is mediated—it is dependent on God's self-disclosure. This knowledge of God is faith-based: it arises from the belief in God's existence and also in God's self-revelation. Doing theology from a Christian perspective requires having confidence in God. To believe or have confidence in God is to trust God as "where I find anchorage of my life, where I find a solid ground, home."[10] Christian theological discussions should be conducted in a manner that enables people to see the relationship between Christian life and theology.

How are we to understand the role of faith in Christian theology? Theologians understand faith in several ways. Broadly speaking, Christian theologians use "faith" in ways that correspond to one of the following two usages.

Faith as a Form of Reason and Inquiry

"Reason" here refers to the act of reasoning that involves drawing conclusions from already established data. The view that sees faith and reason as compatible components of theology also construes faith as launching an individual into a rigorous inquiry concerning the mystery of God. Faith, therefore, does not obstruct or hinder theological inquiry. Faith welcomes theological tensions and paradoxes. Anslem of Canterbury construed faith in this way when, as previously mentioned, he defined theology as "faith seeking understanding."

Theologians, however, disagree on the functions of reason and faith in gaining knowledge about God. Some see faith as *perfecting* the knowledge of God that is acquired through reason alone (Thomas Aquinas). For others, faith *precedes* and also *critiques* the knowledge of God gained through reason (Anselm).

---

10. Williams, *Tokens of Trust*, 6.

Faith as an Antithesis of Reason

People who see faith as an antithesis of reason argue that reason has no relevant place in knowing and experiencing God. In fact, some see reason as an intellectual virus that destroys the knowledge of God gained through faith in God's self-revelation. Faith, for them, is the antidote for theological tensions—it helps the believer grope in the unknown territories of the spiritual world. This understanding of faith's relationship to theology is misleading. A person's faith or belief in the existence of God should not undermine his or her desire to explain how he or she came to such belief. This view of faith is sometimes called *fideism*, the act of accepting "religious beliefs in defiance of or contrary to reason."[11]

The Tasks of Theology

What are the tasks of Christian theology? Theologians have answered this question in different ways. The question about the tasks of theology is ultimately the question about what theology does for humanity. Theology is not just about acquiring knowledge but also concerns practice.

Doxological

Our knowledge of God should lead us to doxology: the act of praising God. Doxology is one of the criteria of adequate theology. A theology that fails the test of doxology is useless for living a Christlike life. Theology must also become an act of worship to God. Glorifying God, and not merely gaining intellectual knowledge about God, is the ultimate goal of theology. In the context of fellowshipping with and worshipping God, theology's function is preparatory. It ought to prepare each believing person and community to grow in relationship with God through obedience to Jesus Christ and in the power of the Holy Spirit. A theology that does not aim to lead people to worship God is wanting. Sadly, many theologies today hardly kindle in people's hearts a passionate and sincere love for God. Christian theology should invoke the search for a response and language to express the mystery of God's love for God's creation.

Our theology, when properly done, should inspire us to revel in God, and this should lead us to exalt God and to glorify God. Theology is an important aspect of Christians' response to a loving God who has given God's

11. Clark, *Return to Reason*, 154.

self ultimately in Jesus Christ "to restore and fulfill all creation." It should not lead only to praise but must in itself become an act of praise to God. In praise, we express our appreciation for something or someone important to us. This involves recognizing the worth of the recipient of our praise. Part of the task of theology, then, is to express the worthiness of God, who is the ultimate recipient of theological praise.

Didactical

Another task of theology is to provide a comprehensive exposition of Christian beliefs and truth-claims. Theologians in this sense are the teachers of the church. In his letter to Timothy, Paul wrote, "What you heard from me, keep as the pattern of sound teaching, with faith and love in Christ Jesus" (2 Tim 1:13, NIV). In the same letter, Paul instructs Timothy to present himself "to God as one approved, a workman who does not need to be ashamed and who correctly handles the word of truth" (2 Tim 2:15, NIV). Christian theologians by definition should become involved in the teaching ministry of the church. Their knowledge and study of God's acts in human history should be motivated by the desire to become good servants of God who correctly explain and communicate the Christian message. A good theologian does not drive people away from God. On the contrary, the theologian inspires people to explore and experience God.

Apologetical

Apologetics focuses on the defense of Christian doctrines against false teachings and against external opposition (competing religions). All Christians should be ready to defend and explain the Christian message. The Apostle Peter instructs Christians to be "prepared to make a defense to anyone who asks for a reason" for their faith and hope in Christ (1 Pet 3:15, ESV). In doing apologetics, we must distinguish the act of defending God and the act of defending our understanding of God. The Scriptures call us to defend our understanding of God and not to defend God. The Christian God defends God's self. Our apologetics should be contextual. For example, if you live in a context that considers rationality as the primary measuring standard, you will need to find ways to logically express the Christian message.

There are, broadly speaking, two interrelated ways of ways of doing apologetics; these are negative apologetics and positive apologetics. *Negative apologetics* seeks to provide responses to the challenges to the truth-claims of a competing religion, and also to remove the potential or actual obstacles to believing the truth-claims. A negative apologist is defensive in his or her tactics. Conversely, *positive apologetics* seeks to provide reasons for supporting the truth-claims of Christianity. A positive apologist plays offense in his or her tactics. Maintaining a balance between positive and negative apologetics is needed for the spiritual and intellectual life of the church.

Praxis

Some theologians see the task of theology as providing ethical guidance for the Christian life. Theologians in this sense are the ethicists of the church. A theology that does not lead people to conform to the life of Christ will risk being irrelevant. Historically, a good number of theologians have pursued theological issues that merely satisfy their intellectual curiosity but fail to strengthen the faith of the majority of Christians who do not have theological training. Such theologians answer the questions their peers ask but ignore the questions lay Christians are asking about how to live and please God in their daily lives. This is one of the reasons many Christians rarely read the works of professional theologians.

Theology and God

God is the main subject matter of theology. In Christian theology, God's identity, modes of existence, and actions are the primary focus. Other topics are considered in relation to the doctrine of God. How can human beings come to know God? Is it possible to speak adequately about God's character, actions, and relationship with the world? Two factors in particular inhibit human beings from having a direct access. First, the truth about God is hidden from us because God's nature is different from human nature. We cannot study finite human beings with the intention to gain reliable and exhaustive knowledge about the infinite God. Second, sin immensely distorts our understanding of God, making it impossible for us to speak effectively and correctly about God's existence without God's help and self-disclosure. One of the greatest effects of sin on human perception, in the words of Pope Benedict XVI (Joseph Ratzinger), is to see ourselves as the "center of things, around which the world and everyone else have to turn." We see "other things and people solely in relation to our own selves, regarding them as satellites, as it were, revolving around the hub of our own self."[12]

12. Ratzinger, *Credo for Today*, 10.

How can these two dilemmas be addressed? The answer is God's self-disclosure. Apart from God's revelation we can only guess or speculate about who God is and what God does. The best theologians can do is interpret and appropriate God's self-disclosure and manifestations in the world. What this means is that theologians cannot be God's custodians, because they have limited knowledge of God. On the contrary, like all people who desire to know and experience God, theologians are to see themselves as God-seekers. They should be willing to learn and to revise their theologies, since theologies are prone to distortions. It is a theological mistake, therefore, to assume that God can be completely known and mastered or that human beings can always explain God's actions in a neat and tidy way. Since God is radically different from us, our knowledge of God is partial. Doing theology can be likened to making a cognitive and experiential journey in which one sometimes encounters what may be unknowable. As finite creatures, there are certain things human beings may never fully know about themselves, about the world, and about God. We may be unable to explain exhaustively some of the things we will come to know about God and God's relationship with the world. We may never know with certainty, for example, the fate of some classes of people who lived and died without hearing the Christian message about Jesus Christ.

EXERCISE 1.2

Which of the following may be knowable, and which may be unknowable? Among those you believe to be knowable, which ones do you think can be explained exhaustively? (*a*) The existence of God; (*b*) the doctrine of the Incarnation; (*c*) the doctrine of the Trinity; (*d*) God's involvement in human affairs; and (*e*) the inspiration of the Scriptures.

Theology's Nature

Theology Is a Human Endeavor

Whereas God, the principal subject matter of theology, is divine, theologians and theologies are human. Some implications of this are noteworthy.

FOCUS QUESTION:
What are the features of
Christian theology?

First, our theologies can be (and often are) inadequate. Theology is fallible because human beings construct them. Since this is the case, theologians should be ready and willing to correct or revise their theologies when necessary. Second, theology cannot encapsulate the mystery of God. Daniel Migliore has rightly noted that "theology is not mere repetitions of traditional doctrines but a persistent search for truth to which they point and which they only partially and brokenly express."[13] Theology should be done in a way that gives room for a fresh encounter with God. Third, our theologies, in the end, will remain approximate and provisional interpretations and appropriations of the mystery of God. They will always fall short of the mystery and glory of God. They should be dynamic and ongoing reflections on God's self-disclosure.

Theology Is Contextual

The word *context* (from which the word *contextual* is derived) is defined broadly to include the experience, history, social location, religious aspiration, language, and culture of an individual or a community. Although not readily acknowledged by many theologians, every theology is contextual insofar as it arises from a specific community and also is designed to address the needs of that community. This is always the case, whether a theologian consciously imagines his or her theology in this way or not. By nature, then, theology has a *context* comprising several other contexts, such as the context of the theologian, the context of the intended recipients of his or her theology, the contexts of the communities that produced the Scriptures, and the contexts of contemporary global Christian communities. These contexts raise questions about theological judgments. How should Christians make theological judgments? Two tests are helpful: the *test of Christian identity* and the *test of relevance*.

The Test of Christian Identity

Where a theology bears the name "Christian," such a theology is obliged to demonstrate its *Christianness* or its Christian identity. Although theologians disagree on the criteria for Christian identity, they tend to focus on three.

The first criterion is *faithfulness to Scripture*. Christian theologians also do not agree on the extent of the authority of the Scriptures and the books that should be included in the Scriptures. But they normally agree that an adequate Christian theology must demonstrate faithfulness to the Scriptures. Of course, what faithfulness to the Scriptures really means is a matter of intense debate. For some, the Scriptures determine whether a specific

---

13. Migliore, *Faith Seeking Understanding*, 1–2.

theology is authentically Christian. Any theology that contradicts or opposes the teaching of the Christian Scriptures is judged to be non-Christian.

The second criterion is *faithfulness to Christian traditions*. Christian theology should also demonstrate its continuity with the earliest Christian theological confessions about God's actions in the world, particularly in the life, teaching, and experience of Jesus Christ. This does not mean that theologians cannot question or revise church traditions. The theologies of the classical ecumenical councils (such as the Council of Nicaea in 325 CE) function as theological guides. They can help theologians today in the quest to construct theologies that are faithful to the Scriptures. It should be recognized, however, that all classical Christian doctrine, which constitutes the tradition of Christianity, was framed with the language and thought forms of specific cultural contexts to answer the questions of Christians of that era.

The third criterion is *Christ-centeredness*. Christian theology should also be Christ-centered. It ought to learn from Jesus Christ's teaching on God's identity and relationship with the world. If "theology is a witness to the gospel,"[14] as the Japanese theologian Kazō Kitamori has reminded us, Christians, as Christ-followers, should construct theologies that learn from and are faithful to Jesus Christ. Any theology that conflicts with or contradicts the life and teaching of Jesus Christ has failed the test of Christian identity. Christian theology ought to be Christ-centered insofar as it seeks to understand God from Jesus' perspectives. Jesus Christ ought to be understood as the *revealer and interpreter* of divinity and humanity—the one who critiques and reshapes our preconceived understandings of God and human beings.

The Test of Relevance

A theology can pass the test of Christian identity and still become irrelevant to a Christian community. Therefore, Christian theology should pass both the test of Christian identity and the test of relevance. Theologians are to explain the Scriptures' testimony about God's actions in the world in a way that engages constructively with the questions arising from the lives of people in their own communities. Here is the summary of the test of relevance. First, we are to become suspicious of any attempt by a theologian to universalize his or her theology or to superimpose the theology on all contexts without subjecting it to a critical evaluation. Second, we should be willing to revise our already constructed theologies when they fail to address the ever-shifting issues that concern our communities. Our

14. Kitamori, *Theology and the Pain of God*, 19.

theologies should improve human conditions by providing both intellectual and practical suggestions on how to deal with the structures and theologies that perpetuate evils in the world. Our theologies should not ignore human misery and suffering. They should contribute to intellectual conversation and offer practical ways to tackle human trafficking, genocide, and dehumanizing economic structures. Third, Christian theology should be an ongoing endeavor that explains and defends Christianity's claims about God's existence and actions.

Theology and the Theologian

Jürgen Moltmann once wrote, "Like the terms *biologists, sociologists,* and so forth, the word *theologian* immediately suggests an educated, academically trained and competent expert."[15] In a sense, this understanding of a theologian is true. Professional theologians spend many years in universities or seminaries studying to obtain a theology degree. However, one must not be led to assume that only those with theology degrees actually do or ought to do theology. This is because, in the words of Moltmann, "Theology is the business of all God's people. It is not just the affair of the theological faculties. . . . The faith of the whole body of Christians on earth seeks to know and understand. If it doesn't, it isn't Christian faith."[16] All Christians are called to seek, experience, converse with, and interpret God's actions in a way that befits their immediate contexts. The function of professional theologians is to guide their communities in this endeavor. They can provide helpful guidance for people in their communities to reflect on the mystery of God and their encounter with God.

Theology and Method

A theological method is a procedure a theologian adopts to accomplish certain theological tasks. Method is incredibly difficult to conceptualize because of its abstract nature. A theological method is an abstract device employed by theologians to interpret and express the mystery and revelation of God. Method relates to the issues of

> FOCUS QUESTION:
> From which sources should a theologian draw insights to construct a theology?

15. Moltmann, *Experiences in Theology,* 10.
16. Ibid., 11.

procedure, selection of sources, and use of sources in the process of theological reflection. In theological discourse, theological method deals with procedure and sources. It asks and answers the following questions: How should a theologian proceed in his or her theological inquiry? Where should the theologian begin? Where should a theologian draw insights for his or her theology? How are the sources to be used?

A theological *method* and the *actual contents* of a given theology should mutually interact when theology is being done. This is important because of the nature of the primary subject matter of Christian theology, namely, God. Since we cannot *master* God, we must allow our theological knowledge to inform our theological method, and vice versa. We must be suspicious of the fallacious assumption that a *right method* guarantees a *right theological knowledge*. Also, we should not necessarily see the various methods as mutually exclusive. Theologians sometimes borrow ideas from different methods when they construct their theologies.

> "Theology not only asks questions but must be self-conscious about the way it does so. This is, in brief, the problem of theological method. While much has been written about theological method in recent years, we are far from any clear consensus. No doubt differences in theological method reflect fundamental differences in understandings of revelation and the mode of God's presence in the world. They also show the limitations of any single method to do all the tasks of theology."
>
> —Migliore, *Faith Seeking Understanding*

Broadly, Christian theology walks three paths: *theocentric* (God-centered), *cosmocentric* (cosmos- or world-centered), and *Christocentric* (Christ-centered). The theocentric pathway (or pathway from "above") views God as the first principle both in the order of being and in the order of knowing.[17] Theologians who follow this pathway begin their theological inquiry from the particularity of Christianity and (generally) move to common human experience. They believe that God inspired the Scriptures and also revealed God's self ultimately in Jesus of Nazareth, the Christ. Tertullian, Augustine, Anselm, and Kwame Bediako are among the numerous prominent theologians who have adopted the theocentric pathway.

The cosmocentric pathway (or pathway from "below") construes the world as the first principle in knowing. Theologians who follow this pathway begin their theological inquiry from a common human experience and (generally) move to the particularity of Christianity. The majority of the theologians who follow this pathway to theology believe God has revealed

---

17. Braaten, "Scripture, Church, and Dogma," 145.

God's self by creating the world. They also argue that one can arrive at knowledge of God through a rigorous study of the world. Paul Tillich and Carl Braaten exemplify those theologians who have followed this pathway.[18]

The Christocentric pathway sees Jesus Christ as God's revelation and also as the person through whom human beings can rethink their understandings of God and humanity. In this pathway, the person and work of Jesus Christ are the focal point of theology, functioning as the "lens" through which we can see, imagine, and explain the person and work of God in the world. Karl Barth is an example of those theologians who have adopted the Christocentric pathway.

Submethods within Theocentric, Cosmocentric, and Christocentric Theological Pathways

These three pathways to Christian theology have several approaches or methods within each. They are the rationalistic-oriented method, dialectical-oriented method, and contextual-oriented method. Each of these submethods can be used in both the theocentric and cosmocentric pathways.

Rationalistic-Oriented Theological Method

The word *rationalistic* does not simply mean "relying on reason" or "being rational." It rather refers to the belief that it is possible for a person (whose cognitive faculty is functioning properly) to reason his or her way to an indubitable, unambiguous, and non-culturally conditioned first principle on which he or she can proceed to erect the edifice of theological knowledge. Theologians who adopt this method are primarily shaped and driven by the quest to provide rational explanation and justification for Christian beliefs, practices, and truth-claims. They assume the following: (*a*) God has revealed God's self both non-propositionally (in nature, in the event of Jesus Christ, etc.) and propositionally (in the Scriptures); (*b*) truth can be accessed through a universally shared law of reasoning; (*c*) it is possible to use history, reason, and natural science to demonstrate the truthfulness and validity of the Scriptures; and (*d*) rationally valid theological knowledge can be built on the Scriptures.

Two submethods (*fundamentalist* and *coherentist*) within the rationalistic-oriented method deserve attention. The fundamentalist approach aims to ground theological knowledge on a set of beliefs that are universal

18. Ibid., 146.

and unquestionably certain. Theologians who use this approach, like their Enlightenment precursors, assume there are universal and non-culturally conditioned shared beliefs (e.g., the law of noncontradiction).[19] They are preoccupied with building theological edifices on foundations that are firm and secure. Many theologians now see the fundamentalist vision as a project that was doomed to failure even from the start. As David Tracy notes, "The fact is that no interpreter enters into the attempt to understand any text without prejudgments formed by the history of that person's culture. No interpreter, in fact, is as purely autonomous as the Enlightenment model promised."[20] Our history and experience shape how we perceive things. There is no theology that is not culturally conditioned. Our theological questions arise from our experiences, aspirations, and agendas, which are conditioned by our contexts.

The coherentist approach, like the fundamentalist approach, argues that there are universally accepted laws such as the law of noncontradiction. It also argues that human beings can identify and express these laws because they cohere in human minds. In the words of Norman Geisler, "The word *systematic* in systematic theology implies that all the teachings of both general and special revelation are comprehensive and consistent. This entails the use of another methodology—logic. Remember, the fundamental law of all thought is the law of non-contradiction, which affirms that A is not non-A. No two or more truths can be contradictory, which is why all biblical and extrabiblical truth can and must be brought into a consistent whole."[21] The coherentist approach, however, drops the idea of erecting theological edifices on first principles or a set of beliefs that are universally accepted and unquestionably certain. On the contrary, coherentists "argue that beliefs are interdependent, each belief being supported by its connection to its neighbors and ultimately to the whole."[22]

Theology should be presented in a coherent way. This does not mean that God's actions in the world can be organized and interpreted in a way that is always neat and tidy. Rather, presenting theology in a coherent manner is necessary in order to see the connectedness and relationship of Christian doctrines. A theologian should be aware of how each aspect of his or her theology impacts other aspects. The theologian needs to show how different Christian doctrines are organically connected and interrelated.

19. The law of noncontradiction states that *A* cannot be *B* and *non-B* at the same time and in the same relation.

20. Tracy, "Theological Method," 40.

21. Geisler, *Systematic Theology*, 1:223.

22. Grenz, "Articulating the Christian Belief-Mosaic," 113.

Dialectical-Oriented Theological Method

The German philosopher G. W. F. Hegel (1770–1831) developed the conceptual framework for interpreting history in which three constants—thesis, antithesis, and synthesis—interact. For him, reality is dialectical; history itself "is nothing other than a dialectical movement toward unity, so that every contradiction and antithesis becomes only a single moment that is later relativized and included in a higher synthesis."[23] The Swiss theologian Karl Barth was a major exponent of the dialectical method in the field of theology. His version of the dialectical method was closer to that of the Danish philosopher Søren Kierkegaard (1813–1855), who developed a dialectical method "in which there is no overarching synthesis, but only the paradoxical tension between a statement and its counter-statement."[24] For Barth, ambiguity underlies God's encounter with humanity, for God remains concealed after disclosing God's self to humanity. "As ministers we ought to speak of God," Barth writes. "We are human, however, and so cannot speak of God. We ought therefore to recognize both our obligation and our inability and by that very recognition give God the glory. This is our perplexity."[25] In practice, theological reflection, in Barth's thinking, involves a back-and-forth movement of yes and no without a preoccupation with the quest for a final resolution or synthesis. Of course, this does not mean that a theologian cannot attain any resolutions. Rather, such resolutions remain provisional. For Barth, theological reflection must create room for internal ambiguities.

Theologians who use the dialectical method anchor their theological reflections on the crisis or tension underlying God's encounter with God's creation, particularly with human beings. Their assumptions can be summarized as follows: (*a*) The dichotomy between God and humanity rules out the possibility of human beings' discovery of God through a prior rationalistic process or contemplative imagination. (*b*) Humanity's knowledge of God depends exclusively on God's self-disclosure, particularly in the event of the person and work of Jesus Christ. (*c*) It is through God's gift of "faith" that human beings can meaningfully encounter God's actions and interaction with the world. (*d*) A permanent dialectical crisis preoccupies all theological reflection as one ponders (through hearing the

23. McKenzie and Myers, "Dialectical Critical Realism in Science and Theology," 49.

24. Ibid., 50.

25. Barth, *Word of God and the Word of Man*, 186.

Word of God) God's revelation and mystery, God's judgment and forgiveness of sinful humanity, etc.[26]

Contextual-Oriented Theological Method

This method, while not opposed to a rational explanation of Christian beliefs and practices, elevates contemporary context to the status of an indispensable source of theology. This method is revolutionary, as Steve Bevans has noted, because it does not construe human contexts as an arena to which theology is adapted and applied. On the contrary, the contextual-oriented method sees the context of a community as an indispensable source of theology. Like the Scriptures and church tradition, the context of a community—the history and experience of its people—must be used in the construction of theology.[27]

Many theologies developed in sub-Saharan Africa, Asia, Latin America, and North America since the 1950s have adopted the contextual-oriented theological method. Examples of such theologies are African theology, liberation theology, black theology, Dalit theology, feminist theology, and womanist theology, to name a few. In the West, some theologians have developed theological methods that can be classified under the contextual-oriented category. An example of such methods is Paul Tillich's *method of correlation.*[28] For Tillich, Christian theology must bring Christianity into dialogue with the human situation and the world at large by listening to and engaging existential questions. Other fields of study such as philosophy, literature, and science can help a theologian to identify the questions the human situation poses to theology.

Contextualization refers to the act of interpreting and appropriating God's actions in a way that concretely interacts and critiques a given human context. All theologies are contextual. "Our language and culture," writes Luis Pedraja, "affect the way we perceive God; therefore they have an important effect upon our theological formation."[29] Theologians must become aware of how their social locations, cultures, and thoughts shape and *ought to shape* their theologies. They should also become aware that while God is universally relevant to all Christian communities, their theologies may never enjoy such status. Theologians who are intentionally contextual study the issues that inspired some of the existing Christian the-

---

26. McCormack, *Karl Barth's Critically Realistic Dialectical Theology*, 212.

27. Bevans, *Models of Contextual Theology*, 16.

28. Tillich, *Systematic Theology*.

29. Pedraja, *Jesus Is My Uncle*, 16.

ologies. Such theologians also explore how the history and experience of their own communities affect their perceptions of classical theologies. They also explore how the experiences of their communities ought to shape their imagination of God and construction of theology.

Theology and Hermeneutics

The term *hermeneutics* comes from the Greek word *hermēneuein*. Its basic meanings are "to explain" or "to interpret"; thus hermeneutics can be defined as the act or practice of interpreting and explaining. Theology involves the interpretation of texts—both written (the Scriptures and the works of theologians) and oral (as articulated in song, prayer, liturgy, ethics, etc).[30] Interpreting the Bible correctly is one of the tasks of a Christian theologian. The Apostle Paul instructs Timothy to become God's workman who "correctly handles the word of truth" (2 Tim 2:15, NIV).

Several issues surround theological interpretation. Two questions are central to these issues: How does a theologian deal with the complexity shrouding the construction of textual meaning? And how does a theologian navigate through the conflict that arises as his or her agenda confronts the agenda of a text? Theologians consciously or unconsciously bring their personal agendas to the Scriptures. Sometimes such agendas can help a theologian gain access to the *meanings and purposes* of a text (illocution) and some *anticipated responses or actions* that are prompted by the text (perlocution). Other times a theologian's personal agendas can lead to a distortion of the meanings and purposes of a text. Theologians disagree on who and what determines the meaning of a text. Is it the author of the text, or the text itself, or the community that reads the text? However one answers these questions, a Christian theologian should seek to establish the intended meaning of the text and the significance of the text for his or her community.

Theology and Its Sources

This is a question about the resources of theology. A theologian's response to this question will vary depending on several circumstances. The religious affiliation, denominational convictions, academic training, school of thought, social location, and personal experience of a theologian will always have a significant effect on his or her choice of theological resources and sources. For example, a theologian whose goal is to demonstrate and defend

---

30. Kevin Vanhoozer defines a text as "an expression of human life that calls for interpretation." See Vanhoozer, *Is There a Meaning in This Text?*, 23.

the rationality of the truth-claims of Christianity and who uses analytical arguments as a tool to achieve this agenda may favor reason over experience. Below are two examples of the sources of theology.

Two Examples of Theology's Sources

JOHN WESLEY (1703–1791)

Many theologians today, particularly in the West, have adopted the quadrilateral (four) theological sources attributed to John Wesley, an English theologian.[31] The chart below describes these sources and how Wesley intended them to be used. Scott Jones has noted that for John Wesley, the fourfold source of theology is to be understood as "a single focus of authority with four unequal parts" in which "all four [sources] are mutually interdependent."[32] In other words, while these sources are needed to do theology, they do not hold equal authority and relevance.

Scripture (Protestant Canon)	Scripture is the primary source and final authority on Christian teaching and practice. Theologians should seek to properly interpret the Scriptures with the help of tradition, reason, and experience.
Tradition	By "tradition," Wesley meant the teaching of Christian antiquity and the early Church of England.* Tradition is subordinate to the Scriptures.
Reason	When used and understood properly, reason testifies to the authority and validity of Scripture.
Experience	Experience refers to the human encounter with God in Christian communities. Experience also refers to the mediated knowledge of God and God's creation gained through practice, study, and observation.

*See Campbell, "Interpretative Role of Tradition," 65.

---

31. See Outler, *John Wesley*; Gunter et al., *Wesley and the Quadrilateral.*
32. Jones, "Rule of Scripture," 42.

John S. Mbiti

The Kenyan theologian John Mbiti talked about four sources or "pillars" of theology.[33] Some of these sources are similar to Wesley's four sources. Although Mbiti discusses these sources in the context of African Christian theology, theologians from Asia and Latin America may find his sources relevant to their contexts.

Scriptures (all canons accepted in Christianity)	When interpreted properly, the Scriptures must be the final authority in all religious matters.
Theologies of Older Churches	These are the theologies of the classical ecumenical councils and the theologies of the Western churches that brought the Christian message to sub-Saharan Africa.
African Indigenous Religious Traditions	On the grounds that God was already present in Africa before the arrival of European missionaries, Mbiti argues that African theologians should use indigenous religious ideas and thought forms to express the Christian message.
Living Experiences of the Present-Day Churches	These include all contemporary socioeconomic, cultural, and religious issues that Christians face daily.

Exercise 1.3

Read 1 Corinthians 15 and identify the sources the Apostle Paul used to construct his theology of resurrection and hope. List all the possible sources that are present in the texts below.

15:1–8: _____

15:9–11: _____

15:12–28: _____

Relationship of the Sources

In doing theology, how are the sources of theology to be used? Christian theologians worry about the relationship between the sources—how the sources ought to interact. For some, the Scriptures alone are the controlling

33. Mbiti, "Some African Concepts of Christology," 51–52.

factor and therefore constitute the ultimate measuring standard for testing the relevance and usage of other sources. Others contend that the Scriptures and church tradition (the classical and official church dogmas that derive from the authorized interpretation of the Scriptures) have the same status of primacy and authority. The Second Vatican Council's Dogmatic Constitution on Divine Revelation articulates this view of the Scriptures and church tradition when it states, "Sacred theology rests on the written Word of God, together with sacred tradition, as its primary and perpetual foundation."[34] Yet others see religious experience (personal and communal) as the final authority in theological matters. Each of these views has significant implications for dealing with the issues of identity (whose theology is it?), validity (is it reliable and authentic?), and relevance (does it adequately work in this context?). These issues are not mutually exclusive. A theologian should continually work out the appropriate relationship of these sources of theology.

Theology and Orthodoxy

Many Christian theologians are concerned with the "center" or the core element or elements that are nonnegotiable and to which all Christian theologies must conform. The center or the core elements are usually construed as constituting *orthodoxy* (i.e., "right beliefs" or "pure beliefs").

In theological discourse, orthodoxy has been used in two interrelated senses. First, orthodoxy refers to the theological positions of the classical ecumenical councils such as the Council of Nicaea. Orthodoxy was understood to be the body of beliefs that derive from the right interpretation of the unchanging gospel. Based on this understanding of orthodoxy, the majority of theologians in the early church and medieval church believed that orthodoxy could not be changed or altered. All that a theologian could do was to deepen or confirm, but not revise, the orthodox theological positions. However, given that some orthodox theological positions were the views of the theologians whose arguments prevailed (sometimes because of their political connections in the church and the empire), one wonders whether using orthodoxy in this sense is not in fact misleading and unhelpful.

The second sense in which orthodoxy is used in theology is in contrast to *heterodoxy*—the innovative and alternative theological positions that were rejected by the classical ecumenical councils on the grounds that they did not adequately convey the teaching of the Scriptures. These views were typically labeled *heretical*—wrong or false opinions. Some of the heterodox

---

34. Second Vatican Council, Dogmatic Constitution on Divine Revelation, 4.24:16.

views were innovative interpretations and expressions of the gospel, while others were actively traditional.

The desire to preserve the purity of Christian doctrines and unity of the church led to the persecution of heretics (those who propounded and held alternative theological positions). Many heretics (for example, the Arians) suffered immensely under the emperor Theodosius (c. 346–395 CE). The majority of them were excommunicated from the church; many were banished from their societies, some were killed, and others were maimed.

This treatment of heretics clearly betrayed the liberative content of the Christian message. Should physical abuse, dehumanization, and death be the penalty of the heretics? Some early church theologians answered this question in the affirmative. As a consequence Christian theology, which ought to proclaim the good news of Jesus Christ, became bad news for many who held theological positions that differed from the theologies of the ecumenical councils.

Some of the earliest ecumenical church councils constructed orthodox beliefs. Historically, none of the councils with the label "ecumenical" united *all* separated Christian communities. Only the Council of Nicaea came close to achieving this enormous task.[35] Christians disagree on which councils merit being called "ecumenical." Carnegie Samuel Calian rightly observed that "no official list of recognized ecumenical councils will be satisfying to all church traditions in the East or the West. We can count as many as twenty-one councils if we are Roman Catholics and zero if we are contemporary Arians, with an interesting and varying range of two for Nestorians, three for the Oriental Orthodox, four for the Reformers, and seven for the Byzantine Orthodox."[36] Of course, the list could go on, and could become even more intriguing when we add the teaching of contemporary independent churches such as the African Independent Churches (AICs) and *Mukyōkai* ("non-church movement") of Japan. Orthodoxy should not obstruct fresh ways of imagining the mystery of God and God's involvement in the world. It should function as a signpost pointing Christians in the direction they ought to be heading in their ongoing reflection on the mystery of God.

Disciplines of Theology

Although the disciplines of theology I will describe below differ in style and form, they intersect. I will describe only biblical theology, contextual

---

35. Calian, *Theology Without Boundaries*, 13.
36. Ibid., 12.

theology, and systematic theology. Other disciplines include dogmatic theology, philosophical theology, practical theology, and historical theology.[37]

Biblical Theology

Biblical theology is concerned with the overarching "theology" of the Bible. A biblical theologian locates the books of the Bible in their own historical settings, that is, in their "own terms, categories, and thought forms."[38] In biblical theology, the issue the author addresses, the purpose of the author, the experience of the author, and the experience of the recipients of each book are of paramount importance. These contexts function as a key to understanding the theological themes in each book. Given the nature of biblical theology, knowing the original biblical languages (Aramaic, Hebrew, and *koinē* or common Greek) is necessary.

Some biblical theologians seek to reconcile the various themes found in both the Old Testament and the New Testament. Usually, these theologians operate with the assumption that an underlying *story* connects all the major themes in the books of the Bible. Biblical theologians, however, disagree on the nature of this story. The majority of these theologians agree, albeit with some modifications, that the story centers on God's redemptive acts that climaxed in God's action in Jesus of Nazareth, the Christ. One of the major criticisms of biblical theology is that the differences of the books of the Bible could be diminished in the process of harmonization.

Contextual Theology

Although every theology is contextual because theology is by nature historically and culturally conditioned, not all theologians consciously do theology in a way that reflects the cultures, social locations, and experiences of the theologian and the recipients of the theology. *Contextual theology* seeks to accomplish two tasks. First, it seeks to uncover how the contexts of the authors of the Bible shaped the contents of their books and also how the contexts of earlier theologians informed their interpretations of the

---

37. *Philosophical theology* uses philosophical techniques to express Christianity's theological claims, beliefs, and doctrines. Philosophical theologians explore questions such as, does God exist? *Historical theology* is concerned with the history of Christian theologies and doctrines. It explores the historical contexts of the major theologies and doctrines that have arisen within different Christian communities. *Practical theology* focuses on Christian praxis—how Christians ought to live and practice their faith.

38. Ladd, *Theology of the New Testament*, 20.

theological themes in the Bible. Second, it imagines how the contexts of present-day Christian communities ought to inform the theologies that are designed for them. Contextual theologians elevate human contexts to the status of a nonnegotiable source of theology. As Stephen Bevans remarks, "Theology that is contextual realizes that culture, history, contemporary thought forms, and so forth are to be considered, along with the Scriptures and tradition, as valid sources for theological expression."[39]

Contextual theologians adopt different theological approaches. Bevans has discussed six of these approaches in *Models of Contextual Theology*.[40] Although these models differ in style and content, what they share is the desire to constructively communicate the mystery of God's identity and actions in a way that is befitting to contemporary human religious traditions, cultures, and experience. Since the 1950s, some non-Western Christian communities have produced theologies that are consciously contextual. These include African theology, liberation theology, and Dalit theology. In the Western world, some theologians have begun to construct theologies that are likewise intentionally contextual. These include feminist theology, womanist theology, and black theology.

One main criticism of contextual theology is the different ways contextual theologians understand the ideas "universal" and "local" in theological discourse. Here are the key questions: Are there theologies that are universally binding? And are there universally accepted criteria for defining an adequate Christian theology? Contextual theologians are aware of how notoriously slippery the concept of a universal core can be. The underlying issue is the place of orthodoxy (right belief) in all Christian theologies. While the majority of contextual theologians are suspicious of the uses of orthodoxy, some reject entirely any notion of a universally binding orthodoxy because of the political and cultural undertones of the theologies of the earliest ecumenical councils.

Systematic Theology

It has become increasingly difficult to define *systematic theology* in the wake of the flowering of definitions and usages of this type of theology. Michael Horton's definition captures the basic notion of systematic theology. He writes, "Systematic theology is like the box top of a jigsaw puzzle, and every believer is a theologian in the sense of putting the pieces together. If we fail to recognize there is a box top (i.e., a unified whole) to Scripture, we will

39. Bevans, *Models of Contextual Theology*, 4.
40. Ibid., 37–137.

have only a pile of pieces."[41] Systematicians (i.e., systematic theologians) assume that the diverse representations of God and God's actions recorded in the Scriptures can be explained and arranged in a coherent, organized, and logical order. While some systematic theologians seek only to identify the relations and implications of a doctrine on another doctrine, others seek to order their thoughts on a given doctrine "in a tightly arranged and geometrically arranged circle, which could be entered in any place and followed round back to the starting point."[42] Many systematic theologians, like philosophical theologians, emphasize the role of rationality or human reason in the construction of theology.

One of the strengths of systematic theology is its emphasis on the relationship and implications of a doctrine on other doctrines. It helps Christians to be consistent in their explications of their beliefs and practices. For example, the belief about God's love for humanity should not be explained in a way that contradicts God's justice. A major problem of systematic theology, especially the way in which it has been imagined by many Western systematic theologians since the Enlightenment, is the assumption that all things cohere in human minds. With this assumption these theologians aim to present their understandings of God's actions in a neat and tidy system, leaving little or no room for a dialectical engagement with the mystery of God.

Diversity, Unity, and Theology

Christianity is interwoven with different threads. Today theologians and historians speak of "African Christianity," "Western Christianity," "Asian Christianity," and "Latin American Christianity." Several subcategories exist within these forms of Christianity. For example, within "Western Christianity" we can speak of "European Christianity," "American Christianity," and "African American Christianity." This categorization of Christianity signals the existence of diverse (and sometimes competing) theologies. The challenge that a student of Christian theology faces is how to articulate the similarities and differences within the various strands of Christianity. The existence of competing theologies within Christianity can be daunting and frustrating. Many Christians and

> FOCUS QUESTION:
> How should the diverse and competing doctrines within Christinaity be approached?

41. Horton, *Christian Faith*, 27.

42. Gunton, "Historical and Systematic Theology," 11.

students of theology wonder whether it is at all possible to know the "right theology" among the myriad competing theologies. The tests of Christian identity and relevance I have already discussed are helpful in this situation. Although competing theologies can be daunting, they are also essential to develop and further our knowledge of God. Every theology, including an inadequate one, can help the theologian refine his or her own thinking about God.

Theology students should be prepared to answer the following two questions: Are there any nonnegotiable truth-claims that define the theology that sees itself as "Christian"? Is there room for internal contradictions in Christian theology? A helpful way to deal with these questions is to categorize Christian theologies as "essential," "important," and "useful." Theologians, of course, disagree on the beliefs that belong to each of these categories.

- *Essential*—rejection entails rejecting the essence of Christianity (nonnegotiable).

- *Important*—rejection may result in a distortion of Christianity but not a rejection of the essence of Christianity (negotiable).

- *Useful*—rejection may result in a distortion of Christianity and unhealthy Christian living (negotiable).

EXERCISE 1.4

Using the categories above and the chart below, classify the following doctrines: belief in the divinity and humanity of Jesus; belief in the Trinity; a clear understanding of the Trinity; the practice of water baptism; the modes of water baptism; the practice of speaking in tongues; the belief in God's self-revelation; the inerrancy of the Bible; and the infallibility of the Bible.

Essential	Important	Useful

Concluding Reflections

Theologians, like those in other fields of study, should aim to make contributions to the conversation on how humanity can attain a religious, peaceful, healthy, and prosperous life. They are to draw insights from all fields of study with the intention to contribute to the alleviation of human misery and oppression, and to the struggle for justice. In other words, theology should become interdisciplinary. If theology has any worthy contributions to make in addressing human suffering, religious conflict, terrorism, the threat of nuclear warfare, failing legal systems, economic instability, and sociopolitical issues, it must begin to converse with and influence other disciplines. This, of course, does not mean that the authenticity of theology depends on its affirmation by other disciplines, since in a true conversation each party negotiates its self-affirmation within the context of the uniqueness and relatedness of others.

Key Terms

Apologetics: subfield in theology that deals with the defense of Christian beliefs, doctrines, and practices.

Biblical Canon: accepted body of books that make up the Scriptures. There are different biblical canons in Christianity.

Contextualization: interpretation and appropriation of the Christian message within a particular context—the history, culture, and experience of a community.

Hermeneutics: the act of interpreting a text with the aim to discover its intended meaning and the actions it hopes to stimulate in readers.

Orthodoxy: right beliefs or pure beliefs. The body of beliefs regarded as the right beliefs or teachings of Christianity.

Review Questions

1. What is the nature of theology?
2. What are the tasks of Christian theology?
3. How does John Wesley's quadrilateral view of the sources of theology differ from John Mbiti's sources of theology?
4. What are the forms of Christian theology?
5. What are the roles of faith and reason in the construction of Christian theology?

Suggestions for Further Reading

Bevans, Stephen B. *Models of Contextual Theology*. Rev. ed. Maryknoll, NY: Orbis, 2002.

Gunton, Colin E. *The Christian Faith: An Introduction to Christian Doctrine*. Oxford: Blackwell, 2002.

Gutiérrez, Gustavo. *A Theology of Liberation: History, Politics and Salvation*. Rev. ed. Maryknoll, NY: Orbis, 1988.

Ott, Craig, and Harold A. Netland. *Globalizing Theology: Belief and Practice in an Era of World Christianity*. Grand Rapids: Baker Academic, 2006.

Placher, William C., editor. *Essentials of Christian Theology*. Louisville: Westminster John Knox, 2003.

2

God's Revelation

This chapter discusses the idea, loci, nature, accessibility, and purpose of God's revelation. The basic definition of revelation (*apokalypsis* in Greek) is "unveiling." Revelation entails the unveiling of what was previously hidden or unknown. Revelation also entails knowledge: the recipient of a revelation attains knowledge of or about the subject of revelation or the revealer.

The relationship between theology and God's revelation is of paramount importance. The relevance of theology depends on whether God truly exists, and if God exists, whether human beings are able to know of God's existence. If God truly exists but human beings do not know about God's existence, theology is ultimately useless and irrelevant. This is because theology, particularly Christian theology, does not merely concern itself with a theoretical knowledge of God; it also concerns itself with ethics. One of the tasks of Christian theologians is to articulate what God expects of human beings.

Can human beings know that God truly exists? By nature, as Christianity teaches, human beings and God do not have the same properties and characteristics. To put it differently, God and human beings possess some characteristics that they do not share in common. Since human beings are not God, how then can they adequately talk about God's nature and expectations? A question of this sort has led some people to conclude that the idea of God is an imaginary and illusionary human construct. Some philosophers and theologians, on the contrary, contend that God truly exists but human beings can only make *negative statements* about God. For them, human beings can only successfully say *what God is not* but are unable to say *what God is*. Many Christian theologians, however, have continued to confess that humans can experience, discuss, and relate to God because of God's self-revelation in Jesus Christ. The author of the book of Hebrews puts it this way: "In the past God spoke to our forefathers through the prophets at many times and in various ways, but in these last days he has spoken to us by his Son, whom he appointed heir of all things, and through whom he made the universe" (Heb 1:1–2, NIV).

The Possibility of Knowing God

The majority of the earliest Christian theologians, like some Greek philosophers and Jewish theologians of their era, recognized the *otherness* of God. On the one hand, they were aware of the chasm between God and human beings. On the other hand, they were also convinced that human beings could come to the knowledge of God because of God's actions (speech and acts) in the world. Yet, they were willing to admit that human beings and human words cannot totally comprehend and express the mystery of God. Christian theology commonly confesses that God is simultaneously hidden and revealed. Many Christians have continued to confess that human beings can know of God because God has taken the initiative to unveil God's self in recognizable and knowable ways. Theologians, however, express this confession in different ways. Pseudo-Dionysius, for example, wrote, "Indeed the inscrutable One [God] is out of the reach of every rational process. Nor can any words come up to the inexpressible Good, this One, this Source of all unity, this supra-existent Being. Mind beyond mind, word beyond speech, it is gathered up by no discourse, by no intuition, by no name."[1] Pseudo-Dionysius' claim exemplifies a *negative theology*—the theology that states human beings and human words can only say what God

FOCUS QUESTION:
How do human beings come to
the knowledge of God?

1. Pseudo-Dionysius, "The Divine Names," in *Pseudo-Dionysius: The Complete Works*, 49–50.

is not.[2] The problem with negative theology, as Thomas Morris has pointed out, is that "rational denial seems clearly to presuppose rational affirmation. Knowledge of what something is not seems to be based upon knowledge of what, to some extent, it is."[3] Saying *what or who God is not* requires some idea of *what or who God is.*

Theologians who distance themselves from negative theology appreciate the critical issue inherent in negative theology, namely, the *otherness* of God. The otherness or distinctiveness of God exerts a significant influence on theological reflections on God's revelation. Human beings do not have direct access to God. They do not see God and cannot take God to a laboratory for an examination. The Christian confession of God's revelation—the claim that God, who was previously hidden, has taken the initiative to reveal God's self to human beings—implies that human beings can have only indirect or mediated access to God. They come to knowledge of God only by means of what God has unveiled about God's self. As human beings we "do not approach God like we engage in the study of objects around us, namely, in an objective, scientific manner or through our own human will. Rather, we come to know God as God gives himself to be known. In the knowing process, therefore, the initiative comes from the divine side."[4]

Since theology is constructed only on a mediated knowledge of God—on what God has revealed about God's self and actions—every theology reflects the aspiration and experience of the theologian who constructs it. This is because the theologian develops his or her theology on the basis of his or her partial understanding of God's self-revelation. Theologians, therefore, must heed the advice of the Apostle Paul: "For we know in part and we prophesy in part, but when perfection comes, the imperfection disappears. . . . Now we see but a poor reflection as in a mirror; then we shall see face to face. Now I know in part; then I shall know fully, even as I am fully known" (1 Cor 13:9–12, NIV). A perfect understanding of God's revelation that functions as a universal law in the court of theology does not yet exist. Our knowledge of God's revelation, and consequently our theologies, will remain fallible until such a time when God, through Jesus Christ, and in the power of the Holy Spirit, completely redeems and perfects us.

Broadly, we have three ways or paths to knowledge—namely, through *revelation, scientific experimentation,* and *contemplative reflection.*

---

2. "Negative theology" is also called "apophatic theology."

3. Morris, *Our Idea of God*, 23.

4. Grenz, *Theology for the Community of God*, 49.

Different Ways of Knowing

Revealed Knowledge	*Means of knowing:* Through revelation—the sort of knowledge that is hidden and may never be known until disclosed or revealed. *Relation to knowledge of God:* Human beings know God only because God has taken the initiative to reveal God's self to them. *Limitations of this way of knowing:* It is too subjective. It is notoriously difficult to ascertain the truthfulness of revealed knowledge, which is not open to independent verification.
Scientific Knowledge	*Means of knowing:* Through experimentation, observation, and reflection on nature. *Relation to knowledge of God:* Some theologians argue that humans can prove God's existence by reflecting upon nature and the world. *Limitations of this way of knowing:* We cannot attain an adequate knowledge of God's personal characteristics merely by studying nature.
Contemplative Knowledge	*Means of knowing:* Through rational intuition and sensuous intuition. *Relation to knowledge of God:* Some theologians contend that it is possible to gain the knowledge of God's existence by engaging in sustained thinking and reasoning. *Limitation of this way of knowing:* It is too subjective. Proving logically that "A" can exist does not mean that "A" exists in reality. Also, a contemplative form of knowledge may never lead a person to a personal and intimate knowledge of God.

Description of God's Revelation

In Christian theology, God's revelation refers to God's disclosure of God's modes of existence and God's relationship with the world. Christian theologians, however, disagree on the form or forms of God's revelation. Theologians propose different answers to the question, Is God's revelation God's self-disclosure (i.e., a direct representation of God's mode of existence) or general disclosures of God's actions in the world, none of which is God's self-disclosure? The primary issue here is whether in Christian theology "revelation" should be used exclusively in the sense of "God's self-disclosure."[5] While some theologians restrict the use of revelation to those special acts in which God revealed God's self, others use revelation broadly to include God's actions, which may or may not be identified with God's self-revelation.[6] Yet, some argue that God's revelation is not the disclosure of God's essence. For them, God's revelation should not be understood as God's *direct self-revelation* but rather as God's *indirect self-disclosure*, which is manifested in God's acts in history.[7]

> FOCUS QUESTION:
> What is God's revelation?

God's revelation is God's gracious act of making God's self known to humanity with the intention to communicate with humanity. God's revelation takes different forms (e.g., words and deeds) that are accessible to human beings. Although theologians disagree on the nature and modes of God's revelation, they agree that God has taken the initiative to reveal God's self to humanity. God's self-disclosure makes it possible for human beings to communicate with God, to be in relationship with God, to talk about God, or to do theology. In the words of Rowan Williams, the archbishop of Canterbury, "In spite of everything, we go on saying 'God.' And since God is not the name of any particular thing available for inspection, it seems that we must as believers assume that we talk about God on the basis of 'revelation'—of what has been shown to us by God's will and action."[8]

The ability of human beings to attain knowledge of God is contingent on two acts of God. First, since human beings and God are radically different, God alone can reveal God's self to human beings. God's revelation must also be in the forms that accommodate human beings' ways of acquiring knowledge (Heb 1:1–2). Second, the radical ontological difference between

---

5. Pannenberg, "Introduction," 4.

6. Ibid., 5.

7. Ibid., 13.

8. Williams, *On Christian Theology*, 131.

God and human beings implies that human beings are in need of a divine help if they are to know God. For Christians, God has given such help by illuminating human minds or by giving them the eyes of faith. Without God's gift of faith human beings will be unable to accept and appropriate God's revelation.

In what ways has God disclosed God's self? This question has haunted and divided Christians for centuries. The issues embedded in this question are the nature of revelation (in what forms has God revealed God's self?), the accessibility of revelation (who has access to God's revelation?), and the purpose of revelation (does God intentionally reveal God's self in order to accomplish any specific objectives?).

The Nature of God's Revelation

What does God's self-revelation or disclosure look like? Where can we find God's revelation? While some theologians believe that God reveals God's self only through auditory speech (i.e., by speaking), others argue that God reveals God's self only through acts or by doing something such as initiating an event.

FOCUS QUESTION:
In what ways has God revealed
God's self to humanity?

Yet some who are influenced by speech-act theory see the dichotomy between *speaking* and *doing* as misleading and unwarranted on the grounds that God's communicative acts can be verbal. In other words, "saying too is a doing, and . . . persons can do many things by 'saying.'"[9] Using Avery Dulles' classifications, I turn now to the major views or models of God's revelation.

Avery Dulles' Classifications

In *Models of Revelation*, the Jesuit theologian Avery Dulles presents six helpful typologies or models of revelation.[10] The following sections contain a summary and critique of these models. I have followed Dulles' arrangement.

9. Vanhoozer, *First Theology*, 130.
10. Dulles, *Models of Revelation*.

Revelation as Doctrine or Propositional Statements

Description: "Revelation as doctrine" dates to the early Reformation or late medieval eras. Carl F. H. Henry claims that the "historical Christian view is that revelation is given in the form of verbal truths inerrantly conveyed in the inspired prophetic-apostolic writings."[11] Some traces of the components of this view can be found in the ideas of inspiration of the Bible propounded by theologians since the second century CE. However, it was in the works of the nineteenth-century Roman Catholic neo-scholastic theologians (such as Christian Pesch) and Protestant Orthodox theologians (such as B. B. Warfield) that this view of God's revelation was most clearly articulated. Many Evangelicals hold this view today. Although some variations exist in the manner in which Evangelicals and Roman Catholics understand the propositional nature of God's revelation, they share the view that God's revelation "is embodied in definite written statements" that constitute Christianity's sacred text—the Bible.[12]

The propositional view argues that God's revelation comes in the form of rational statements and assertions. It sees God as the "infallible teacher who communicates knowledge by speech and writing."[13] Proponents of this view claim that God, who previously revealed God's self through deeds, miraculously supervised some prophets and apostles to preserve God's deeds and words in inerrant and infallible written records. They divide revelation into natural (or general) and supernatural (or special). Natural revelation is embedded in God's creation. This form of revelation can help human beings "even in their present fallen condition to know by reason the existence of the one personal God, creator and last end of all things."[14] However, due to the effect of sin on the human intellect and will (sin corrupts them), human beings cannot attain an accurate knowledge of God through reason and contemplation on nature without God's help. A supernatural or a special revelation is "absolutely necessary in order for anyone to know strict mysteries, such as the doctrines of the Trinity and the Incarnation."[15] God's revelations, which Jesus Christ brought to a climax through his miraculous deeds and teaching, are preserved in the Bible—God's speech to human beings. The Bible "transmits revealed information about God's will and purpose."[16]

---

11. Henry, "Priority of Divine Revelation," 78.

12. Dulles, *Models of Revelation*, 40.

13. Ibid., 33.

14. Ibid., 41.

15. Ibid., 42.

16. Henry, "Priority of Divine Revelation," 77.

The majority of the proponents of this view argue that the Bible—God's revelation in written form—is universally binding and is the judge for all events attributed to God. While some contend that God no longer reveals God's self at all, some grant that God may choose to reveal God's self but that such revelations cannot compete with or improve God's written revelation, the Bible.

Contributions: The major contribution of the propositional view of God's revelation is its perception of the Bible as the sacred text where people in postapostolic times can encounter God's words and actions. The Bible has remained the primary text that unifies Christian communities from all ages and cultures. It defines the identity of Christians. Although it is interpreted and appropriated in diverse and sometimes competing ways, the Bible remains the cord that binds Christians. They derive their confessions, beliefs, and theological explications of God's relation to the world from the Bible. The status of authority the Bible enjoys in Christian communities cannot be justified if the Bible does not have any real connection with God.

The major theological difference between the Protestant and Roman Catholic views of the propositional revelation centers upon the role of the Bible in the formulation of Christian beliefs and practices. Many Protestant theologians who see God's revelation as God's rational assertions argue that the Bible alone is the *final authority* in matters of faith, practice, history, and science. The majority of Roman Catholic theologians, on the contrary, contend that the Bible and the *magisterium* (the official teachings of the church that derive from the Bible) constitute the final authority in matters of faith and practice.

Problems: One of the major problems of the propositional view of God's revelation is its assumption that the Bible is a collection of propositional statements that proceed from the mind and mouth of God. This assumption fails to account properly for the diverse genres of the books of the Bible and diminishes the humanity of the Bible. Human beings wrote the books of the Bible, albeit under the guidance of the Holy Spirit, from their own understanding and experience of God. Another problem within the propositional view of God's revelation is the belief that the Bible is a source of scientific and historical information. This belief is misleading because the books of the Bible were written primarily from a theological perspective. Although there are some historical and scientific materials in the Bible, the authors of the Bible did not intend to write scientific and historical textbooks. They wrote to attest to God's actions in the world, particularly in their own communities.

The text below is an excerpt from Carl F. H. Henry's *God, Revelation and Authority*. Henry (1913–2003) was an American theologian who stood in the tradition of neo-evangelicalism. Neo-evangelicalism or new evangelicalism was a movement that was started by figures such as Henry and Harold J. Ockenga, who aimed to rid the "old" fundamentalism of its anti-intellectualism and sectarianism. Henry's view of divine revelation continues to reverberate in the works of many theologians who construe divine revelation as divine propositional assertions or statements.

The decisive question concerning the interrelation between theology and philosophy is whether the governing content of one's philosophy is derived from revelation, or whether the governing content of one's philosophy is the secondary instrument of revelation—and hence considered another final authority—alongside the Word of God. Revelation is not a possibility of man but solely of God in his self-disclosure. Does human reasoning pretend itself to supply—even if unconsciously—the structure and function and content of theology, and to constitute in some respects an ultimate source in the sphere of revelation? If so, the divine is engulfed by the human. There is no ultimate justification for the secular philosopher's insistence that divine revelation always gets mixed up in human reasoning, for that is simply a denial of divine revelation. Not unrelated to this denial is the notion that universal truths are implicit in divine revelation, but that revelation looks to the eschaton, so that we presently misunderstand rather than understand its propositional content.

The theologian needs the truth of revelation—which is truth of the same kind as any other truth, even if it involves its distinctive object and method—to purge his own thought from philosophical misunderstandings. The Scriptures not only challenge the secular assumptions that frustrate man's belief in the reality and purpose of God and his acceptance of the gospel. They also controvert any theologian's claim, or pope's claim, that what any modern man says supplies the normative meaning of revelation.

But since revelation is itself conceptual and verbal, no arbitrary boundary can be erected between philosophy and theology, and philosophy can enrich itself from the content of revealed theology. For theology and philosophy are active on the same terrain. . . .

Reason and faith are not antithetical. Faith without reason leads to skepticism and reason without faith does so also. Human knowledge is possible only on the basis of divine revelation; Augustine rightly held that all knowledge is faith. . . . Rationality permeates the revelational outlook: the Logos [God's Word] is at the beginning and center and climax of divine disclosure. Christianity has never offered itself as a refuge from rationality; rather it emphasizes the rational difficulties and inconsistencies of alternative views of reality and life. Christian theologians of the past fearlessly solicited reason; God summons man to think thoughts after him. But revelation lifts human reason beyond restrictions of intellect limited by finitude and clouded by sin through the knowledge it conveys of man's Maker and Redeemer.[17]

Question: How does Henry justify his view of revelation as propositional truths or statements?

Revelation as History

Description: This view of God's revelation, which became prominent in the nineteenth century, argues that God's self-disclosure does not come to us in the form of propositional statements but rather in the form of *actions*: "God reveals himself primarily in his great deeds, especially those which form the major themes of biblical history."[18] God intentionally unveils God's identity and character by intervening in human history. Some theologians who see God's revelation as *history* argue that God's revelatory acts extend to the prophets' and the apostles' interpretations of God's revelation. Others reject this notion and insist that God's revelatory manifestations in history must be distinguished from human interpretations of such events.

Those events that are God's revelatory actions are notoriously difficult to know and verify. Some theologians who construe God's revelation as *history* deal with this difficulty by arguing that God's revelation "is not to be found in a special segment of history but rather in universal history—the history of the whole world as it moves to its appointed consummation."[19] Others argue that God's revelation is only found in the segments of human history that relate to *salvation history*—the "story of God's redemptive dealings with his elect people, issuing in a message of salvation to be carried to the ends of the earth."[20] Events such as God's deliverance of the people of Israel from the Egyptian bondage belong to the category of special redemptive events. The birth, life, teaching, death, resurrection, and ascension of Jesus Christ are viewed as the climax of God's redemptive or salvific events in human history.

17. Henry, *God, Revelation and Authority*, 1:199–201.
18. Dulles, *Models of Revelation*, 27.
19. Ibid., 59.
20. Ibid., 56.

Contributions: The view of God's revelation as *history* emphasizes God's involvement and active role in shaping the course of human history. "Just as actions are said to be the proper language of love," Avery Dulles writes, "so the deeds of God manifest his attitudes more powerfully than mere words could ever do, and evoke deeper personal response. In times of fear and confusion, this type of theology inspires trust in God's providential care."[21] Also, viewing God's revelation as what occurs in historical events and what must be distinguished from human interpretations of such events makes God's revelation a phenomenon that is open to interpretation. People from all ages and cultures will interpret God's revelatory manifestations in the ways that resonate and befit their experience of God. Paul Bekye, in *Divine Revelation and Traditional Religions*, puts it this way: "The divine-human encounter not only presupposes but actually occurs within the historical, social and cultural conditions of people where such an encounter necessarily takes place. Naturally, also, the human response to the divine involvement is given from within the same historical, social and cultural nexus which express the human existential reality."[22] God invites all people to encounter God's revelation and also to discover the message God is seeking to convey through God's actions in the world. The intended message and its meaning are "capable of being formulated in many ways according to the perspectives and thought-forms of varying cultures, and [are] constantly subject to reconceptualization."[23]

Problems: A major criticism of this view is the lack of a universal criterion for determining salvific events. How can humans know that God actually intervenes in human history or know that an event *is* or *conveys* God's self-disclosure? Another criticism of this view is that it does not account for God's revelatory speeches, which are recorded in several places in the Old Testament and a few places in the New Testament. For example, God reveals God's name to Moses through speech (Exod 3:14). God undoubtedly acts and speaks. Dulles correctly notes that "God's word is a creative power that calls being into existence. Any act of God, expressing a divine intervention, possesses features of word and of deed alike."[24]

The following excerpt is taken from Wolfhart Panneneberg's *Systematic Theology*. Pannenberg presents one of the major versions of the view of revelation as *history*.

21. Ibid., 61.
22. Bekye, *Divine Revelation and Traditional Religions*, 3.
23. Dulles, *Models of Revelation*, 61.
24. Ibid., 66.

In general God is not the content of the Word [*logos* in Greek, see John 1:1–2], and this has to be taken into account when appeal is made to biblical ideas of the Word on behalf of the thought of God's self-revelation. When we think of God's self-revelation we have to think of it as mediated by his action, for that is always the content of biblical ideas of the Word of God, whether it be God's action in creation, his historical action as it was intimated in the prophetic word, or the action in Jesus of Nazareth to which the primitive Christian kerygma made reference. The only exception in this regard is the word of the law, which has human action in view, but which for its part is again integrated into the larger context of divine action in view of its incompatibility with the demand of law.

The fact that the various experiences of revelation which are transmitted in the biblical writings, including the prophetic reception of the word, but also the revelation of the law at Sinai, do not have God as their direct content—a fact which hardly promotes the understanding of revelation as God's self-revelation—this very fact makes possible a uniform understanding of the event of revelation which still leaves proper room for the variety of the biblical experiences of revelation. All of these contribute to God's making himself known in his deity, and to that extent they are all factors in the history of the divine action which along the lines of the prophetic word of demonstration has as its goal the achievement of a knowledge of God not merely by Israel but by all peoples. Thus the thesis of the indirectness of God's self-revelation has the systematic function of integrating the various experiences of revelation to which the biblical writings bear witness.

If we had direct self-revelation, i.e., God's making himself known directly by special communication, in all these various forms and in association with all the various recipients and events, then inevitably their claims would be in competition with one another. The divine Self might be revealed in one special communication as distinct from another. But if the communications come directly from God, yet are only indirectly communications about God himself which make known his nature and deity, i.e., to the degree that they have God as their Author, then we can view the various events of revelation as components parts of the one all-embracing event of self-revelation to which each of them makes its own specific contribution. Along these lines there need be no rivalry between the OT and the NT witness to revelation....

As the revelation of God in his historical action moves towards the still outstanding future of the consummation of history, its claim to reveal the one God who is the world's Creator, Reconciler, and Redeemer is open to future verification in history, which is as yet incomplete, and which is still exposed, therefore, to the question of its truth. This question is given an ongoing answer in the life of believers by the power of revelation to shed light on their life experiences. In theological thinking, then, the question finds provisional answer in the assurance that our own reality and that of our world are to be seen as determined by the God of revelation.[25]

Question: How does Pannenberg construe the ideas of God's revelation and God's self-revelation?

Revelation as Inner Experience

Description: This view sees God's revelation as "a privileged interior experience of grace or communion with God."[26] It relocates the locus of God's revelation from external speech and acts to internal psychological and mystical experience. It rejects the view that God reveals God's self in deeds and words. Proponents of this view propose that God's revelation "is not only to be found in experience but that it consists in an immediate experience of God who inwardly communicates with each believer."[27] Revelation occurs when God makes God's self "present to the consciousness of the individual in a way that minimizes the need for mediation through created signs."[28] It is the consciousness of an individual, and not a written text or a historical event, that is the locus of revelation. The German theologian Friedrich Schleiermacher (1768–1834) was one of the major proponents of this view. In *The Christian Faith*, Schleiermacher argued that Christian theology arises when an individual encounters God or experiences the feeling of being absolutely dependent on God.[29] While external objects such as sermons on the life of Jesus Christ may arouse the God-consciousness in an individual, God's revelation actually takes place within the individual.

Some theologians who see revelation as an *inner experience* view religion as a phenomenon rooted in humanity's experience of God-consciousness. Rosemary Radford Ruether writes, "By *revelatory* we mean breakthrough experiences beyond ordinary fragmented consciousness that provide interpretative symbols illuminating the means of the *whole* life. Since consciousness is ultimately individual, we postulate that revelation

---

25. Pannenberg, *Systematic Theology*, 1:243–44, 257.

26. Dulles, *Models of Revelation*, 27.

27. Ibid., 69.

28. Ibid.

29. Schleiermacher, *Christian Faith*, 1:12.

always starts with an individual."[30] Given the subjective, mystical, and experiential nature of God's revelation, E. Bọlaji Idowu argues that no single religion encapsulates the mystery of God. All religions, he contends, have the capacity to lead people into fellowship with God, who has left God's mark upon the created order and God's witness within human beings.[31]

Contributions: Three key contributions of the *inner experience* view of divine revelation are noteworthy. First, it "relieved Christians of the burden of having to justify the whole system of inherited beliefs" in the universal court of reason.[32] It opposes the Enlightenment and modernist projects that established human reason or rationality as the arbiter of truth. Exponents of the experiential view of revelation argue that knowledge need not pass a scientific test in order to be authentic and reliable. The validity of Christian doctrines and truth-claims does not depend on a Christian's ability to demonstrate their rational and scientific warrants. Of course, this does not mean providing rational warrants for Christian beliefs is of no value.

Second, the view of revelation as an inner experience distinguishes God's self-revelation from the phenomenon of religion. Since God's self-disclosure is different from its interpretation and appropriation by human beings, proponents of this view contended for a "more positive attitude toward the nonbiblical religions than had been customary for Christians."[33] No religion can exhaustively explain the mystery of God's relationship to the world. Sin compromises and distorts humanity's perceptions and understandings of God's revelation.

Third, the view of revelation as an inner experience can promote personal and communal piety. It can bridge the gap between abstract theology and human religious experience. As Dulles notes, "The life of prayer and mystical experience, which had been shunted off from the main thoroughfare of theology, appeared once again as central themes. Works of devotion and spiritual autobiography became primary loci for the study of revelation."[34]

Problems: A major criticism against the *inner experience* view of revelation is its subjectivity. Religious experience is notoriously slippery. What religious experience actually means and looks like is highly debated. If God's revelation occurs only in the consciousness of an individual, then how is

---

30. Ruether, *Sexism and God-Talk*, 13.
31. Idowu, *African Traditional Religion*, 56.
32. Dulles, *Models of Revelation*, 77.
33. Ibid., 78.
34. Ibid.

the origin and source of the experience to be evaluated? An experience purported to be a *religious experience* may be a "hallucinatory experience or an experience that occurs as a result of mental disorder."[35] Another problem of this view is its failure to account for or its disregard of the uniqueness of the Bible. Construing the Hebrew Bible as the codified collective experience of the Jewish people and the New Testament as the codified collective experience of Jesus' followers, as Rosemary Ruether suggests,[36] can lead to the assumption that the Christian Bible is *truly human* but *barely God's inspired* book. If this were to be the case, the Bible would be a collection of compromised and distorted appropriations of certain individuals' experience of God's consciousness. As such, we can conclude that the Bible contains inadequate and unreliable "answers to the deep human questions about the origin and ultimate destiny of humanity and the world."[37]

As stated above, Schleiermacher was among those who articulated the view of revelation as inner experience. The following passage is taken from his *Christian Faith*.

> The words "reveal," "revealed," "revelation," present still further difficulties, since even originally they sometimes signify the illumination of what was obscure, confused, unobserved, and sometimes rather the disclosing and unveiling of what was hitherto concealed and kept secret, and still further confusion has been introduced by the distinction between mediate and immediate (direct and indirect) revelation. To begin with, all will at once agree that the word "revealed" is never applied either to what is discovered in the realm of experience by one man and handed on to others, or to what is excogitated in thought by one man and so learned by others; and further, that the word presupposes a divine communication and declaration. And in this sense we find the word very generally applied to the origin of religious communions. For of what religious mysteries and varieties of worship, either among the Greeks or among the Egyptians and Indians, would it not be asserted that they originally came from heaven or were proclaimed by Deity in some way which fell outside the human and natural order? Not seldom, indeed, we find even the beginning of civic communities ... traced to a divine sending of the man who first gathered the tribe together into a civic union, and so the new organization of life is based on a revelation. Accordingly, we might say that the idea of revelation signifies the *originality* of the fact which lies at the foundation of a religious communion, in the sense that this fact, as conditioning the individual content

35. Ezigbo, *Re-imagining African Christologies*, 114.

36. Ruether, *Sexism and God-Talk*, 12.

37. Dulles, *Models of Revelation*, 79.

of the religious emotions which are found in the communion, cannot itself in turn be explained by the historical chain which precedes it.

Now the fact that in this original element there is a divine causality requires no further discussion; nor does the fact that it is an activity which aims at and furthers the salvation of man. But I am unwilling to accept further definition that it operates upon man as a cognitive being. For that would make the revelation to be originally and essentially *doctrine*; and I do not believe that we can adopt that position, whether we consider the whole field covered by the idea, or seek to define it in advance with special reference to Christianity. If a system of propositions can be understood from their connexion with others, then nothing supernatural was required for their production. But if they cannot, then they can, in the first instance, only be apprehended . . . as parts of another whole, as a moment of the life of a thinking being who works upon us directly as a distinctive existence by means of his total impression on us; and this working is always a working upon the self-consciousness. Thus the original fact will always be the appearing of such a being, and the original working will always be upon the self-consciousness of those into whose circle he enters.[38]

Question: What does this text say about Schleiermacher's view of the relationship between God's revelation and human experience of God?

Revelation as Dialectical Presence

Description: The "dialectical presence" view of God's revelation originates from the "dialectical" (or "crisis") theology of Karl Barth and other theologians who emphasized the dialectical nature of revelation. On the grounds that God is "wholly other" and also the inability of sinful human beings to grasp God's revelation without divine help, these theologians argued that God's presence could not be straightforwardly "discovered within the realms of historical fact, doctrinal statements, or religious experience."[39] In order for divine revelation to occur, God essentially does two interrelated things.

First, God makes God's self known to humanity. Second, God quickens and enables human beings to recognize the vehicles God uses to reveal God's self. God's revelation is a gift to humanity. This is because, in the words of Barth, "God does not belong to the world. Therefore He does not

38. Schleiermacher, *Christian Faith*, 1:49–50.
39. Dulles, *Models of Revelation*, 85.

belong to the series of objects for which we have categories and words by means of which we draw the attention of others to them, and bring them into relation with them."[40] However, this does not mean that God is absent from the world. Rather, God in some sense remains concealed or hidden to humanity, even in the gift of self-disclosure.

Wherein, then, is God's revelation to be found? For Barth, the primary locus of God's revelation is Jesus Christ. The tools (such as the Bible and the church's proclamation) that God uses to help human beings attain knowledge of God's self-disclosure will accomplish their tasks only when they are brought into "alignment with [the] primary locus of God's revealing."[41] God, for dialectical theologians, unveils God's self through God's word. The written or the spoken word is not intended here, but rather the word in person, namely, Jesus Christ.

Contribution: God's otherness is clearly articulated and emphasized in dialectical theology. The Scriptures speak of the creatureliness of human beings and their inability to understand God's ways or to discover God without God's help. Theologically, the holiness of God expressed in the Bible does not refer primarily to God's moral rectitude but rather to God's otherness and distinctiveness. Through revelation God bridges the chasm between divinity and humanity without obliterating completely the chasm.

The christological focus of the dialectical theologians is highly commendable. Jesus Christ is undoubtedly the center and circumference of Christians' expressions of God's mystery and revelatory presence. The claim that God (the Son) chose to identify with humanity by becoming a human being is the ground on which Christianity's uniqueness rests. The emphasis on Jesus Christ as the locus of God's revelation helped in the rediscovery of the earliest Christians' devotion to Jesus and also the orthodox Christology that described Jesus as fully God and fully human. Some dialectical theologians, particularly Barth, were highly critical of liberal theologians who denied that Jesus Christ was ontologically divine.

Problems: Avery Dulles notes that theologians from both the Roman Catholic and Protestant camps were highly suspicious of the dialectical interpretation of God's revelation. One major criticism leveled against this view is the ambivalence that surrounds the way proponents of this view work out the dialectic between God and human beings. "With apparent boldness," Dulles writes, "these theologians insist on the word of God as the norm that judges all human words, but then they add that the word of God is

---

40. Barth, *CD*, 1/2, 750.

41. Hart, "Revelation," 46.

never accessible except in deficient human words."[42] Dialectical theologians are accused of inconsistency and incoherence. If God remains hidden, a mystery and wholly other even after God has revealed God's self, then can we say that divine revelation has occurred at all? According to Dulles, the dialectical view of revelation seems to have failed to bridge the chasm or the "'infinite qualitative difference' between God and creatures; it leaves God unrevealed."[43]

Some versions of the dialectical presence view fail to account for God's revelatory acts in the form of speech. The Old Testament is filled with instances of God introducing God's self and God's expectations for humanity through words. The earliest followers of Jesus Christ also believed that God sometimes unveils God's self and God's relationship with Jesus Christ through speech (Mark 1:11; 9:17). Barth, whose view of God's revelation and God's word are influential in many theological communities, addresses some of these criticisms, as the excerpt below demonstrates.

> God reveals Himself. He reveals Himself *through Himself*. He reveals *Himself*. If we really want to understand revelation in term of its subject, i.e., God, then the first thing we have to realize is that this subject, God, the Revealer, is identical with His act in revelation and also identical with its effect....
>
> According to Scripture God's revelation is God's own direct speech which is not to be distinguished from the act of speaking and therefore is not to be distinguished from God Himself, from the divine I which confronts man in this act in which it says Thou to him. Revelation is *Dei loquentis persona* [the person of God speaking].
>
> From the standpoint of the comprehensive concept of God's Word it must be said that here in God's revelation God's Word is identical with God Himself. Among the three forms of the Word of God [preached, written, revealed] this can be said unconditionally and with strictest propriety only of revelation. It can be said of Holy Scripture [the *written* word of God] and Church proclamation [the *preached* word of God] as well, but not so unconditionally and directly. For if the same can and must be said of them too, we must certainly add that their identity with God is an indirect one. Without wanting to deny or even limit their character as God's Word we must bear in mind that the Word of God is mediated here, first through the human persons of the prophets and apostles who receive it and pass it on, and then through the human persons of its expositors and preachers, so that Holy Scripture and proclamation must always become God's Word in order to be it. If the Word

42. Dulles, *Models of Revelation*, 94.
43. Ibid.

of God is God Himself even in Holy Scripture and Church proclamation, it is because this is so in the revelation to which they bear witness. In understanding God's Word as the Word preached and written, we certainly do not understand it as God's Word to a lesser degree. But we understand the same Word of God in its relation to revelation. On the other hand, when we understand it as revealed, we understand it apart from such relations, or rather as the basis of the relations in which it is also the Word of God. We thus understand it as indistinguishable from the event in virtue of which it is the one Word of God in those relations, and therefore as indistinguishable from God's direct speech and hence from God Himself. It is this that—we do not say distinguishes, since there is no question of higher rank or value—but rather characterizes revelation in comparison with Holy Scripture and Church proclamation.[44]

Question: What does this text reveal about Barth's view of God's revelation and also his view of the relationship between the threefold Word of God?

Revelation as New Awareness

Description: Revelation, according to this view, is "a transcendent fulfillment of the inner drive of the human spirit toward a fuller consciousness."[45] It is a "divine summons to transcend one's present perspectives."[46] In other words, divine revelation is not something an individual *receives* as a passive participant in God's act of revealing but rather something an individual *discovers.* The difference between *revelation as new awareness* and *revelations as inner experience* is that in the latter God intrudes or breaks into the consciousness of an individual in order to reveal God's self to the individual. In the former, an individual progressively recognizes and discovers divine presence. Dulles writes, "Revelation, then, should not be understood as an insertion of fully articulated divine truths into the continuum of human knowledge, but rather as the process by which God, working within history and human tradition, enables his spiritual creatures to achieve a higher level of consciousness."[47]

Founders of religions are, according to the new awareness view of revelation, individuals whose consciousness of God rose to the level where they experienced God in extraordinary ways. John Hick puts Jesus Christ

44. Barth, *CD* 1/1, 296, 304–5.
45. Dulles, *Models of Revelation*, 98.
46. Ibid., 187.
47. Ibid., 100.

in this category. He writes, "I see the Nazarene, then, as intensely and overwhelmingly conscious of the reality of God. He was a man of God, living in the unseen presence of God, and addressing God as *abba*, father. His spirit was open to God and his life a continuous response to the divine love as both utterly gracious and utterly demanding. He was powerfully God-conscious that his life vibrated, as it were, to the divine life; and as a result his hands could heal the sick, and the 'poor in spirit' kindled to new life in his presence."[48]

In the new awareness view of revelation, an individual will realize his or her full potential as a human being when his or her consciousness is raised to discover new vistas and horizons for responding to life's ultimate questions: How are we here? What is humanity? Does life possess meaning and purpose? In the new awareness view, revelation is ongoing. And as an ongoing process, "revelation has no fixed content. . . . It activates the imagination and thereby contributes to the restricting of experience and to the transformation of self and world."[49]

Contributions: The major contribution of this view to Christian theology is its answers to the question, does God reveal God's self outside of the Scriptures? The other views impose a limitation on the timing of God's revelation. The *new awareness* view rejects this limitation and contends that God's revelation occurred in the past, is happening in the present, and will continue to happen. If God's revelation is closely related to God's offer of salvation to humanity, and it is possible that God saves people today who do not have access to the Bible, it follows that God's self-revelation is not limited to the revelatory acts of God that are witnessed in the Bible. Christians who belong to denominations that emphasize religious experience of the divine, prophetic utterances, and visions will resonate with this view. In Africa, for example, the churches that are growing numerically are the churches that emphasize these forms of religious experience.

Problems: This view is undoubtedly too subjective. Like the *inner experience* view, it is grounded in personal religious experience. Given how hard it is to define the nature of religious experience and also to independently verify a religious experience, it is extremely difficult to see how revelation, as construed in this view, can function as a reliable and universal reference point for interpreting God and God's relationship with the world. The *new awareness* view of revelation presents us with a form of Christianity that lacks a concrete reference point. "It seems to imply," Dulles argues, "that Christians

48. Hick, "Jesus and the World Religions," 172.
49. Dulles, *Models of Revelation*, 109.

today can no longer be satisfied by the revelation given in biblical times, and that the early Christians had only a preparatory revelation in comparison with modern Christians."[50] When pushed to its logical conclusion, the *new awareness* view can lead to a vision of religious pluralism that threatens the uniqueness of Christian claims about God's revelation in Jesus Christ. Also, as Dulles has pointed out, this view confuses God's revelation with human beings' experience of God: "The prophets and apostles sharply distinguish between divine revelation and the deliverances of their own consciousness. For them, revelation is closely identified with a specific message, which is to be proclaimed as the word of God."[51]

Revelation as Symbolic Mediation

Description: After examining the preceding five views, Avery Dulles offers symbolic mediation as a better way of understanding the self-disclosure of an invisible and transcendent God. For Dulles, the revelation of a transcendent God is always mediated through symbols. He argues that "revelation never occurs in a purely interior experience of an unmediated encounter with God. It is always mediated through symbols—that is to say, through an externally perceived sign that works mysteriously on the human consciousness so as to suggest more than it can clearly describe or define. Revelation symbols are those which express and mediate God's self-communication."[52] Dulles defines a symbol as a "sign pregnant with a plentitude of meaning which is evoked rather than explicitly stated."[53] He argues that in the religious sphere three types of symbols exist. They are "cosmic or natural symbols (such as the sun), personal or historical symbols (such as David and Davidic monarchy [or Jesus Christ and the cross]), and artistic symbols (such as temples and icons)."[54]

Contributions: The strengths of the symbolic mediation view of revelation lie in its understanding of the purpose of revelation. Dulles describes four characteristics of a symbol that synchronize with the characteristics and tasks of revelation. First, he argues that the word *symbol* gives a participatory knowledge because it draws the observer into a wide range of meanings and values that it opens up.[55] This characteristic of a symbol, Dulles

50. Ibid., 112.
51. Ibid., 111–12.
52. Ibid., 131.
53. Ibid., 132.
54. Ibid., 133.
55. Ibid., 136.

contends, is relevant to revelation because an act of self-disclosure demands participatory knowledge. "To accept the Christian revelation," he writes, "is to involve oneself in a community of faith and thus to share in the way of life marked out by Jesus."[56]

Second, a symbol has the capacity to transform the seeker that encounters it. Like a symbol, revelation "is transformative, for it introduces us into a new spiritual world, shifts our horizons, our perspectives, our point of view."[57] An icon of the Trinity that reflects the life of fellowship of God the Father, the Son, and the Holy Spirit has the capacity to transform a worshipper's understanding of a life of fellowship within Christian communities.

Third, a symbol empowers and motivates people to make commitments. For example, the call to arise and the quest for unity symbolically embedded in the post-apartheid national anthem of South Africa has the capacity to inspire people within and outside of South Africa to stand up against injustice and dehumanization. In a similar manner, revelation "has an impact on the commitments and behavior of those who receive it."[58] Christians who encounter God's self-sacrificing love in and through Jesus Christ may be inspired (and ought to be inspired) to give themselves as gifts in order to become good news to others who may not share their religious convictions.

Fourth, a symbol also has the capacity to "introduce us into realms of awareness not normally accessible to discursive thought."[59] As humans, we have the ability to experience things that may lose their vividness and sense of awe when we attempt to express such experiences with words. Dulles argues that "revelation gives insight into mysteries that reason can in no way fathom. . . . Revelation is itself a mystery inasmuch as it is the self-communication of the God who 'dwells in unapproachable light' (1 Tim 6:16)."[60]

Problems: Three major criticisms can be marshaled against Dulles' *symbolic mediation* view of revelation. First, it is not entirely clear, at least in the way he articulates this view, how it differs substantively from the other views of revelation he examined. This view and the preceding five views are not mutually exclusive. With slight modifications, the views can adapt to and also utilize the *symbolic mediation* view. Second, William Thompson has pointed out Dulles' failure to articulate clearly a satisfying theory of "how the Divine and the human coparticipate in the drama of experience, and of

56. Ibid., 138.
57. Ibid.
58. Ibid.
59. Ibid., 137.
60. Ibid., 138.

how this coparticipation engenders varying kinds of symbolism or symbolic differentiation."[61] Third, the exclusivity underlying Dulles' *symbolic mediation* view is troubling. He fails to explain whether prior to the establishments of Judaism and Christianity, God revealed God's self and enabled people to live, however distorted their understanding of God's revelation might have been, in accordance with God's intended purpose. Dulles does not explain whether people living and dying today without any access to Christianity and Judaism have been barred from birth to encounter and experience God's revelation. The key question here is: Is God's self-disclosure limited to the mediated symbols that are in the Christian Bible and expressed by the Christian church?

The Accessibility of God's Revelation

The issue of the accessibility of God's self-revelation is central to Christian theology because it touches on key Christian doctrines, such as God's love and human salvation. Who has access to God's self-disclosure? Christian theologians, especially Roman Catholics and Protestants, are accustomed to classifying God's revelation into the categories of "general" and "special." However, Protestant and Roman Catholic theologians differ in the ways they imagine the nature and purpose of general and special revelation.

FOCUS QUESTION:
Do all people have access
to God's revelation?

General (or Natural) Revelation

The word *general* is used in two related senses in this context. First, it refers to the loci of this form of revelation, namely, nature and human conscience. These loci are open to all people to see and use. Second, the word *general* is used to describe the broad and non-intimate nature of the information about God gained through this form of revelation.

General revelation refers to God's revelatory acts embedded in God's creation. This view of God's revelation operates with the assumption that the economy of God's self-disclosure begins with the creation and moves toward redemption and consummation. Theologians who defend general revelation cite the words of the psalmist in Psalms 8 and 19 and the words of the Apostle Paul in Romans 1:18–38. These texts, they argue, show that

61. Thompson, review of *Models of Revelation*, 358.

the creation, which is God's handiwork, bears witness to God's existence and sovereignty. *General revelation* is imprinted in nature as a whole and in human beings who, as the image-bearers of God (Gen 1:26–27), are created with a sense of divinity (*sensus divinitatis*). In other words, the idea or concept of God is innate in all human beings. The sixteenth-century French theologian John Calvin was one of the key figures who appealed to the existence of a *sensus divinitatis* in their defense of general revelation. Calvin writes, "Men of sound judgment will always be sure that a sense of divinity which can never be effaced is engraved upon men's minds. Indeed, the perversity of the impious, who though they struggle furiously are unable to extricate themselves from the fear of God, is abundant testimony that this conviction, namely, that there is some God, is naturally inborn in all, and is fixed deeply within, as it were in the very marrow."[62] Sin has distorted the innate knowledge of God in human beings but has not eradicated completely the ability of human beings to know God (Acts 14: 16–17). Human beings can recognize the existence of God because they are born with the capacity to do so; they can also exhibit some characteristics that point them in the direction of God's character because they are created in God's image (Gen 1: 26).

By reflecting on nature, human beings may be able to discern that God exists and also discover some of God's characteristics. However, the awareness of God and the knowledge of God gained through reflection on nature do not lead the observer to an intimate knowledge of God or salvation. John Calvin articulated this view in its clearest form. In his discussion on Romans 1:20, Calvin contends, "We conceive that there is a Deity; and then we conclude, that whoever he may be, he ought to be worshipped: but our reason here fails, because it cannot ascertain who or what sort of being God is."[63] In order for the observer of nature to gain personal and intimate knowledge of God, he or she must encounter God's special revelation.

Special Revelation

Special revelation, unlike general revelation, is not found in every aspect of God's creation. It is located in select events and actions of God. In this form of God's revelation, God unveiled God's self through speech (through the prophets) and by means of *theophanies* (God's appearance in humanlike or non-humanlike forms—e.g., an angel, a "flame of fire," a whirlwind; see Gen 16:13; Exod 3:2; Job 38:1). Also, God's intervention to undo human misery (such as the liberation of the people of Israel from their Egyptian

62. Calvin, *Institutes of the Christian Religion*, 1.3.3.
63. Calvin, *Commentaries*, 19:71.

slave masters) is included in this category. The life and work of Jesus Christ is considered the climax of God's special self-disclosure. However, the Bible, because of God's involvement in its composition, retains the status of final authority and the norm for God's revelatory acts. The table below is a comparison of general and special revelation.

General Revelation	Special Revelation
Meaning of "general": It is intended to be accessible to all people and to reveal general things about God.	*Meaning of "special"*: It is not intended to be accessible to all. It refers to the specific ways in which God has chosen to reveal God's self.
Loci: The natural order of creation and human consciousness	*Loci*: God's special acts (such as the liberation of the people of Israel from their oppressors, and the Incarnation) and God's inspired Word (the Bible).
Means of access: Intuition and rational deduction (Rom 1:20)	*Means of access*: Illumination of the Holy Spirit (1 Cor 2:14)
Purpose: To unveil God's existence, power, providence (Acts 14:16–17), and judgment (Rom 1:18–32)	*Purpose*: (*a*) To reveal God personally, (*b*) to reveal God's remedies for human sin, and (*c*) to provide the appropriate outlook to interpret general revelation
Limitations: (*a*) It is distorted by sin; (*b*) it does not have the capacity to redress humanity's inability (a result of sin) to adequately understand God's relationship with the world; (*c*) it does not reveal God personally; and (*d*) it leads people to merely guess at the identity of the maker of the world.	*Limitations*: It is not available to all people. Although there is no consensus on the actual scope of special revelation, the majority of people who use this classification argue that, again, it is not available to all.

The Purpose of God's Revelation

Salvific

Discussions on the nature of God's revelation normally occur in the context of salvation. In such discussions, the relationship between God's act of unveiling God's self and God's act of healing and saving sinful human beings is defined. While some theologians believe that God's revelation is inherently salvific, others

FOCUS QUESTION:
What does God intend to achieve by disclosing God's self to humanity?

distinguish God's revelation from God's salvific acts. Some theologians, however, argue that God's revelatory acts point a class of people to *God's judgment* but lead others to *God's salvation*.

Many Protestant thinkers contend that general revelation does not have the capacity to bring salvation to humanity (i.e., it is non-salvific). It merely leads people to knowledge *about* God. "The revelation of God that is apprehended by looking at the expanse of the heavens," James Hoffmeier writes, "or any part of God's creation, is limited to providing veiled information about God's creation, but not what is necessary to know God in any intimate or salvific sense."[64] For many theologians, general revelation neither reveals God's relational nature nor communicates what God expects from human beings. General revelation leads people to guess who God really is and what God desires for humanity but does not lead to a saving knowledge, which can be attained only by means of special revelation. General revelation also renders sinful humanity (including those who do not have access to special revelation) guilty before God. While God's revelation manifested in creation cannot lead sinful human beings to an intimate and salvific knowledge of God, it does render them inexcusable before the bar of God. "It hence clearly appears," John Calvin writes, "what the consequence is of having this evidence—that men cannot allege any thing before God's tribunal for the purpose of showing that they are not justly condemned."[65]

Some theologians, on the contrary, argue that general revelation can provide sufficient knowledge of the nature and character of God. This is the assumption of those theologians who propound and defend natural theology, which contends that rational human beings may gain true and intimate knowledge of God through *reason alone* and without a prior knowledge of the Bible. Such theologians, as Millard Erickson observes, insist that the "truth about God is actually present within creation, not projected upon it by a believer who already knows from other sources, such as the Bible."[66] They also contend that human beings (even in their sinful state) have the ability to correctly interpret God's acts by reflecting upon creation. This ability, in the words of Emil Brunner, is dependent upon God's "preserving grace," which "does not abolish sin but abolishes the worst consequences of sin."[67]

Some theologians admit the existence of general or universal revelation but reject natural theology. They argue that sin has affected general

---

64. Hoffmeier, "Heavens Declare the Glory of God," 17.

65. Calvin, *Commentaries*, 19:71.

66. Erickson, *Christian Theology*, 181.

67. Brunner, "Nature and Grace," 28.

revelation in two ways. First, it attracted God's curse (Gen 3:17–19). Since creation is under God's curse, creation's testimony about God is distorted.[68] Second, sin has impaired the ability of sinful human beings (who do not yet have access to special revelation) to correctly understand and interpret the witness of nature to God's existence. Therefore, God's special revelation is required in order for sinful human beings to achieve adequate understanding of God's revelation. Against the validity of natural theology, some of these theologians argue that even if any of the *theistic arguments* (arguments presented as proofs of God's existence constructed apart from Scripture) survive all rebuttals, natural theology still will be unable to say convincingly whether a personal being created the world. Also, it certainly will be unable to demonstrate convincingly that the God who created the world is the God whose mode of existence includes the Incarnation, the act of God's *Logos* (Word) becoming a human being—Jesus of Nazareth, the Christ.

Some theologians deny both general revelation and natural theology, among them Karl Barth. In a now famous exchange with his colleague Emil Brunner, Barth said "no" to general revelation and natural theology. According to Barth, "[T]he image of God in man is totally destroyed by sin. Every attempt to assert a general revelation has to be rejected. There is no grace of creation and preservation. There are no recognizable ordinances of preservation. There is no point of contact for the redeeming action of God. The new creation is in no sense the perfection of the old but rather the replacement of the old man by the new."[69] Barth goes on to state that natural theology is, in fact, no real theology. He writes, "Really to reject natural theology means to refuse to admit it as a separate problem. Hence the rejection of natural theology can only be a side issue, arising when serious questions of real theology are being discussed."[70] God is not a part of nature that human beings can know by reflecting upon it. The otherness of God prevents human beings from coming to knowledge of God apart from God's gracious acts and gifts of *self-disclosure* and *faith*. Knowledge of God, for Barth, involves simultaneously encountering God's modes of being and acts, particularly God's self-revelation in Jesus Christ.[71]

Although God's creation *may say* something about God (just as a painting may say something about the painter), it is not in itself God's self-disclosure. Any knowledge of God gained by reflecting upon nature (assuming that this is possible), therefore, does not derive from God's self-revelation. Why did Paul say that human beings are inexcusable (Rom 1:20)?

---

68. Erickson, *Christian Theology*, 195.

69. Barth, "No," 74.

70. Ibid., 75–76.

71. Barth, *CD* 1/2, 25.

Was it because they failed to acknowledge God's revelation manifested in God's creation? Or was it because they failed to trace creation back to its rightful Creator after reflecting on nature? It is helpful to make a distinction between knowledge gained through reflection on creation (which technically should be classified as a form of *knowledge achieved by discovery*) and knowledge gained through *revelation*. The problem with humanity that Paul describes in Romans 1 is not that they did not come to the idea of a creator after reflecting on creation, but rather their failure to recognize its rightful Creator and to offer praise and thanks (Rom 1:18, 21). Paul locates this attitude of human beings in human selfishness, egotism, and mistrust of God (Rom 1:18, 21–22). God's self-disclosure is therefore God's gracious speech-act that enables human beings to recognize God and also to be in relationship with God. God's self-disclosure is the remedy of the problem of humanity that Paul expresses in Romans 1.

Epistemic

A primary goal of revelation is to unveil what is hidden. Human beings can have knowledge of God's existence and actions because God reveals God's self. Christian theologians, however, almost unanimously agree that sin has distorted the ability of human beings to know God. Some theologians who use the categories of special and general revelation have argued that sin hinders human beings from gaining true and salvific knowledge of God through general revelation. Some argue that God has partially removed the effects of sin so that human beings can gain knowledge of God's existence and character through intuition and reflection on nature. While some maintain that the knowledge of God gained through general revelation is not salvific, others contend that it has the capacity to lead people to God's saving knowledge and have called for special revelation to be reconciled with the knowledge of nature gained through natural sciences such as physics.

Caution must be exercised whenever we make the adventurous attempt to reconcile theological knowledge with scientific knowledge. Although human beings can talk theologically about nature and God's providential acts, equating such a theological exercise with the knowledge of the world gained through the natural sciences is unnecessary. Theology and the natural sciences operate with disparate assumptions. Therefore, in the attempt to reconcile theology and natural science, their unique tasks and assumptions should not be overlooked or confused.

Some theologians, particularly those interested in apologetics and the project of defending the existence of God without recourse to the Scriptures, argue that God is the ultimate rational Being who chose to create rational human beings. For these theologians, *rationality* and *morality* are the key components of the *imago Dei* (image of God) spoken about in Genesis 1:26. Focusing on rationality, they argue that human beings can come to knowledge of God by using their rational capacity to reflect on God's creation. This argument is built on two assumptions. The first assumption is, as Emil Brunner puts it, "Wherever God does anything, he leaves the imprint of his nature upon what he does. Therefore the creation of the world is at the same time a revelation."[72] The second assumption is that human beings, as the image-bearers of God, have the capacity to recognize the imprint of God in the creation. Norman Geisler puts it in this way: "According to the Bible, human beings are made in God's image (Gen 1:27), and, therefore, they are like him in that, among other things, they are rational and moral beings. Such beings are capable of receiving a rational and moral revelation from God."[73]

To sum up, these theologians believe a *point of contact* exists between God and human beings on the grounds that there is an analogy or similarity between God and human beings. For them, human beings can come to non-intimate knowledge of God through *reason alone*. Thomas Aquinas was one medieval theologian who held this view. He argued that faith *perfects* but does not suppress reason. Without denying the necessity of *faith* in gaining knowledge of some acts of God (such as the Trinity and Incarnation), he argued that reason is a reliable means to attain the knowledge of God. For him, knowledge of God gained through faith *perfects* knowledge of God acquired through reason. He writes:

> Whatever likeness might be impressed on the human intellect would not suffice to make his essence known since it infinitely exceeds any created form; that is why God is not accessible by the intellect through created forms, as Augustine says. Nor can God be known by us in this life through purely intelligible forms which might be some likeness of him because of our intellect's connaturality with phantasms, as has been said. . . . Thus the human mind approaches knowledge of God in three ways, though it never attains to knowledge of what he is, but only that he is. First, insofar as his effectiveness in producing things is more perfectly known. Second, insofar as he is known as cause of more noble effects, which since they bear some likeness to him better display his eminence. Third, in this that he is known to be more and more distant from all those things which appear in his effects. . . . In this pursuit of this knowledge the human

72. Brunner, "Nature and Grace," 25

73. Geisler, *Systematic Theology*, 1:65.

mind is especially helped when its natural light is strengthened by a new illumination, such as the light of faith and the gifts of wisdom and understanding through which the mind is said to be raised above itself insofar as it knows God to be everything that it naturally comprehends.[74]

A similar idea is found in the teaching of the Second Vatican Council (1962–1965), which, in agreement with the First Vatican Council (1869–1870), concluded the following: "God, the beginning and end of all things, can be known with certainty from created reality by light of human reason (Rom 1:20); but the synod teaches that it is through His revelation 'that those religious truths which are by their nature accessible to human reason can be known by all men with ease, with solid certitude and with no trace of error, even in the present state of the human races.'"[75]

While some theologians cite the presence and effect of sin as the primary reason for human beings' inability to attain an undistorted knowledge of God, others focus on the otherness of God. Karl Barth was one of the key theologians who construed God's otherness as the primary reason for the inability of human beings to attain knowledge of God without God's help. Since God is "wholly other," God remains hidden even after revealing God's self. As Bruce McCormack notes, God's otherness, for Barth, entails that "in revealing himself, God makes himself to be indirectly identical with a creaturely medium of that revelation."[76] McCormack also notes that "Barth makes it quite clear that if revelation is self-revelation (and it is), then revelation means revelation of God in his entirety—*but* the whole being of God is *hidden* in a creaturely veil. Nothing of God is known directly; God remains altogether hidden. And yet, where God is truly known in his hiddenness, it is the whole of God which is known and not 'part' of God."[77] For Barth, it is God's revelation that simultaneously separates and unites God and human beings. God's revelation unveils God's *otherness* and human beings' *creatureliness*. Barth writes, "Revelation itself is needed for knowing that God is hidden and man blind. Revelation and it alone really and finally separates God and man by bringing them together. For by bringing them together it informs man about God and about himself, it reveals God as the Lord of eternity, as the Creator, Reconciler and Redeemer, and characterizes man as a creature, as a sinner, as one devoted to death."[78]

74. Aquinas, "Theology, Faith and Reason," 116–17.

75. Second Vatican Council, Dogmatic Constitution on Divine Revelation, 4.

76. McCormack, *Orthodox and Modern*, 110.

77. Ibid.

78. Barth, *CD* 1/2, 29.

Incarnational

In the chapter on Christology (discourse on the person, work, and significance of Jesus Christ) I will discuss the Incarnation in detail. Here we need say only that the doctrine of the Incarnation, as constructed by the earliest Christian ecumenical councils, states that God's *Logos* (Word), or the second person of the Trinity, became one with humanity by becoming a real human being in the person of Jesus of Nazareth. As Barth has reminded us, God's revelation must be imagined from the perspective of God, whose mode of being is Trinitarian. He writes, "The doctrine of God's three-in-oneness gives the answer to the question about the subject of the revelation attested in Holy Scripture. This answer may be summarized by saying that the revelation attested in Holy Scripture is the revelation of the God who, as the Lord, is the Father from whom it proceeds, the Son who fulfills it objectively (for us), and the Holy Spirit who fulfills it subjectively (in us)."[79] For Barth, recognizing God's self-disclosure is not grounded in a prior *analogia entis* (analogy of being) but rather in God's gracious gift of faith. God's revelation rests on God's gracious acts of unveiling God's self and the gift of faith.

The incarnational purpose of God's self-disclosure lies in God's choice to bridge the chasm between God and humanity by becoming a human being. Immanuel ("God with us"), a title given to Jesus Christ, expresses this theological claim. Christians confess that God's presence is embodied by Jesus of Nazareth, the Christ. God's revelation is intended not only to undo humanity's ignorance of God's existence and identity but also to reveal God's presence in a concrete manner that closely identifies with human beings' form of existence.

The place of Jesus in understanding God's revelation cannot be underestimated. The Scriptures expect us to imagine God's revelatory acts and interpret them in light of Jesus Christ. The author of the Epistle to the Hebrews envisages this: "In the past God spoke to our forefathers through the prophets at many times and in various ways, but in these last days he has spoken to us by his Son, whom he appointed heir of all things, and through whom he made the universe" (Heb 1:1–2, NIV; cf. Matt 11:27; John 6:46–49; Phil 2:6–8). Creatures of God can find their ultimate purpose only in God's self-revelation in the person of Jesus Christ.

---

79. Ibid., 1.

Concluding Reflections

God's revelation is God's act that is designed to reveal God's self, God's work, and God's expectations for humanity. God's revelation is God's act of unveiling or disclosing God's being, character, and action in order to accomplish a given purpose. It occurs in different modes and forms. God is the one who takes the initiative to make God's self known to humanity. We only know God because God desires so and wants to be in fellowship with us. And since God reveals God's self to us from *God's own perspective* (in the ways and forms God chooses), while we have sufficient knowledge of God, we may never have access to an exhaustive knowledge of God's self-revelation (Rom 11:33–36; 1 Cor 2:10–12). God's revelation does not guarantee an exhaustive knowledge of God. God's nature and relationship to the world cannot be known exhaustively. We need to exercise caution when speaking about the accessibility of God's revelation. We may never know with certainty who and who is not able to access God's revelation. God's revelation may challenge and query our preconceived and usually "clear" and "logical" perceptions of God.

Key Terms

Divine Revelation: God's disclosure of God's self through various means that climax in God's self-revelation in Jesus Christ.

General Revelation: the knowledge of God accepted through the natural order.

Natural Theology: holds that human beings can gain sufficient and salvific knowledge of God through the study of nature.

Special Revelation: the knowledge of God accessed through the Scriptures and redemptive acts of God.

Review Questions

1. What are the six models of revelation that are articulated by Avery Dulles?

2. How does special revelation compare to and contrast with general revelation?

3. What are the modes of God's revelation?

4. In what ways have Christians construed the accessibility and purpose of God's revelation?

Suggestions for Further Reading

Barth, Karl. *Church Dogmatics* 1/1. *The Doctrine of the Word of God.* Translated by G. W. Bromiley. 2nd ed. 1975. Reprint, Peabody, MA: Hendrickson, 2010.

Ruether, Rosemary Radford. *Sexism and God-Talk: Toward a Feminist Theology.* London: SCM, 1983.

Second Vatican Council. Dogmatic Constitution on Divine Revelation. Washington, DC: National Catholic Welfare Conference, 1965.

Warfield, Benjamin B. *The Inspiration and Authority of the Bible.* Philadelphia: Presbyterian & Reformed, 1948.

3

Christian Scripture

Many religions have sacred books or Scriptures. Christianity's sacred book is commonly known as the Bible.[1] Christians read the Bible (Scripture) not only to learn from the human authors but most importantly to hear from God. But what exactly distinguishes this book from other books written by Christians? Why are the books of the Bible regarded as sacred writings? What makes them sacred? These questions influence the discourse on the doctrine of the Bible.

"Jesus loves me—this I know, for the Bible tells me so" sums up the general attitude of Christians toward the Bible.[2] In my undergraduate days at ECWA Theological Seminary Igbaja (ETSI), in Nigeria, the question "Is it biblical?" functioned as the primary watchword students used as the test of an adequate theology. I have also encountered many Christians in Europe and North America who asked similar questions with a similar intention as my contemporaries at ETSI. Christians honor the Bible because they believe that God speaks to humanity in and through it. As Stanley Grenz has said, "Scripture is one aspect of the Spirit's mission of creating and sustaining spiritual life. He both authors and speaks through the Bible, which is ul-

---

1. "Scripture" and "Bible" are used interchangeably in this chapter.

2. These are the opening words of the popular Christian hymn "Jesus Loves Me," the lyrics of which were written by the American Anna Bartlett Warner.

timately the Spirit's book. By means of Scripture he bears witness to Jesus Christ, guides the lives of believers, and exercises authority in the church."[3]

Yet the Bible has continued to be a source of division within Christianity. Many Christians believe that the Bible is of divine origin but disagree on the extent and nature of its divineness. They also believe that it is a human book because human beings wrote it but disagree on the extent of its humanness. They derive their theological ideas from it but their theologies differ and sometimes are irreconcilable. They agree that the Bible ought to regulate the beliefs and practices of followers of Jesus Christ of all times but disagree on its specific roles in the formation of Christian identity. They also disagree on the number of books that are inspired by God. The irony of these disagreements is that they are rooted in the quest for an adequate representation of the characteristics, functions, and authority of the Bible. These issues will be discussed in this chapter.

The Characteristics of the Bible

The Bible speaks of itself in a variety of ways. Therefore, the Bible itself is an appropriate place to begin the search for its characteristics and features.

Inspired

Inspiration is a popular term that the majority of Christians readily associate with the Bible. The word *inspiration* derives from the Greek word *theopneustos*, which some translations (including the NIV, quoted below) render "God-breathed." Although the theological ideas subsumed in the word *inspiration* can be traced

> FOCUS QUESTION:
> What are the essential and distinctive features of the Bible?

to several passages in the Hebrew Bible (Old Testament) and the New Testament, it is only in Paul's second letter to Timothy that the word appears.[4] "All Scripture is God-breathed," Paul writes, "and is useful for teaching, rebuking, correcting and training in righteousness, so that the servant of God may be thoroughly equipped for every good work" (2 Tim 3:16–17, NIV) Among many other things these verses express (*a*) the origin of the (Old Testament) Scripture and (*b*) its functions in the life of the community of the people of God.

---

3. Grenz, *Theology for the Community of God*, 379.

4. Other relevant biblical texts are 2 Sam 23:2 and Acts 1:16.

Several issues need to be carefully examined before theological con-clusions are drawn from these verses. First, does Paul intend the Greek word *pasa* to be understood as "every" or "all"? The issue here is whether Paul says that the whole Bible is inspired, or instead that some sections of the Bible are inspired. If "every" is intended, each verse or portion of the Bible is inspired and therefore is "useful for teaching, rebuking, correcting and training in righteousness, so that the servant of God may be thoroughly equipped for every good work." If "all" is adopted, taken as a whole, the Bible will accomplish the preceding functions. It also suggests that some sections of the Bible may not be inspired by God and, as a result, may not be useful to Christians. Second, since in 2 Tim 3:16 the Greek verb *esti* ("is") was not used in the Greek text, should it be placed after "Scripture" ("All Scripture *is* God-breathed . . .") or after "God-breathed" ("All Scripture God-breathed *is* . . .")? If the former translation is adopted, the Bible in its entirety is inspired. But if the latter translation is adopted, only the portions of the Bible that are inspired by God will be profitable.[5] Third, the exact nature of God's act of *breathing* is not readily clear in 2 Tim 3:16–17. The relation-ship between God and Scripture, therefore, requires explanation. Did God *breathe out* the words of the Bible? Or did God *breathe into* the words of the Bible? If the former, one could conclude that the words and the content of the Bible proceeded from God or were exhaled by God. If the latter, a pos-sible conclusion is that the words of the Bible were human words that God later inspired. This means that God did not coauthor the book of the Bible. He only supervised the process. And it can also mean that the words of the Bible only *become* inspired.

Paul's intended meaning in this passage may not be totally resolved by reflecting only on these verses. A good theological practice is to look for help elsewhere in the Bible (and outside the Bible) where similar issues are discussed. In the New Testament, another passage that deals with the divine origin of the Bible is 2 Pet 1:20–21. In these verses, Peter wrote, "Above all, you must understand that no prophecy of Scripture came about by the prophet's own interpretation. For prophecy never had its origin in the will of man, but men spoke from God as they were carried along by the Holy Spirit" (NIV). The question that confronts the reader of these verses is, Was Peter's focus on the *origin of prophecy* or on the *origin of the interpretations of the prophecy*? The NIV leans more in the direction of the former. Con-versely, the English Standard Version (ESV) leans more in the direction of the latter: "knowing this first of all, that no prophecy of Scripture comes from someone's own interpretation" (2 Pet 1:20).

5. Knight, *Pastoral Epistles*, 444.

Clearly, Peter is attacking what he considered a bad theology. But what exactly is the theological position of Peter's opponents? Did they teach that prophecy came from human volition? Or did they resist the apostolic interpretation of some (christological) prophecies in the Bible and propound an alternative interpretation that suited their own views? Thomas Schreiner argues in favor of the latter. He writes, "Verses 16–21 fit together well as an argument if in v. 20 the opponents questioned the apostolic interpretation of prophecy, so that they rejected the parousia of Christ."[6] If Schreiner's reading of verse 20 is correct, then "both the origin of prophecy and its subsequent interpretation [by the apostles] stem from God himself."[7] Richard Bauckham, on the contrary, argues that Peter's opponents may have doubted the divine origin of prophecy and not its subsequent interpretations. "Since v. 20 is certainly aimed polemically against the opponents' charge that prophecy was only the prophet's own interpretation of their visions," Bauckham argues, "it is quite possible that the negative clause in v. 21 is also a specific denial of the false teacher's assertion that prophecy is of human origin."[8]

Bauckham and Schreiner agree that Peter locates the origin of the Bible in the will of God and not in the will of human beings. In another passage Peter states that Paul wrote "with the wisdom that God gave him" (2 Pet 3:15, NIV). Peter goes on to depict the writings of Paul as Scripture: "He writes the same way in all his letters, speaking in them of these matters. His letters contain some things that are hard to understand, which ignorant and unstable people distort, as they do other Scriptures, to their own destruction" (2 Pet 3:16, NIV). Peter's expectation from his readers, as Millard Erickson has noted, is "to pay heed to the prophetic words, for it is not simply humans' word, but God's word."[9]

God's inspiration of the Bible does not obliterate its humanness. Human beings who lived at certain times and in specific cultures wrote the books that now make up the Bible. Any view that denies the *humanness* of the Bible is *docetic*—it makes it a divine text containing only God's words, which *appear* to be human words. The involvement of God and human beings in the production of the Bible is analogous to the Christian belief in the human and divine natures of Jesus Christ. The primary problem of a docetic Christology (that is, a docetic doctrine of Jesus Christ) is that it denies the true humanity of Jesus Christ. It claims that Jesus Christ was a true divine being who only appeared to be a human being.

---

6. Schreiner, *1, 2 Peter, Jude*, 323.

7. Ibid., 324.

8. Bauckham, *Jude, 2 Peter*, 234.

9. Erickson, *Christian Theology*, 227.

Denying the humanity of the Bible confuses two compatible yet different constants that are at work in the writing of the books of the Bible. The first constant is the Holy Spirit. In the words of Peter, the human authors of the Bible "were carried along by the Holy Spirit" as they wrote their works. The involvement of the Holy Spirit in the writing of the Bible is the grounds for identifying the Bible with God. The Bible "repeats, conveys, or reflects the words of the living God."[10] The second constant is human agency. The Bible is also a truly human work. The following observation from Stephen Fowl is helpful: "The original texts which comprise the Bible were written by a variety of human authors (known and unknown) in diverse historical, linguistic, and cultural settings."[11]

Theologians disagree on the exact relation of the two constants (divine and human agencies) in the writing process. Are the two constants complementary? Does one of them enjoy the status of "primary" (and the other "secondary")? And how exactly did the inspiration occur? Was it mechanical or organic? These questions have given rise to a number of theories of the inspiration of the Bible. I will now summarize five major theories, outlining what each says about the role of God, the role of human beings, and the method of inspiration.

Five Theories of Inspiration

THE DICTATION THEORY

God's Role: The dictation theory states that the Holy Spirit dictated the words of the Bible and ensured that human writers wrote down exactly what was dictated to them. God suspended the cognitive activity of the writers of the Bible at the moment of writing and introduced ideas, concepts, and words into their consciousness. Louis Gaussen, for example, has contended, "It is not, as some will have it, a book which God employed men, whom he had previously enlightened, to write under his auspices. No—it is a book which he dictated to them; it is the Word of God; the Spirit of the Lord spake by its authors, and his words were upon their tongues."[12] Although many Christian theologians reject this view of inspiration, some premodern Christians accepted it as the most natural and adequate way to express God's involvement in the writing of the Bible.

---

10. Fowl, "Scripture," 346.

11. Ibid.

12. Gaussen, *Divine Inspiration of the Bible*, 49.

Human Role: Human beings were "secretaries" or "copyists" who had no freedom to alter what was dictated to them by the Holy Spirit. Adherents of this view usually reference numerous prophetic passages, especially in the Old Testament, where the prophets prefaced some of their utterances with the expressions "This is what the sovereign LORD says" (Isa 49:22) or "The sovereign LORD has given me an instructed tongue" (Isa 50:4).

Mode of Inspiration: The Holy Spirit was the primary and active agent. Human beings were passive instruments or tools in the hands of the Holy Spirit. The method of inspiration was mechanical—through dictation. This process or method of inspiration ensured that nothing God did not intend made its way into the Bible.

Criticism: This view fails to account for the unique cultural and linguistic features of the books of the Bible. For example, some of the books of the Bible were written in an elegant and polished style, while others were not. The books of the Hebrew Bible (the Old Testament) were written in archaic, standard, or *late* Hebrew dialects. If the Holy Spirit authored the entirety of the Bible through dictation, then how do we explain these differences? This view of the Bible is also *docetic*: it denies the true humanity of the Bible.

THE VERBAL AND PLENARY THEORY

God's Role: This view claims that the words of the Bible originally existed in the mind of God. Through divine revelation (understood in the propositional sense) God miraculously conveyed the words to the minds of the writers of the Bible and guided them to write down God's thoughts in their own languages. The Holy Spirit controlled the human writers of the Bible and also chose their thoughts and their words. In the words of Harold Lindsell, "Inspiration extends to all parts of the written Word of God and it includes the guiding hand of the Holy Spirit even in the selection of the words of Scripture."[13]

Human Role: In this view, the role of human beings is elevated a little higher than in the dictation theory. God was the primary agency; human beings were the secondary agency. Although God did not dictate the words of the Bible, God meticulously guided and guarded the minds and thoughts of the human authors even in their choice of words. The Holy Spirit "superintended the process of word selection and word order to the extent that

---

13. Lindsell, *Battle for the Bible*, 31.

they are capable of communicating the intended meaning of the text."[14] The guidance of the Spirit overrides and supersedes the fallibility and limitations of the human authors.

Mode of Inspiration: The process of inspiration in this view can be described as semi-mechanical. Human beings were partly passive agents. Although they used their minds, they wrote down only *what God guided them to write*. This mode of inspiration guarantees that "Scripture is not only in its content but also in its form the Word of God written."[15]

Criticism: This view, like the dictation theory, fails to account properly for the humanity of the Bible. If this theory of the Bible is adopted, the Bible is *truly* divine and *barely* human. Although theologians who hold this view have consistently argued that it differs from the dictation theory, the two views are in fact not entirely different. Both construe the sovereignty of God in a way that overrides the limitations and fallibility of the human authors at the moments they wrote down the words of the Bible. "On the original parchment," W. A. Criswell writes, "every sentence, word, line, mark, point, pen stroke, jot, and title were put there by inspiration of God."[16] Even though Criswell does not use the word *dictation*, his words seem to imply that that is what occurred.

THE DYNAMIC THEORY

God's Role: In the dynamic theory of inspiration, God ensured that human beings wrote down what God intended for them to write without choosing the words for them. The Bible, therefore, is the product of both the Holy Spirit and human beings.

Human Role: The human authors of the Bible were active in the process of divine inspiration. They chose their own words and expressed their thoughts from their experience and culture, albeit under the supervision of the Holy Spirit. As Millard Erickson writes, "The Spirit of God works by directing the writer to the thoughts or concepts, and allowing the writer's own distinctive personality to come to play in the choice of words and expressions. Thus, the writer will give expression of the divinely directed thoughts in a way uniquely characteristic of that person."[17]

14. Grenz, *Theology for the Community of God*, 398.

15. Horton, *Christian Faith*, 160.

16. Criswell, *Why I Preach that the Bible Is Literally True*, 40. See also Pierson, *Inspired Word*, 68–69.

17. Erickson, *Christian Theology*, 232.

Mode of Inspiration: This view argues that the Scripture is simultaneously truly human and truly divine.[18] The method of inspiration is *organic*—that is, God intervened in the writing process by sanctifying "the natural gifts, personalities, histories, languages, and cultural inheritance of the biblical writers."[19]

Criticism: Although this view seeks to preserve the involvement of God and human beings in the production of the Bible, it remains to be seen how it can effectively deal with the issue of primacy. Whose involvement was primary? Could any of the human authors have written anything that was not approved and sanctified by the Holy Spirit? Our answers to these questions will have significant impact on how we approach, use, and view the authority of the Bible. For example, if the Holy Spirit did not infringe upon the freedom of the human authors, it is reasonable to believe that some of them might have written down what the Holy Spirit did not authorize. If this were the case, it is also reasonable to assume that some contents of the Bible were not inspired by God. The difficulty here, of course, is how we are to determine what was and what was not approved by the Holy Spirit.

THE INTUITION THEORY

God's Role: The intuition theory of inspiration argues that God had no role whatsoever in the writing of the Bible. The authors of the Bible were geniuses who wrote from their natural capacities.

Human Role: The words of the Bible were truly human words. The authors neither needed nor used any divine assistance. Individual writers and redactors wrote or compiled their materials solely from their own experiences without any divine assistance. Since the books of the Bible are primarily religious texts, the authors' religious experiences informed the content of their books. They also had a high degree of religious insight.

Mode of Inspiration: Divine inspiration of the Bible is denied in this view. The authors of the Bible wrote their works without any supernatural help.

Criticism: This view of the Bible fails to account for the biblical passages that teach God's inspiration of the Bible (2 Tim 3:16–17; 2 Pet 1:20–21).

18. Vanhoozer, *First Theology*, 139.
19. Horton, *Christian Faith*, 163.

THE ILLUMINATION THEORY

God's Role: This view of inspiration argues that God's involvement in the production of the Bible was limited to the role of heightening the spiritual experience and intellectual abilities of the human authors.[20] In this view, then, the words and content of the Bible do not originate from God.

Human Role: Human beings were the primary authors of the books of the Bible. The words, contents, and ideas of the Bible existed in and originated from the minds and experiences of the human authors.

Mode of Inspiration: The mode of inspiration, according to this view, is illumination—God's acting, through the power of the Holy Spirit, to enable, empower, and raise the mental capacities of the human authors beyond their normal mental capacities. These acts of the Holy Spirit are necessary because sin has affected human beings' ability to adequately describe their experiences and understandings of God. However, God intervened by overcoming the effects of sin.

Criticism: The major criticism of this view is that it confuses inspiration with illumination. While these two acts of the Holy Spirit are not mutually exclusive, they are nonetheless different. Inspiration relates to the divine origin of the Bible; illumination relates to God's assistance of the readers to perceive and draw out fuller implications of the content of the Bible.

20. Erickson, *Christian Theology*, 232.

TABLE 3.1 THEORIES OF INSPIRATION

	Dictation	Verbal/Plenary	Dynamic	Intuition	Illumination
God's Role	Sole originator of the Bible	Sole originator of the Bible	Co-originator of the Bible	None—God played no role at all	A *helping role* in the production of the Bible
Human Role	Mere "secretaries"	Writers who were controlled by the Holy Spirit	Co-originator of the Bible	Sole originator of the Bible	Sole originator of the Bible
Mode or Method	Mechanical	Semi-mechanical	Organic	None	Semi-organic
Criticism	Denies the humanity of the Bible	Underemphasizes the humanity of the Bible	Does not effectively deal with the issue of primacy in the divine-human authorship	Does not properly account for what the Bible says about its divine origins	Confuses inspiration and illumination

The Inerrancy and Infallibility Views of the Bible

Although in the works of some earlier theologians "inerrancy" and "infallibility" may have been used synonymously, this is certainly no longer the case. These terms now describe two disparate views on the nature and function of the Bible. An inerrantist, one who believes that the Bible contains no factual errors in all the matters it affirms, by implication believes that the Bible does not mislead or lie in such matters. But not all theologians who believe that the Bible is infallible (trustworthy and not misleading) accept that it is inerrant (without factual and grammatical errors) in all the matters that it addresses and affirms.

Inerrancy

Inerrantists teach that the Bible is completely free from factual errors in its *autographs* (original manuscripts) in all matters it affirms, including theology, history, and science. This view was championed by Princeton theologians such as Charles A Hodge, Archibald A. Hodge, and Benjamin B. Warfield in the 1800s and 1900s. However, the view may have preceded them. Augustine of Hippo, in his letter to Jerome, warned, "For it seems to me that most disastrous consequences must follow upon our believing that anything false is found in the sacred books: that is to say, that the men by whom the Scripture has been given to us, and committed to writing, did put down in these books anything false. It is one question whether it may be at any time the duty of a good man to deceive; but it is another question whether it can have been the duty of a writer of Holy Scripture to deceive: nay, it is not another question—it is no question at all."[21] Several inerrantists share Augustine's concern.[22]

> "The Bible does not appear to be a textbook of history, science, or mathematics; yet when the writers of Scripture spoke of matters embraced in these disciplines, they did not indite error; they wrote what was true."
>
> —Lindsell, *The Battle for the Bible*

The inerrantist view incorporates a variety of subviews or positions. *Strict inerrantists* argue that the Bible is without any factual errors (in its autographs) on any matters it addresses, including science, measurement, history, and geography. For them, no factual or content errors mar the autographs. The inspiration of the Holy Spirit prevented such errors from

21. Augustine, *Letters*, 28.3 (*NPNF*[1] 5:252).
22. Ryrie, *Basic Theology*, 88.

entering the original texts. Strict inerrantists contend that apparent errors in the Bible are resolvable. *Moderate* or *limited inerrantists*, however, claim that the Bible is without errors in its autographs whenever it speaks about issues relating to faith and practice. For them, the main purpose of the Bible is to lead humanity to God's salvific acts. It follows that the Bible may contain even in its autographs discrepancies or errors on subjects such as history, science, and geography.

Harold Lindsell, an advocate of the strict inerrantist position, describes the essential claims of inerrancy in this way: "The Bible in all of its parts constitutes the written Word of God to man. The Word is free from all error in its original autographs. . . . It is wholly trustworthy in matters of history and doctrine. However limited may have been their knowledge, and however much they may have erred when they were not writing the sacred Scripture, the authors of Scripture, under the guidance of the Holy Spirit, were preserved from making factual, historical, scientific, or other errors."[23] God's involvement in the writing of the books that make up the Scripture ensured that it was completely error-free.

For the inerrantists, the reliability of the Bible is at stake when its inerrancy is denied. Should Christians trust that God has spoken and is speaking through the Bible if it contains factual errors? I will return to this question later. Here I will highlight the arguments inerrantists put forward in support of their position.

First, *God's infallibility requires an inerrant autographic Scripture.* Christians believe and have confidence in God's faithfulness, trustworthiness, and infallibility. God has not failed and cannot fail in any way (Titus 1:2). For the inerrantists, the Bible that God breathed out (or inspired) could not err. Some claim that the inspiration extends to all matters—theological, grammatical, moral, historical, and scientific. If this were not the case, then the Bible merely contains the Word of God and cannot in itself be the Word of God. But God's character is at stake, the inerrantists argue. Since God cannot err, the people whom God inspired to speak on God's behalf cannot err.[24] To put it differently, the words of the Bible in the autographs are God's words. If they contained any errors then we should have to conclude that God could err. Inerrantists warn that this is a slippery slope. They contend that since God inspired or breathed out the words of the Bible, it is inerrant; God breathed out the Scripture that was textually and factually error-free.

Second, *God's sovereignty warrants an inerrant autographic Scripture.* Some inerrantists also argue that God's sovereignty overrides or

---

23. Lindsell, *Battle for the Bible*, 30–31.

24. Boyd and Eddy, *Across the Spectrum*, 18.

overshadows the involvement of human authors. The freedom of the human authors was not absolute. It was freedom within the boundary of God's sovereignty and power. Although fallible human beings wrote the books of the Bible, the sovereignty of God ensured that their fallibility did not have any negative impact on its content. Some inerrantists accept grammatical errors but reject content errors in the Bible. Some limit inerrancy only to matters of salvation and revelation.

Third, *Scripture may contain apparent errors but not real errors.* Some inerrantists concede that the Scripture contains apparent errors or discrepancies in the extant manuscripts but deny that genuine errors exist in the autographs. Since there are no extant autographs it is difficult to judge whether the discrepancies were of the copyists' making. What is clear, however, is that the extant manuscripts contain discrepancies and errors. As Warfield observes, "Everybody knows that no book was ever printed, much less hand-copied, into which some errors did not intrude in the process; and as we do not hold the author responsible for these in an ordinary book, neither ought we to hold God responsible for them in this extraordinary book which we call the Bible. It is the Bible that we declare to be 'of infallible truth'—the Bible that God gave to us, not the corruptions and slips which scribes and printers have given us, some of which are in every copy."[25]

The Bible contains some historical and numerical discrepancies. Let me highlight two examples—one from the Old Testament and the other from the New Testament. First, while Gen 1:11–12 states that God created vegetation on the third day (which implies that the creation of vegetation preceded the creation of Adam and Eve), Gen 2:5 indicates that vegetation appeared after Adam was created. Second, although the Gospel of Matthew records the account of Jesus healing two blind men at Jericho (20:29–34), the Gospel of Mark, which in all likelihood was written before Matthew, states that Jesus healed a blind man named Bartimaeus as Jesus and his disciples were leaving Jericho (10:46–52).

Many inerrantists take the apparent errors or discrepancies in the Bible seriously. They devote enormous time to the task of explaining the errors in the Bible. Some suggestions on how to deal with the apparent errors or discrepancies include (*a*) recognizing that the authors of the Bible wrote *phenomenologically*—that is, they wrote down God's revelation in the ways things appeared to them; (*b*) recognizing that the authors used uninspired sources in their books; and (*c*) learning to patiently explore all possible explanations before coming to the conclusion that there are irreconcilable contradictions in the Bible.

25. Warfield, "Inerrancy of the Original Autographs," 270.

Theologians who reject the inerrantist view of the Bible have pointed out several problems with it. Three are noteworthy. First, the inerrantist view assigns to the Bible some tasks that it is not designed and intended to perform, such as to speak authoritatively on scientific matters. Since the authors wrote primarily from and for their religious contexts, one could argue that the Bible was written exclusively for theological and moral matters. Second, the inerrantist view is an example of (or comes dangerously close to) the error of docetism in that it strips the Bible of its true humanity. In other words, it renders the Bible truly divine but barely human. It fails to account properly for the fallibility of the human authors who wrote the Bible. Third, some theologians have argued that the inerrantists erroneously identify the Bible with God's self-revelation. Karl Barth, for example, rejects the identification of God's revelation with the Bible. He argues that the Bible witnesses and points humanity to God's self-revelation (Jesus Christ).[26]

Infallibility

The infallibilist view rejects the inerrantists' belief in the absence of factual errors in the autographs. However, like the inerrantist view, the infallibilist view argues that since God does not lie (Titus 1:2), inspiration (2 Tim 3:16–17; 2 Pet 1:21) ensures that the Bible is a trustworthy and unfailing guide for faith and practice. Infallibilists concede genuine errors and contradictions in the Scripture, which may be attributed to the authors of the Bible. Since fallible human beings authored the Bible, it is reasonable to conclude that it has a capacity for error. Below I summarize the major arguments in support of the infallibility position.

First, *God's infallibility guarantees the Bible's trustworthiness in matters of faith and practice alone.* For many infallibilists, God inspired the Bible in order to make the reader wise enough to receive salvation (2 Tim 3:15; cf. Rom 15:4–6; 1 Cor 10:6–13). The Bible unerringly leads people to God. To extend the task of the Bible beyond this scope is misleading and counterproductive. The authors of the Bible, because of their limited knowledge of certain issues or subject matters, expressed and also affirmed some erroneous historical accounts and false scientific statements as true. But this should not make the reader distrust the Bible, because it is not designed to be a scientific or historical text. The authority of the Bible does not depend on its inerrancy but rather on God, who inspired it and who continues to use it, through the Holy Spirit, to speak to the reader about God's providence and involvement in the world.

26. Barth, *CD* 1/1, 111.

Second, *the Bible does not teach inerrancy*. This does not simply mean there are no scriptural proof-texts, that is, passages in the Bible that explicitly state "there are no errors in the Bible." Rather, taken as a whole, the Bible does not presuppose or make any indirect claims to its inerrancy. As Stephen Davis argues, "The Bible does not teach inerrancy, nor does inerrancy seem to be presupposed or implied by what it does teach."[27] It is a mistake to assume that the inspiration of the Bible necessarily warrants or presupposes its inerrancy. Given what we know about the origins of the Bible—the authors freely used preexisting sources ("older documents, public registers, literary or liturgical sources, oral tradition")—it is unwarranted to conclude that the Bible is inerrant in all matters it affirms because it is inspired.[28]

Third, *God speaks through fallible means*. The Bible does not lose its authority because it contains some errors. The authority of the Bible lies primarily in God's gracious act of speaking to the reader through its words, enabling him or her to experience God's act of reconciling the fallen creation to God's self. God can declare or make holy what is impure and use it to accomplish what God desires. God can use a fallible text to accomplish God's purposes. We may call this divine act "imputed sanctification" to indicate that it is God who ultimately makes something holy. Protestant theologians use a similar concept—"imputed righteousness"—to describe God's act of declaring a sinner to be righteous on account of the righteousness of Jesus Christ (Rom 3:21–22).

The charges against the infallibilist view of the Bible may be summarized as follows. It may lead to a rejection of the authority and trustworthiness of the Bible. If the Bible contains factual errors in any of the matters the authors address and affirm, then how can one determine whether it speaks truthfully about any matters relating to God's revelation and God's work of salvation? Inerrantists contend that the infallibilist view also undermines the sovereignty, veracity, and infallibility of God. "The charge that Scripture teaches error," Clark Pinnock writes, "is tantamount to a denial of inspiration. For if God, who does not lie, is the Author of it, the text possesses complete veracity."[29] If God inspired (breathed out) a text that is errant, it follows that God also is fallible. The Bible, however, attests to God's veracity and infallibility (John 17:17; Heb 6:18).

Some theologians are critical of both the inerrancy and infallibility views, which aim to present the Bible as a trustworthy or inerrant text containing the deposit of God's revelatory message. Stanley Grenz, for

---

27. Davis, *Debate about the Bible*, 61.

28. Ibid., 62.

29. Pinnock, *Biblical Revelation*, 79.

example, argues that the views of inerrancy and infallibility misconstrue how the words of the Bible can function as divine speech. They run the risk of "collapsing the Spirit into words of the Bible, or more specifically, into our exegesis of the words of the Bible."[30] Grenz argues that a Christian theology of the Bible must avoid exchanging "the dynamic of the ongoing movement of the Spirit speaking to the community of God's people through the pages of the Bible for our attempts to exegete and synthesize its contents."[31] The Bible, for him, is authoritative not because "it is either inspired or inerrant" but rather because it is an instrument of the Holy Spirit that provides the interpretative framework for the lives of the people of God.[32] The Holy Spirit uses the words of the Bible to call sinful humanity into the new humanity God has enacted and inaugurated in the person of Jesus Christ. "Through Scripture," Grenz argues, "the Spirit works to shape our identity and existence as the community of Christ and as individual members of that people. And the Spirit seeks to guide us as to how we should respond to the situations of life in our world."[33]

The Canonicity of the Bible

Self-identity and hermeneutics (a way of interpreting a text) were central in the process of the formation of the biblical canon. Both in rabbinic Judaism and early Christianity, self-identity (or self-definition) and hermeneutics functioned as the two interrelated grids for the selection or rejection of the writings that were considered for the status of *authoritative sacred texts* or Scriptures.[34] One's view of what a Christian community should be and one's reading (or interpretation) of the writings of the earliest leaders of rabbinic Judaism and early Christianity, for example, will influence greatly one's view of the biblical canon. Michael Holmes has pointed out that the hermeneutics of Marcion (c. 85–160) "led him to accept as authoritative only a limited number of Christian documents (and only in a revised form), a collection that is widely considered the first 'canon' of Christian writings."[35]

FOCUS QUESTION:
What criteria were used for the selection of the books of the Bible?

30. Grenz, "Agenda for Evangelical Theology in the Postmodern Context," 10.
31. Ibid.
32. Ibid.
33. Ibid., 11.
34. Holmes, "Biblical Canon," 417.
35. Ibid..

The issue of canonization informs theologians' discussions on the nature of the Bible. Although originally in its Semitic root it means "reed" or "stalk" (from the Hebrew *qāneh*), the word *canon* has come to mean, when applied to the Bible, the accepted body of books believed to be inspired by God, which Christians should use for ethical, theological, and moral guidance. While some Christians use *canon* to express the idea of the list of authoritative religious writings, others use *canon* to express the idea of an authoritative list of religious writings. Many Christians also use the word *canon* to indicate the closure of God's inspired books, signaling that no books may be added to the already closed and fixed collection of sacred books. The early church theologians also spoke of the "canon of faith" or "canon of truth" to describe the "core beliefs that identified the Christian community, its understanding of the will of God, and it mission."[36]

The canonization process was a messy one, which partly explains the differences in the existing biblical canons. Christians borrowed the idea of canonical texts from the Jews, who read certain texts during worship in the synagogue. The process of the Jewish canonization of sacred books was also a messy one. Historians have disagreed in their conclusions as to when the Alexandrian Jews and the Palestinian Jews assembled their canons. But in spite of this messiness, theologians, biblical scholars, and historians have pointed out some criteria that might have been used by the ancient Jews and early Christian churches in deciding which books made the list of normative books, the canon.

Although some scholars cite Matt 23:34–35 and Luke 11:48–51 as evidence of a complete and fixed Jewish canon that followed a tripartite formula—Law, Prophets, and Writings—many reject this conclusion. Lee Martin McDonald has argued that these New Testaments passages only "give evidence for an emerging tripartite biblical canon in the first century BCE" and that the full development of these three categories became "a reality for Judaism in the second century CE and even later for the church."[37] The canon of the Jewish or Hebrew Bible was most probably assembled in the mid-second century BCE.

Paul Wegner has argued that at least four important criteria determined the Old Testament canon. First, *non-internal contradiction*—the books must not contain internal contradictions. Second, *prophetic authorship*—the book should be written by a prophet or someone recognized as having divine authority. Third, *claim to inspiration*—the book must be believed to have originated through inspiration from God. Finally, *universal acceptance*—the

36. McDonald, *Biblical Canon*, 50.
37. Ibid., 100.

book must have been accepted "by the Jews as authoritative material."[38] The books that met all or the majority of these criteria were considered for the canon. These criteria, however, should not suggest an unequivocal process in the conception and selection of the Jewish Scriptures. Michael Holmes, for example, has argued that "during the Christian movement's early years, there apparently did not exist a 'closed' canon of Hebrew scriptures for it to take over."[39]

The formation of the New Testament canon, like that of the Jewish (or Old Testament) canon, was a long and messy process. Several early church leaders quoted from or alluded to some of the New Testament books as authoritative texts in their writings. For example, Clement of Rome (c. 60–100 CE) made references to about six New Testament books, namely, Acts, Romans, 1 Corinthians, Ephesians, Titus, Hebrews, and 1 Peter.[40] Eusebius of Caesarea (c. 260–340 CE) in his *Life of Constantine* reveals that Constantine (r. 306–337 CE) sent a letter to him, directing him to produce and send fifty copies of the Bible to Constantinople.[41] Emperor Constantine's request suggests the existence of a biblical canon. Unfortunately, Eusebius did not enumerate the books that constituted the Bible during this period. Athanasius (c. 296–373 CE), the Alexandrian theologian, included all twenty-seven books of the New Testament in his canon. He enumerated them to his parishioners in 367 CE in his thirty-ninth Festal (Easter) Letter.[42] The references to some lists of books in the writings of these church leaders, however, could well represent circumstantial accumulations rather than deliberate accumulations.[43]

Wegner has articulated four criteria that were used to determine the New Testament canon.[44] First, *apostolic authorship*—the books that were written by the apostles were accepted, partly on the grounds that they were eyewitnesses of the life and ministry of Jesus Christ. Second, the *rule of faith*—the accepted body of apostolic teachings, some of which were recorded in the earliest writings of the apostles (such as the undisputed letters of Paul and the Gospels), was used to evaluate the authenticity of other books. Third, *universal acceptance*—in the early church, Christian

---

38. Wegner, *Journey from Texts to Translations*, 117.

39. Holmes, "Biblical Canon," 409.

40. Wegner, *Journey from Texts to Translations*, 141.

41. Eusebius, *Life of Constantine*, 4.36:166–67. The letter might have been written around 315 CE.

42. Wegner, *Journey from Texts to Translations*, 144.

43. Holmes, "Biblical Canon," 415–16.

44. Wegner, *Journey from Texts to Translations*, 147–50.

leaders in the Western Roman Empire and in the Eastern Roman Empire often disagreed with each other on theological issues. The books that were accepted as authoritative by Church leaders from both empires were considered during the process of canonization. Lastly, *self-authentication*—the books that claimed divine inspiration or showed sufficient evidence to have been inspired by the Holy Spirit were also considered for the canon. This criterion is immensely subjective. As a result, it should be used in conjunction with other criteria.

In Table 3.2, I have listed the books that are in the Protestant, Roman Catholic (follows the Vulgate), Greek Orthodox (follows the Septuagint), and Ethiopian Orthodox canons. These four canons are similar, as the table shows, yet there are significant differences. Some books in the Protestant canon are given different names in the other canons. Also, some books in the Roman Catholic, Greek Orthodox, and Ethiopian Orthodox canons have more chapters than the corresponding books in the Protestant canon. Some books in the Roman Catholic and Greek Orthodox canons are not in the Protestant and Ethiopian canons. The Ethiopian canon contains books that are not included in the other three canons. The arrangement of the books differ as well.

Many students of theology worry about the differences between the canons. Some are preoccupied with the question, which canon is the most reliable? This is a very important question because many students do not want to treat any book that is not inspired as an inspired text. I offer the following suggestions. The Bible (all canons included) should not be elevated to the status of God. Elevating the Bible to a divine status or allowing the Bible to replace God is idolatry. Ultimately, the Bible cannot replace God. It should be recognized that the process of canonization was very messy. Some inspired books may have not been included in any of the existing canons. Whatever criteria were used in the selection process are fallible and prone to errors. Within Protestantism, for example, Martin Luther was not thrilled by the inclusion of the book of James in the Protestant canon.[45] Finally, many theologians continue to use books that are not included in the canons of their churches in their theological works. They consider some of these books highly relevant in historical and theological matters.

---

45. For further discussion of Luther's view of the book of James, see his view of the Bible in this chapter.

TABLE 3.2 OLD TESTAMENT BOOKS IN SOME CHRISTIAN CANONS

Brackets indicate additional verses or a different name.

Book	Protestant	Roman Catholic	Greek Orthodox	Ethiopian Orthodox
Genesis	X	X	X	X
Exodus	X	X	X	X
Leviticus	X	X	X	X
Numbers	X	X	X	X
Deuteronomy	X	X	X	X
Joshua	X	X	X	X
Judges	X	X	X	X
Ruth	X	X	X	X
1 Samuel	X	X	X	X
2 Samuel	X	X	X	X
1 Kings	X	X	X	X
2 Kings	X	X	X	X
1 Chronicles	X	X	X	X
2 Chronicles	X	X	X	X
Prayer of Manasseh			X	[Pt. of 2 Chronicles]
Ezra	X	[1 Esdras]	[Esdras B]	X

Book	Protestant	Roman Catholic	Greek Orthodox	Ethiopian Orthodox
Nehemiah	X	[2 Esdras]	[Esdras B]	X
1 Esdras		[3 Esdras]	[Esdras A]	[2 Ezra]
2 Esdras		[4 Esdras]		
Apocalypse of Ezra (2 Esdras 3–14)				X
Tobit		X	X	X
Judith		X	X	X
Esther	X	[with additions]	[with additions]	[with additions]
1 Maccabees		X	X	
2 Maccabees		X	X	
3 Maccabees			X	
Job	X	X	X	X
Psalms	X	X	X	X
Psalm no. 151			X	X
Proverbs	X	X	X	X
Ecclesiastes	X	X	X	X
Song of Songs	X	X	X	X
Wisdom of Solomon		X	X	X
Ecclesiasticus		X	X	X

Book	Protestant	Roman Catholic	Greek Orthodox	Ethiopian Orthodox
Isaiah	X	X	X	X
Jeremiah	X	X	X	X
Lamentations	X	X	X	X
Baruch		X	X	X
4 Baruch				X
Epistle of Jeremiah		Baruch (ch. 6)	X	X
Ezekiel	X	X	X	X
Daniel	X	X	X	X
Hosea	X	X	X	X
Joel	X	X	X	X
Amos	X	X	X	X
Obadiah	X	X	X	X
Jonah	X	X	X	X
Micah	X	X	X	X
Nahum	X	X	X	X
Habakkuk	X	X	X	X
Zephaniah	X	X	X	X
Haggai	X	X	X	X
Zechariah	X	X	X	X
Malachi	X	X	X	X

The Ethiopian canon also contains Enoch, Jubilees, and
1, 2, and 3 Maccabees

The Authority of Scripture

In 2008 members of the Biblical and Theological Studies Department of Bethel University, where I currently teach, asked me to lecture on the authority of Scripture in a Christian theology class as a part of their interview process. The invitation to lecture on this topic was frightening because it is a highly controversial (and hotly debated) one in Christianity. It was even more frightening as I pondered the rationale for the department's choice of topic. I recall asking myself, "Why has the department chosen the authority of Scripture out of all other possible theological topics?" I assumed they wanted to know something about my theological position on one of the most important doctrines in Christianity.

FOCUS QUESTION:
What sort of authority does the Scripture have, and what is its role in the formation of Christian identity?

The authority of Scripture reverberates in Christian families, institutions, businesses, universities, and churches. Christians sometimes are willing to appeal to the authority of Scripture during theological discussions. In any case, it permeates their thinking. The Bible occupies an important place in the life of many Christians and is expected to perform certain functions because of its authority. Christians see it as the primary point of reference for theological reflection and Christian living. As a divinely inspired collection of books, the Bible is expected to speak authoritatively to Christian communities on matters of belief and practice. Some Christians, as we have already seen, extend its authority to the fields of history and science.

The authority of the Bible has come under severe attack since the dawn of postmodernism. Carl Braaten describes this situation as "a crisis of authority."[46] It has become increasingly difficult to associate the Bible with the word *authority* in an age of immense suspicion and incredulity toward any claim to a *universal* authority. The reasons for this suspicion are not without merit. The quest for power and status has informed the understanding of scriptural authority in many Christian communities. Historically, some Christian communities have committed atrocities under the guise of scriptural authority. To cite a few examples, some Christians in South Africa appealed to the Bible and used it in the construction of the theological warrants for apartheid. In the United States, Christians in both the South and the North used the Bible to support slavery. Some Indian Christians who continue to uphold the caste system also seek biblical justification for what is a dehumanizing social and religious system. Many Christian communities continue to use the Bible as an authoritative source in rationalizing their

46. Braaten, "Shared Dilemma," 67.

mistreatment and subjugation of women, both in the church and in society. Unfortunately, in these cases the Bible has been employed as an oppressive tool rather than as a liberating text.

To say that the Bible is authoritative implies that it has the capacity to perform certain functions within the communities that profess to be Christian. However, Christians disagree on its exact functions and on the source of its authority. This disagreement is to be expected given that Christianity has found a home in many cultures that are vastly different from the cultures of the communities that produced the Bible. Yet, the Bible is expected to speak authoritatively to new cultures. As Stanley Grenz has noted, "The [Holy] Spirit's work within Scripture did not end in the distant past. Throughout history he continues to act, speaking to people through the Bible."[47]

Granted, the Bible is expected to function as an authoritative text within Christian communities of all times because it is God-breathed and also because the Holy Spirit speaks through it. But what does this mean in practice? Should Christians believe everything in the Bible? Should they follow all of the instructions found in it? For instance, on the basis of 1 Tim 2:11, should women remain silent during theological discussions when men are present? I chose this question because of its potential impact on global Christianity. Christians continue to wrestle with the implications of their answers to this question. Undoubtedly, a Christian's answer to this question will expose his or her ability to navigate through the complex process of interpretation and appropriation as his or her culture encounters the cultures of the writers and original recipients of the books of the Bible. What is at stake here is not primarily the skill of the individual that reads the Bible. It is rather the authority of the Bible and, by extension, the authority of God who inspired it.

Protestant and Roman Catholic theologians have continued to disagree on the criteria for determining an authoritative interpretation of the Bible. Roman Catholic theologians reject the Reformation principle of *sola scriptura* ("Scripture alone"), insisting that it is the church that determines an authoritative interpretation of the Bible. In Roman Catholic teaching, the Bible and tradition are the two indispensable sources of authority. Protestant theologians reject the Roman Catholic claim to an infallible ecclesiastical magisterium (the official teaching of church). They contend that the Bible is self-interpreting and self-authenticating. But for some independent churches, such as African independent churches (AICs), it is God who *makes* the Bible authoritative. This occurs when God uses it as a tool in the hands of a true worshipper to dismantle diabolical works and powers. The

47. Grenz, *Theology for the Community of God*, 382.

majority of the members of AICs use the Bible, particularly the Old Testament, to justify their recovery and affirmation of some traditional beliefs and taboos in their worship and theology.[48]

In what follows I will discuss the views of some key theologians that represent, broadly speaking, the understandings of the nature, function, and authority of Scripture in Christian communities around the globe.

Martin Luther

Martin Luther (1483–1546) was the most famous of the first generation of Protestant reformers. His experience in the midst of a thunderstorm on July 2, 1505, on his way back to the University of Erfurt had a great and lasting impact on his life.[49] The experience compelled him to rethink his eternal destiny: "When lightning struck nearby, Martin feared for his life. The terror over his eternal destiny engulfed him, and in a final effort to save himself he cried out to St. Anne. 'Help me, St. Anne! I will become a monk!' he shouted. When Martin survived the storm, the matter, as far as he was concerned, was decided."[50] He later joined the Augustinian monastery in Erfurt. But his desire to live righteously in order to please God ended in despair. This and other experiences inspired him to participate in the reformation of the Roman Catholic Church's doctrines of the authority of Scripture, salvation, God's grace, and righteousness. Luther's theologies have influenced several churches today, including those who disagree with his theological stipulations and conclusions.

The Nature and Function of Scripture

As one of the reformers, Luther's goal was to establish the Bible as the final authority in matters of faith and practice. For Luther, the Bible alone—and not the leaders of the church or official church doctrine—is the sole authority. This view of the Bible conveys the idea of the Reformation principle of *sola scriptura*.

Luther rejects the elevation of the official teaching of the church to the status of an authority equal to the Bible. He argues that the Bible derives its authority from the content of the gospel, namely, Jesus Christ. Thus, for Luther, there is "a canon within the canon": Jesus Christ is lord over the Bible and as such is the one who bestows on the Bible its authority. "And

48. Mbiti, "Role of the Jewish Bible in African Independent Churches," 223.

49. Robinson, *Martin Luther*, 8.

50. Ibid.

this is the true test by which to judge all books," Luther writes, "when we see whether or not they inculcate Christ. . . . Whatever does not teach Christ is not yet apostolic, even though St. Peter or St. Paul does the teaching. Again, whatever preaches Christ would be apostolic, even if Judas, Annas, Pilate or Herod were doing it."[51] In his "Lecture on Galatians," Luther declares that Jesus Christ is Lord over the Bible and that it is the servant of Christ.

Luther acknowledges that the Bible performs several functions in the community of believers. For him, its primary function is to convey or promote Christ. He considers this function of the Bible as the criterion for judging all books of the Bible. Those books that do not communicate the liberating work of Jesus Christ hold a low position in Luther's theology of the Bible. It is for this reason that he describes the book of James as "an epistle of straw."[52] The relevance and authority of the Bible must be viewed in the light of how it witnesses to Jesus Christ, who is its content.

Luther also warns against viewing the Bible as primarily a book of legal codes. In his theology, the theme of justification by faith reigns supremely and is used to buttress the liberating work of Jesus Christ, on whose account God declares a sinner righteous. Of course, this does not mean that Luther does not view the Bible as the text that provides guidance for the Christian life.

Assessment of Luther's View of Scripture

The major problem with Luther's view of the Bible is his failure to clearly describe the criteria for determining what "inculcates Christ." For example, does the book of James, which occupied a low position in his classification of the biblical canon, inculcate Christ? Luther's preoccupation with God's justification, understood in a legal or forensic sense, may have tainted his understanding of the functions of the Bible.

Another criticism of Luther's theology of Scripture is directed against the Reformation principle of *sola scriptura*. The Bible is never truly "Scripture alone," never read by one with a completely neutral mindset. Christian individuals and Christian communities interpret the Bible in the light of their own experiences and aspirations. People read the Bible with different agendas. Some read it *theologically*—with the aim to discover what God's says to the reader through the words of the Bible. Others may read it *exegetically*—with the aim to discover the authorial intent. And still others read it

---

51. Luther, "Preface to the New Testament," in *Luther's Works*, 35:396.
52. Luther, "Preface to the New Testament," 117.

mystically—with the aim to discover and experience the hidden power of God encoded in the words of the Bible.

The following excerpts highlight some of the major ideas in Luther's theology of the Bible.

"Preface to the Old Testament (1523, Revised 1545)"

There are some who have little regard for the Old Testament. They think of it as a book that was given to the Jewish people only and is now out of date, containing only stories of past times. They think they have enough in the New Testament and assert that only a spiritual sense is to be sought in the Old Testament. Origen, Jerome, and many other distinguished people have held this view. But Christ says in John 5[:39], "Search the Scriptures, for it is they that bear witness to me." St. Paul bids Timothy attend to the reading of the Scriptures [1 Tim 4:13], and in Romans 1[:2] he declares that the gospel was promised by God in Scriptures, while in 1 Corinthians 15 he says that in accordance with the Scriptures Christ came of the seed of David, died, and was raised from the dead. St. Peter, too, points us back, more than once, to the Scriptures.

They do this in order to teach us that the Scriptures of the Old Testament are not to be despised, but diligently read. For they themselves base the New Testament upon them mightily, proving it by the Old Testament and appealing to it, as St. Luke writes in Acts 17:11, saying that they at Thessalonica examined the Scriptures to see if these things were so that Paul was teaching.

"Preface to the New Testament (1522, Revised 1546)"

See to it, therefore, that you do not make a Moses out of Christ, or a book of laws and doctrines out of the gospel, as has been done heretofore and as certain prefaces put it, even those of St. Jerome. For the gospel does not expressly demand works of our own by which we become righteous and are saved; indeed it condemns such works. Rather the gospel demands faith in Christ: that he has overcome for us sin, death, and hell, and thus gives us righteousness, life, and salvation not through works, but through his own works, death, and suffering, in order that we may avail ourselves of his death and victory as though we had done it ourselves.[53]

Question: What does this text tell us about Martin Luther's view of the relationship between the OT and NT, and what ought to be their functions in Christian communities?

---

53. Lull, *Martin Luther's Basic Theological Writings*, 115, 118–19.

Karl Rahner

Karl Rahner (1904–1984), a German Jesuit theologian, was one of the greatest Christian thinkers in the twentieth century. Some of his theological works were groundbreaking and greatly influenced the theologies of the Second Vatican Council (1962–1965), to which he served as a theological consultant. His theology of the Bible demonstrates, on the one hand, continuity with classical Roman Catholic theology and, on the other hand, a rigorous interaction and affinity with the modern historical consciousness of his era.[54]

The Nature and Function of Scripture

For Rahner, the Bible is the collection of the records and testimonies of the apostolic church's understanding of God's revelation. The early (apostolic) church was the initial recipient of God's revelation, which culminated in Jesus Christ, and therefore is the irreplaceable foundation of the later Christian churches. In order for the apostolic church to function in this capacity, God enabled it to express its faith and experience in writing—a durable and dependable way to preserve a body of knowledge.[55] The Bible consists of the writings of ancient Israel and the apostles. It expresses the faith of the apostolic church preserved for later Christians.

Informed by ecclesiocentrism (church-centeredness), Rahner sees *inspiration* as God's activity in the life of the apostolic church—God enabled it to express its experience of God's revelation in written form. He writes, "This inspiration does not consist in the fact that the Scriptures have been accepted as canonical by the Church, nor solely in the fact that they inerrantly record the divine revelation." He continues, "Inspiration consists in God supernaturally enlightening the human author's mind in the perception of the content and essential plan of the book, and moving his will to write no more and no less than what God himself wants written, God providing him with special assistance to ensure that the work, thus conceived and willed, be correspondingly carried into effect."[56] Against the danger of diminishing the true humanity of the Bible, Rahner argued that the human authors were not "mere secretaries taking down divine dictation."[57] On the contrary, they were true authors who wrote down, albeit under the supervi-

---

54. Dulles, "Scripture," 10.

55. Ibid., 11.

56. Rahner, *Inspiration in the Bible*, 11–13.

57. Ibid., 14.

sion of God, their experiences of God's revelatory actions in the world. For Rahner, the human and divine elements of the Bible must be upheld if it is to be meaningful to humanity. "God's transcendental causality of the Bible alone is not sufficient to make him the author; if he is to be truly its author, his operation itself must be within the world, within salvation history, as it is in the case of the prophetic inspiration and the Incarnation."[58]

Rahner argues that the role of God in the Bible also extends to its canonicity. God empowered the post-apostolic church to compile and establish the canon of Scripture. As Avery Dulles notes, "The canon, for Rahner, is the necessary correlative of inspiration, which is given precisely in order that there may be canonical books. The revelation of the canon is not an act distinct from the inspiration of the Bible. In reaching a decision concerning the canon, the church of the early centuries did not have to rely on apostolic authorship or on explicit apostolic testimonies. Gifted with the Spirit of Christ, the church was able to recognize through 'connaturality' those writings of the foundational period that purely expressed its own faith."[59]

Given God's involvement in life of the church, Rahner believes it is the church that has the right and is also properly equipped to protect the Bible from misinterpretation. It is the church or its infallible ecclesiastical magisterium that determines the meaning of the words of Scripture. Here, Rahner demonstrates his allegiance to the Council of Trent (1545–1563). The church also determines the implications of the Bible for churches today. The Orthodox Church in some ways shares a similar understanding of the role of the church in the interpretation of the Bible. Bishop Kallistos Ware of the Greek Orthodox Church has argued for the reading of the Bible "in communion with all the other members throughout the ages."[60] He goes on to say, "The final criterion for our interpretation of Scripture is the mind of the Church. And this means keeping constantly in view how the meaning of Scripture is explained and applied in Holy Tradition: that is to say, how the Bible is understood by the Fathers and the saints, and how it is used in liturgical worship."[61]

Assessment of Rahner's View of Scripture

Although Rahner has attempted to reconcile the relationship between the authority of the Bible and the ecclesiastical magisterium, while maintaining

58. Ibid., 16.
59. Dulles, "Scripture," 11.
60. Ware, *Orthodox Way*, 110.
61. Ibid.

the necessity of both sources of authority, many Protestants and Roman Catholics do not accept his resolution. Some Protestants continue to hold that the Bible, in order to retain its status as the final authority in matters of faith and practice, must be self-sufficient and self-interpreting. For these Protestants, the Reformation principle of *sola scriptura* cannot be negotiated. Many Roman Catholics continue to see the two sources of authority as indispensable elements in the continual existence and meaningfulness of the church. Another criticism relates to Rahner's vague description of inspiration. He does not clearly articulate the difference between God's act of inspiring the Bible and God's enactment of the church. He argues that the Bible is inspired because God enacted the apostolic church that authored it. In his attempt to explain the uniqueness of the apostolic church and the grounds for which it reserves the sole right to author the Scripture, Rahner does not clearly explain the distinctiveness of these two acts of God.

The excerpt below, from Rahner's *Inspiration in the Bible*, provides helpful clues to Rahner's theology of the Bible.

The Bible, too, belongs to the constitutive elements of the Apostolic Church which was the qualitatively unique work of God and permanent "canonical" origin of the later Church. We say "among," because the essentially constitutive elements of the Apostolic Church must include all those things which are considered elements of the Church in general (believing possession of the transmitted revelation, the *ius divinum* of the primacy and apostolic succession, sacraments, socially organized unity of the faithful), in addition to numerous other elements peculiar to the Apostolic Church (Peter, the apostles, their functions as bearers of revelation). What we mean to say is this: granted the priority within the Apostolic Church, as the Church's initial stage, of the oral *paradosis* possessing both authority and infallibility, God freely, but for reasons into which we can gain some insight, made the Bible a constitutive element of the Apostolic Church.

The facts involved in this proposition are not open to question. For (a) the Holy Scriptures exist, and (b) they are essentially the Church's book; they are recognizable as sacred only through her, they are given to her, only she can interpret them and thus bring their inner nature to actualization.

This proposition needs no further proof, but it does need some explanation. In its origin and essence the Bible is undeniably God's word to man, but it is just as fundamentally the Church's self-expression of her faith, a written record of the Apostolic Church's faith and of her self-constitution. To deny this would be to deny that the New Testament writers were real authors and would be to reduce them to mere transmitters of a message from above. This would go counter to the concrete character of these writings: their *genus litterarium* is that of a testimonial to belief, not merely a record of revelation. It is not true that in some way and in some place or other a book was composed *Deo auctore*, and that the Church, subsequently recognizing this book as a communication to her from God, took it over, authenticated it, and adopted it as a textbook in the faith. The origination of the New Testament writings was a vital operation of the Church herself: they are the written embodiment of that which she transmitted and preached as her faith. They are writings which came into existence as manifestations of the Church's life, as letters, exhortations, sermons, and so on. This means that, from the very beginning, a fundamental character of the Scriptures is the fulfillment of the role which we have in general ascribed to the Apostolic Church as distinct from the later Church: to be not only the earliest phase in time, but also the permanent source, the Canon and norm for the Church of later eras.[62]

Question: How does Rahner understand the relationship between the authority of Scripture and the authority of the Church?

Benjamin Breckinridge Warfield

Benjamin Breckinridge Warfield (1851–1921) ranks as one of the most influential American orthodox Protestant theologians. His interests in both science and theology reflect on his theologies. Like other Princeton theologians such as Archibald Alexander Hodge, Warfield defended the Reformation's principle of *sola scriptura* against what he considered threats coming from the Roman Catholic Church's doctrine of the ecclesiastical magisterium. Warfield also rejected the form of liberal theology that viewed the Bible as human-made rather than God-breathed. He equally criticized neo-orthodox theologians for rejecting a direct identification of the Bible with God's revelation. Warfield's view of the Scriptures continues to be held in many Protestant communities, especially among American Evangelicals.

The Nature and Function of Scripture

Like his Princetonian forebears, Warfield contends that the Bible is God's inspired, authoritative, and inerrant revelation of God. The Bible is self-attesting, self-sufficient, and self-interpreting, and therefore its authority need

---

62. Rahner, *Inspiration in the Bible*, 49–51.

not be certified by an ecclesiastical authority. Part of Warfield's agenda, of course, was to establish the Bible as the sure and trustworthy foundation on which a Christian theologian could erect a theological edifice. For Warfield, God's inspiration of the Bible elevates it to an oracular status: whatever the Bible says, God says. He writes, "Our Lord and his apostles looked upon the entire truthfulness and utter trustworthiness of that body of writings which they called 'Scripture,' as so fully guaranteed by the inspiration of God that they could appeal to them confidently in all their statements of whatever kind as absolutely true; adduce their deliverances on whatever subject with a simple 'it is written,' as the end of all strife; and treat them generally in a manner which clearly exhibits that in their view 'Scripture says' was equivalent to 'God says.'"[63] Warfield appeals to the Bible's testimony about itself and the views of Jesus and the apostles to buttress his argument for the trustworthiness and authority of the Bible: "That the Scriptures are throughout a Divine book," he argues, "created by the Divine energy and speaking in their every part with Divine authority directly to the hearts of the readers, is the fundamental fact concerning them which is witnessed by Christ and the sacred writers to whom we owe the New Testament."[64]

Warfield's unique contribution to the theological discussion on the nature and authority of the Bible consists in his conceptualization of the *concursive* (from the Latin *concurrere*, "to run together") mode of inspiration. He employs the word *concursus* to explain the involvement of God and of human beings in the production of the Bible. Warfield writes, "Justice is done to neither factor of inspiration and to neither element in the Bible, the human or the divine, by any other conception of the mode of inspiration except that of *concursus*, or by any other conception of the Bible except that which conceives of it as a divine-human book, in which every word is at once divine and human."[65] By imagining the mode of inspiration in this way, he aims to preserve the divine and human constants in the writing of the books of the Bible. The concursus mode of inspiration, according to him, guarantees that the "Scripture is the product of divine activities which enter it, however, not by superseding the activities of the human authors, but confluently with them; so that the Scriptures are the joint product of divine and human activities . . ."[66] He rejects the dictation theory of inspiration. For him, although the writers of the Bible were God's "instruments," they nonetheless left their marks on the final product. Yet the human authors did not have

---

63. Warfield, "Inerrancy of the Original Autographs," 269.

64. Warfield, "Inspiration," 285.

65. Warfield, "Divine and Human in the Bible," 278.

66. Ibid.

the freedom to include words and thoughts that God did not approve. He writes, "It has always been recognized that this conception of co-authorship implies that the Spirit's superintendence extends to the choice of the words by the human authors (verbal inspiration), and preserves its product from everything inconsistent with a divine authorship—thus securing, among other things, that entire truthfulness which is everywhere presupposed in and asserted for Scripture by the Biblical writers (inerrancy)."[67] Although the view of scriptural inerrancy predated Warfield, he brought it to the center stage in the American Protestant and Evangelical communities.

Assessment of Warfield's View of Scripture

Warfield is praised in Evangelical communities as one of the key theologians who audaciously defended the authority and veracity of the Bible in the midst of severe attacks. Many Protestant theologians today, with little or no modification, use his view of the concursus mode of inspiration. The criticisms against Warfield's view of the Bible can be summarized as follows. First, his conception of the concursus mode of inspiration and his view of inerrancy diminish the true humanness of the Bible. If the human authors did not have the freedom to choose their own words and freely express their thoughts, it follows that Warfield's concursus mode of inspiration is not substantially different from a mechanical mode of inspiration. Second, as we have already seen, some theologians today maintain that the Bible does not teach inerrancy. Third, Warfield's view of inerrancy presupposes that the Bible is a collection of divinely given *facts* (propositional statements that correspond to facts), which Christians are to believe. This understanding of the Bible fails to account properly for the diverse genres of the books. The excerpt below captures Warfield's view of concursive inspiration.

---

67. Warfield, *Revelation and Inspiration*, 17.

There is probably no problem more prominently before the minds of the Bible students of today than the one which concerns the relation between the divine and human elements in the Bible....

Justice is done to neither factor of inspiration and to neither element in the Bible, the human or the divine, by any other conception of the mode of inspiration except that of *concursus*, or by any other conception of the Bible except that which conceives of it as a divine-human book, in which every word is at once divine and human.

The philosophical basis of this conception is the Christian idea of God as immanent as well as transcendent in the modes of his activity. Its idea of the mode of the divine activity in inspiration is in analogy with the divine modes of activity in other spheres—in providence, and in grace wherein we work out our own salvation with fear and trembling, knowing that it is God who is working in us both the willing and the doing according to his own good pleasure. The biblical basis of *concursus* is found in the constant scriptural representation of the divine and human co-authorship of the biblical commandments and enunciations of truth, as well as in the constant scriptural ascription of Bible passages to both the divine and the human authors, and in the constant scriptural recognition of Scripture as both divine and human in quality and character.

The fundamental principle of this conception is that the whole of Scripture is the product of divine activities which enter it, not by superseding the activities of the human authors, but by working confluently with them; so that the Scriptures are the joint product of divine and human activities, both of which penetrate them at every point, working harmoniously together to the production of a writing which is not divine here and human there, but at once divine and human in every part, every word and every particular.

As full justice is done to the divine element as is done by those who deny that there is any human element in the Bible, for of every word in the Bible it is asserted that it is inspired by God and has been written under the direct and immediate guidance of the Holy Spirit. And full justice being done to both elements in the Bible, full justice is done also to human needs.... Because it is the word of man in every part and element, it comes home to our hearts. Because it is the Word of God in every part and elements, it is our constant law and guide.[68]

Question: How does Warfield's concept of concursive inspiration explain the relation of the divine and human elements in the production of the Bible?

---

68. Warfield, "Divine and Human in the Bible," 51–58.

Karl Barth

Karl Barth was one of the most famous Protestant theologians of the twentieth century. He was an outstanding thinker, outclassing many of his contemporaries. Numerous doctoral dissertations and books have been written on aspects of his theological works. Several premier universities have established research centers and lectureship positions in honor of his contributions to Christian theology. Barth is known, especially in Protestant Evangelical circles, as a neo-orthodox theologian. The term *neo-orthodoxy* is applied to "a twentieth-century development in theology, which is 'orthodox' inasmuch as it emphasizes key themes of Reformed theology, but 'neo-', i.e., 'new', inasmuch as it has taken serious account of contemporary cultural and theological developments. It originated with continental theologians: Barth, Brunner, Bultmann and Friedrich Gogarten . . ."[69] The theological positions of those theologians who are classified as "neo-orthodox" sometimes differ and compete. An example is Karl Barth's debate with Emil Brunner on God's revelation and natural theology.[70] These differences have led several Barthian scholars to reject the association of Barth with neo-orthodoxy.

The Nature and Function of Scripture

Barth's major contribution to theological discussions on the Bible is his exclusive association of God's revelation with Jesus Christ and also his view of Scripture as the text that witnesses to God's revelation. "The Bible is God's Word," Barth writes, "as it really bears witness to revelation . . ."[71] Barth vigorously rejected any direct identification of God's revelation with the Bible. For him, God's revelation is not subject to or reducible to mere speech and propositions. God does not unveil God's self in ink and paper. God is a being-in-act that discloses or reveals God's self in flesh—in Jesus Christ. The relationship of the Bible with God's revelation is limited to the role of witness or attestation. In Barth words, "The promise of this Word is thus Immanuel, God with us—with us who have brought ourselves, and continually bring ourselves again, into the dire straits of not being able to be with God. Holy Scripture is the word of men who yearned, waited and hoped for this Immanuel and who finally saw, heard and handled it in Jesus Christ. Holy Scripture declares, attests and proclaims it. And by its declara-

---

69. C. A. Baxter, "Neo-orthodoxy," in Ferguson, Wright, and Packer, *New Dictionary of Theology*, 456.

70. See Brunner and Barth, *Natural Theology*.

71. Barth, *CD* 1/1, 111.

tion, attestation and proclamation it promises that it applies to us also and to us specifically."[72]

The Bible itself, according to Barth, is not God's self-revelation. The Bible is comprised of of human words. However, the Bible can properly be regarded as the "Word of God written" because, although it is a text containing human speech about God,[73] its truthfulness and trustworthiness are grounded in the truthfulness and trustworthiness of God's speech.[74] The Bible (human speech-act) can also *become* God's Word (God's speech-act) when God uses the words of the Bible to speak to the hearer or reader, confronting him or her with the event of Jesus Christ (the Word of God). Barth writes, "The Bible is God's Word to the extent that God causes it to be His Word, to the extent that He speaks through it."[75] This is a miraculous act of God. Barth emphasizes that it is God who accomplishes the tasks of using the words of the Bible to point the reader or hearer to the event of Jesus Christ. In the words of Barth, "The fact that God's own address becomes an event in the human word of the Bible is, however, God's affair and not ours. This is what we mean when we call the Bible God's Word."[76]

Given Barth's view of the Bible's relationship with God's revelation, a radical redefinition of *inspiration* is anticipated: it is the promise of God to be present among God's people when they listen to the words of the Bible.[77] Bruce McCormack has noted that for Barth "knowledge of God occurs when and where God takes up the language of the biblical witness and bears witness to himself in and through its witness (the objective moment) *and* awakens in us the faith needed to comprehend that witness (the subjective moment)."[78] Since the Bible is a collection of human documents that are written by fallible human beings, the Bible has a capacity for error. This (potential) condition of the Bible does not denigrate it or devalue its significance for the church. Barth maintains that the Bible is a unique text of the church because (*a*) it imposes itself upon the church as the canon, and (*b*) its content is a witness to God's revelation of God's self in Jesus Christ.[79]

---

72. Ibid., 108.

73. Ibid., 99–110.

74. Ibid., 132–33. According to Barth, the Word of God (that is, God's speech-act) has taken three distinct and yet related forms or modes of existence. They are *preached* (its oral form conveyed by the prophets, apostles, and present-day preachers), *written* (the Bible), and *revealed* (that is, the Word of God in flesh, namely, Jesus Christ). See Barth, *CD* 1/1, 88–124.

75. Ibid., 109.

76. Ibid.

77. Kelsey, *Uses of Scripture in Recent Theology*, 212.

78. McCormack, *Orthodox and Modern*, 112.

79. Barth, *CD* 1/1, 107.

Barth, however, does not focus so much on the frailty of the human authors of the Bible and the weakness of their words, but rather on what God accomplishes through the words of the Bible as it is proclaimed by the church.

Barth speaks about the supremacy and authority of the Bible. He contends that the "Bible cannot be taken prisoner by the Church."[80] As the canon—that on which the church's proclamation about God is to be founded—the Bible must be allowed to address the church. He writes, "Already as a text the canonical text has the character of a free power. All the Church needs to do is just this: After any exegesis propounded in it, even the very best, it has to realize afresh the distinction between text and commentary and to let the text speak again without let or hindrance, so that it will experience the lordship of this free power and find in the Bible the partner or counterpart which the Church must find in it if it is to take the living *successio apostolorum* [apostolic succession] seriously."[81] The authority and normative status of the Bible derive from the Bible's primary content, namely, the promise of God's self-disclosure in Jesus Christ. The Bible is also authoritative because God addresses humanity in and through it. The Bible is "a human word which has God's commission to us behind it, a human word to which God has given Himself as object, a human word which is recognized as accepted by God as good, a human word in which God's own address to us is an event."[82]

Assessment of Barth's View of Scripture

Barth's view of the Bible recaptures the true humanness of the Bible and also its significance as a text that points sinners to God's revelation. There are problems with his theology of the Bible, however. He does not account properly for those sections of the Bible that present God as speaking directly to the prophets. If the Bible only becomes the Word of God at the moment when God uses it to point people to God's revelation of God's self in Jesus Christ, the prophets who declared "This is what the LORD says . . ." are misleading and untrustworthy. Also, Barth's view of inspiration is seriously wanting. He does not explain properly the involvement of the Holy Spirit (2 Pet 1:20–21) in the writing of the books of the Bible. The inspiration of the Bible cannot be limited only to God's act of "inspiring" or "becoming" present through the words of the Bible when God chooses to use it to point to God's revelation.

80. Ibid., 106.
81. Ibid., 107.
82. Ibid., 109.

The excerpt below is taken from volume 1 of Barth's *Church Dogmatics*.

The Bible is the concrete means by which the Church recollects God's past revelation, is called to expectation of His future revelation, and is thus summoned and guided to proclamation and empowered for it. The Bible, then, is not in itself and as such God's past revelation, just as Church proclamation is not in itself and as such the expected future revelation. The Bible speaking to us and heard by us as God's Word, bears witness to past revelation. . . . Thus the decisive relation of the Church to revelation is its attestation by the Bible. Its attestation! Once again, the Bible is not in itself and as such God's past revelation. As it is God's Word it bears witness to God's past revelation, and it is God's past revelation in the form of attestation. When the Canon, the staff which commands and sets moving and points the way, is moved by a living stretched-out hand, just as the water was moved in the Pool of Bethesda that it might thereby become a means of healing, then it bears witness, and by this act of witness it establishes the relation of the Church to revelation, and therewith its proclamation as true proclamation. By its witness! Witnessing means pointing in a specific direction beyond the self and on to another. Witnessing is thus service to this other in which the witness vouches for the truth of the other, the service which consists in referring to this other. . . .

The direct identification between revelation and the Bible which is in fact at issue is not one that we can presuppose or anticipate. It takes place as an event when and where the biblical word becomes God's Word, i.e., when and where the biblical word comes into play as a word of witness, when and where John's finger does not point in vain but really indicates, when and where we are enabled by means of his word to see and hear what he saw and heard. Thus in the event of God's Word revelation and the Bible are indeed one, and literally so.

But for this very reason one needs to see that they are not always the same and also to what extent they are not always the same, to what extent their union is really an event. Purely formally, the revelation to which the biblical witnesses direct their gaze as they look and point away from themselves is to be distinguished from the word of the witnesses in exactly the same way as an event itself is to be distinguished from even the best and most faithful account of it.[83]

Question: How did Barth define the relationship between God's revelation and the Bible, and what function did he ascribe to the Bible?

83. Barth, *CD* 1/1, 111–13.

Phyllis Trible

Trible is a well-known American biblical and feminist scholar whose approach to the Bible has inspired many to rethink the very nature of the Bible and its estimation of women. She has written several books and numerous essays on the subject. Her contribution to feminist theological and biblical discourses merits a close examination.

The Nature and Function of Scripture

The Bible, Trible writes, is "a pilgrim wandering through history to merge past and present. Composed of diverse traditions that span centuries, it embraces claims and counterclaims in witness to the complexities of existence."[84] This nature of the Bible allows the reader to interpret it from different perspectives and with different agendas. Trible's agenda is to "read selected biblical texts" from the perspective of feminism.[85] She describes feminism broadly as the "critique of culture in light of misogyny" in a way that engages with the "issues of race and class, psychology, ecology and human sexuality."[86] It is a form of feminism that announces itself as a "prophetic movement, examining the status quo, pronouncing judgment, and calling for repentance."[87]

> "The Bible is not a single-minded document; rather it teems with diverse voices and points of view. Despite attempts to harmonize it, by ancient redactors working within it for canonization or by modern commentators working from the outside to establish and reestablish its authority, the Bible itself comes to us full of struggles, battles, contradictions and problems. It refuses to be the captive of any one group or perspective."
>
> —Trible, "Eve and Miriam"

Trible construes the Bible as a work of literature and adopts rhetorical criticism as a method of inquiry into the meaning of the text embedded in its interlocking structure of words and motifs. In this approach, the text must be allowed to speak for itself. Through a careful analysis of some texts from Genesis and other Old Testament passages, Trible concludes that the Bible presents both male and female imageries and motifs, but notes that for too long the female motif and imagery have been underemphasized and

---

84. Trible, *God and the Rhetoric of Sexuality*, 1.

85. Ibid., 8.

86. Ibid., 7.

87. Trible, *Texts of Terror*, 3.

in some circles completely lost.[88] But the parable of the lost coin should become our guide, she proclaims. Using feminist hermeneutics, she seeks "to recover old treasures and discover new ones in the household of faith."[89]

Trible does not, however, exonerate the negative impact of patriarchy on the communities that produced the Bible. In *Texts of Terror*, she writes, "In this book my task is to tell sad stories as I hear them. Indeed, they are tales of terror with women as victims. Belonging to the sacred scriptures of synagogue and church, these narratives yield four portraits of suffering in ancient Israel: Hagar, the slave used, abused, and rejected; Tamar, the princess raped and discarded; an unnamed woman, the concubine raped, murdered, and dismembered; and the daughter of Jephthah, a virgin slain and sacrificed."[90] Yet Trible is convinced that the Bible contains a "critique of patriarchy" (a hidden treasure!) that must be explored with the intent (*a*) to expose the horror of the sufferings of women in ancient Israel and the early church, and (*b*) to interpret the stories of outrage on behalf of the female victims "in order to recover a neglected history, to remember a past that the present embodies, and to pray that these terrors shall not come to pass again."[91]

Among the many contributions Trible has made to biblical scholarship, her articulation of the "non-patriarchal principle" of the Bible is most unique. Other feminist biblical scholars and theologians have developed their theologies of the Bible along the line of this principle. Trible rejects the notion that the Bible is irrecusably patriarchal. This does not mean, of course, that she underestimates the imposing presence of patriarchy in the Bible. As she notes, "The Bible was born and bred in a land of patriarchy; it abounds in male imagery and language. For centuries, interpreters have explored and exploited this male language to articulate theology; to shape the contours of the church, the synagogue and the academy; and to instruct human beings, male and female, in who they are, what roles they should play, how they should behave."[92]

Trible shares the vision of those feminist scholars who are "unwilling to let the case against women be the determining word" and who, on the contrary, "insist that the text and its interpreters provide more excellent ways."[93] As she contends, "the Bible can be redeemed from the bond-

---

88. Trible, *God and the Rhetoric of Sexuality*, 200.

89. Ibid., xvi.

90. Trible, *Texts of Terror*, 1.

91. Ibid., 3.

92. Trible, "Eve and Miriam," 7.

93. Ibid., 8.

age to patriarchy; that redemption is already at work in the text; and the articulation of it is desirable and beneficial."[94] However, in order for this task to be accomplished, the Bible must be reinterpreted. According to Trible, this reinterpretation recognizes (*a*) "the polyvalency of the text: that any text is open to multiple interpretations," and (*b*) "that all Scripture is a pilgrim wandering through history, engaging in new settings, and ever-refusing to be locked in the box of the past."[95] To illustrate her point, Trible argues that the reader who interprets Genesis 2–3 with a patriarchal lens sees Eve as Adam's derivative, helper, and seducer who must be blamed for their disobedience against God.[96] But the reader with a non-patriarchal lens may see the woman as "alert, intelligent and sensitive," whereas "the man comes off as passive, bland and belly-oriented."[97]

Assessment of Trible's View of Scripture

Trible, like many other feminist theologians, calls the attention of Christians to the nature of the books they hold to be sacred, inspired, and authoritative. She highlights the diversity of genres in the books of the Bible and also the plurality of views expressed therein. She equally points out that the Bible has capacity for several meanings without endorsing the assumption that it is only the reader who ultimately determines what a text says. Reinterpretation of the Bible, as she imagines it, "does not mean making the Bible say whatever the reader wants it to say. It does not hold that there are no limits to interpretation and that the text can, in effect, be rewritten."[98]

Some of the criticisms of Trible's view of the Bible center on her project of "reinterpretation," which aims to unearth the non-patriarchal principle in the Bible. Some feminist theologians and biblical scholars doubt that her revisionist hermeneutics have properly convicted the Bible of its sin of misogyny and androcentrism.[99] The question is, has Trible, in the attempt to rescue the Bible from its patriarchy, underemphasized its negative impacts on the life of women in both ancient Israel and the apostolic church? Also, some biblical scholars have questioned Trible's reinterpretation of Genesis 2–3, labeling it a complete distortion of the text.[100] Her claim

94. Ibid.

95. Ibid., 8–9.

96. Ibid., 10.

97. Ibid., 11.

98. Ibid., 8.

99. See Schottroff, Schroer, and Theres-Wacker, *Feminist Interpretation*, 38–48.

100. See Kawashima, "Revisionist Reading Revisited," 46–57.

that *ha adam* (Hebrew, literally "the human") in Gen 2:7 does not refer to the first man (or male creature) but rather to an "earth creature" that was not sexually differentiated is viewed by many as a misreading of Genesis creation narratives.[101]

Concluding Reflections

A few observations are noteworthy. First, the Bible should not be uprooted from the Christian communities that produced it. This implies that any understanding of the Bible that either denies or diminishes its humanness (which is reflected in the diversity of views, genres, contexts, and styles of the books) is inadequate. An adequate view of the Bible will simultaneously hold and emphasize the true humanity and divinity of the Bible. Kevin Vanhoozer notes that "Scripture is neither simply the recital of the acts of God nor merely a book of inert propositions. Scripture is rather composed of divine-human speech acts that, through what they say, accomplish several authoritative cognitive, spiritual and social functions."[102]

Second, to say that the Bible is inspired by God is a confession of faith that is rooted in the disposition of the believing communities' confidence and trust in the God who speaks and acts. It also derives from the Christian belief in God's interaction with God's creation, particularly God's involvement in the affairs of humanity. Inspiration is a divine miraculous act. While 2 Tim 3:16 and 2 Pet 1:21 tell us that God inspired the Bible, they do not tell us precisely the mode of this divine act. Inspiration should be understood as God's miraculous act, which is not subject to scientific explanation.

Third, Christians are to constantly negotiate their self-understanding and identity in the light of the Bible. No Christian community should ignore and relegate the Bible to nonuseful status. Whatever its limitations, the Bible, when properly interpreted, should function as the text that shapes and informs the Christian understanding of God's acts of reconciling creation to God's self.

Fourth, God was not only actively involved in the apostles' and prophets' articulation and interpretation of God's activities in human history, which some of them committed to writing, but God is also actively involved in helping the readers of the Bible understand and apply it to their lives (2 Tim 3:16–17; 2 Pet 1:21). The Christian community that reads the Bible should (*a*) seek to establish what the authors intended their texts to convey to the original recipients, and also (*b*) seek to discover what God is saying

101. Trible, *God and the Rhetoric of Sexuality*, 75–105.
102. Vanhoozer, *First Theology*, 131.

to their own communities through the text. The Holy Spirit's enablement of the reader of the Bible to understand its meaning is regarded by theologians as *illumination* (Job 32:8; 1 Cor 2:10–16; 2 Cor 14–17). The Spirit inspires fresh meanings and enables us to understand these meanings as we earnestly seek to appropriate what the Spirit of God intends to communicate to us in Scripture. Daniel Migliore has noted that "the same Spirit of God who guided the prophets and apostles must again be active in the preaching and hearing of their witness if what is spoken and heard is to be received as the Word of God."[103] The Holy Spirit continues to help people understand and apply the Bible to their lives. "God does not say exactly the same thing to every historical context," Clark Pinnock argues, "and we muzzle the power of Scripture when we refuse to ask how the Lord wants to use this Scripture in our hearing now. God has spoken in the Scriptures, but he also speaks through them today in ways that the original writer may not have intended. In saying this, we are simply confessing our faith in the Spirit as alive and active in bringing out from the Bible the ever-relevant Word of the Lord."[104] Christian communities of all times should seek the guidance of the Holy Spirit in discovering new ways to appropriate God's acts recorded in the Bible.

Key Terms

Autograph: the original texts or manuscripts of the books of the Bible.

Ecclesiastical Magisterium: the official teaching of the Roman Catholic Church that is believed to be an infallible guide for faith and practice.

Infallible: in the context of the discourse on the Bible, refers to the claim that the Bible is trustworthy and does not mislead the reader in matters of faith and practice.

Inerrancy: in the context of the discourse on the Bible, refers to the claim that the autographs contained no factual errors in all that they affirmed.

Inspiration: although variously understood, this term is used to convey the involvement of God through the Holy Spirit in the production of the books of the Bible.

---

103. Migliore, *Faith Seeking Understanding*, 48.
104. Pinnock, *Scripture Principle*, 57.

Review Questions

1. In your view, what are the major differences in the views of the Bible expressed by Luther, Rahner, Warfield, Barth, and Trible? What are their strengths and weaknesses?

2. What does it mean to say that the Bible is authoritative? How is the authority of Scripture construed in Christianity?

3. What does the process of the canonicity of the Bible tell us about the role of the church in the construction of the authority of the Bible?

Suggestion for Further Reading

Bacote, Vincent, Laura C. Miguélez, and Dennis L. Okholm, editors. *Evangelicals and Scripture: Tradition, Authority and Hermeneutics.* Downers Grove, IL: InterVarsity, 2004.

Trible, Phyllis. *God and the Rhetoric of Sexuality.* Philadelphia: Fortress, 1978.

Vanhoozer, Kevin J. *First Theology: God, Scripture and Hermeneutics.* Downers Grove, IL: InterVarsity, 2002.

4

Trinity

The Christian God

A t the beginning of my lecture on the doctrine of the Trinity, I usually ask my students to share their initial perceptions of the doctrine. Here are some of the responses I have heard over the years: "confusing," "contradictory," "nonsensical," "clumsy mathematics," "mystery," "God is three-in-one," "the Christian view of God," and "a difficult doctrine to understand." After listening to their responses, I normally ask this follow-up question: Is the doctrine of the Trinity essential to Christianity? Many of them stare in confusion, some audaciously say no, and a few timidly say yes. These answers may not be too far from the responses of the majority of Christians. On the one hand, the Trinity is Christianity's greatest and most unique contribution to the discussion on God in the religious market. On the other hand, it is a doctrine that is framed with theological concepts and words that are extremely difficult to explain. Many theologians find the words of the North African-born theologian Augustine most helpful in their explication of the doctrine of the Trinity: "And I would make this pious and safe agreement with all who read my writings, as well in all other cases as, above all, in the case of those which inquire into the unity of the Trinity, of the Father and the Son and the Holy Spirit; because in no other subject is error more dangerous, or inquiry more laborious, or the discovery of truth more profitable."[1] Undoubtedly, Augustine has given a wise counsel.

Since the Trinitarian idea of God found its way into the theology and liturgy of the church, Christians have struggled to deal with the theological and practical problems associated with the Trinity. They have wrestled with the following questions, among others: What does it mean to say that God is "triune"? How are we to meaningfully describe the divine persons—Father, Son, and Holy Spirit? Should the emphasis be on the "threeness" or on the "oneness"? Are the Father, Son, and Holy Spirit "a community of gods," as the Nigerian theologian A. Okechukwu Ogbonnaya has proposed?[2] Should we continue to describe God with predominantly male language?

The Trinity—the belief that the "one" God exists in three distinct yet interrelated persons—is a major doctrine of God that was propounded by some theologians in the early church. Among the numerous difficulties Christians face when they speak about God, these questions are highly formative: Is God knowable? Can human beings experience God? Is it humanly possible to speak meaningfully about God? What is God's gender? Is God actively involved in the world? In what ways does God relate to the world? What is the identity of God? These are samples of the questions that shape the discussions on the doctrine of the Trinity.

Christianity teaches that the world exists and subsists because God has brought it into existence and is preserving it. Christians claim that human beings know God because God has revealed God's self to humanity. They have also learned, in the words of Langdon Gilkey, that "the idea of God remains the most elusive, the most frequently challenged, the most persistently criticized and negated of all important convictions."[3] Christians, however, have not shied away from the difficulty of teaching about God's existence and actions.

In chapter 2, we saw that Christians believe that human beings can know and experience God because God has revealed God's self to humanity. They also frequently describe God as a *mystery*—that which can only be known when revealed. God remains concealed in God's self-disclosure to humanity. Therefore, anyone who aims to explain God's modes of existence and acts faces two related challenges. The first challenge is to avoid an intellectual idolatry—reducing God to *what we want God to be* or describing

1. Augustine, *On the Trinity*, 1.3.5.
2. Ogbonnaya, *On Communitarian Divinity*, 23.
3. Gilkey, "God," 88.

God in a manner that *contradicts* God's self-revelation. The second challenge is to correctly interpret and appropriate God's self-disclosure *kerygmatically*—the proclamation that God was in Jesus Christ reconciling the world to God's self (2 Cor 5:19).

A direct study of God's divine nature eludes humanity. Human beings can study only God's self-disclosure; we can study, interpret, and explain only what God has revealed about God's self. One successful approach to the study of God is *naming*. In most cases, the names given to God are metaphors believers use to describe their understandings and experiences of God. Three observations are noteworthy.

First, naming God should be an attempt to describe God's identity and acts in our limited ways and should not be an attempt to construct a God after our own image and likeness. Christians' naming of God should not contradict the expressions of God's identity in the Bible. Second, no single name for God can encapsulate the mystery of God. Since the divine names in the Bible are not exhaustive, we should not shy away from naming God afresh. Third, people name, and ought to name, God from their encounter with God. In Gen 16:13, Hagar named God *El Roi*, "the God who sees me," after God spoke to her in the desert. Upon seeing God's provision of a ram for sacrifice, Abraham called God *Yahweh yireh*, "Jehovah will provide" (Gen 22: 14). The Igbo people of southeast Nigeria call God *O loro ihe loro enyi* (literally, "the One who swallows a being that has swallowed an elephant") when they want to describe the strength and power of God. The *Trinity* is a Christian name for God that expresses, albeit non-exhaustively, the God of the Bible who calls people into a relationship through the life and work of Jesus Christ and through the Holy Spirit.

In this chapter, I will discuss some major Christian beliefs about the identity and work of God, focusing on the meaning, nature, and implications of the doctrine of the Trinity.

Imagining the Trinity

Christians confess that God is one, a confession they learned from Judaism (Deut 6:4). Unlike adherents to Judaism, they also confess that God exists as Father, Son, and the Holy Spirit. As attested by some of the earliest ecumenical church councils, these three "persons" share divine nature and divine attributes. Stanley Grenz notes that Christianity teaches that

FOCUS QUESTION:
What does it mean to say that God is triune?

"there is no God but the triune God; God is none other than Father, Son, and Holy Spirit."[4] The greatest difficulty with the doctrine of the Trinity is how to simultaneously explain God's oneness and God's threeness. Is God three persons who are one? Or are the Father, Son, and Holy Spirit three "aspects" of a single being? For some critics of the Trinity, it is contradictory, unwarranted, and unjustifiable to construe God as three-in-one. Yet many Christian theologians have continued to proclaim the Trinity as the key to understanding the God who is described in the Bible.

The core of Christian theology can be summarized thus: *God was in Jesus of Nazareth reconciling creation to God's self in the power of the Holy Spirit* (2 Cor 5:19; Gal 4:4–6). But how are we to understand the doctrine of the Trinity? What exactly do Christians hope to convey when they speak of God as triune? What are the implications of thinking of God simultaneously in terms of oneness and threeness? Although we do not know exactly when a Trinitarian idea became part of the liturgical and theological life of the earliest Christian communities, we do know that by the second century CE Christians freely spoke about God in connection with Jesus Christ and the Holy Spirit. A Trinitarian idea was clearly present "in the liturgy, in baptism, and the Eucharist" of the earliest Christian communities.[5] As the early church began to iron out its theological identity, the doctrine of the Trinity became one of its unique theological hallmarks. It became the distinct way of speaking about God that set Christianity apart from other religions. As Karl Barth says, "The doctrine of the Trinity is what basically distinguishes the Christian concept of revelation as Christian in contrast to all other possible doctrines of God or concepts of revelation."[6] Barth goes on to say that the content of the doctrine of the Trinity should be "decisive and controlling for the whole of dogmatics" or Christian theologies and beliefs.[7] Nowadays the majority of Christian theologians accept the importance of the doctrine of the Trinity for the identity of Christianity. Some continue to be skeptical about the importance of the doctrine. But whether one accepts the importance of the doctrine of the Trinity, "faith in the risen Christ and testimony to the outpoured and indwelling Spirit require a theological explication of the monotheistic confession that is consistent with the awareness of a more pluralist dimension to the saving action of God and the graced recognition of the same in worship and doctrine."[8]

4. Grenz, *Theology for the Community of God*, 66.

5. Jenson, *Triune God*, 11.

6. Barth, *CD* 1/1, 301.

7. Ibid., 303.

8. Del Colle, "Triune God," 122.

The Origin and Development of the Doctrine of the Trinity

At an astonishingly early period, Christians faced a tremendous challenge—to explain their understandings of Jesus' relationship to God, both of whom they worshipped. The religious context in which they lived intensified this challenge. Most followers of Jesus Christ were adherents of Judaism who confessed that "the LORD our God, the LORD is one" (Deut 6:4, NIV). In the context of Judaism, Christians needed to demonstrate that they were not polytheists and blasphemers. In the context of the Greco-Roman religions, Christians were compelled to show that they were not atheists—those who were impious and did not believe in the Greco-Roman gods. From the second century CE onward, Christians faced the challenge of explaining their understandings of the relationship between God (the Father), Jesus Christ, and the Holy Spirit as expressed in the Bible (Matt 28:19; Rom 15:30; 2 Cor 13:14; Gal 4:4–6; Eph 1:3–14).

Since the expressions "three-in-one" and "triune" are not used in the Bible, many have wondered why this doctrine developed in the first place. Others have wondered if it is biblical—that is, if the doctrine of the Trinity maintains fidelity to the ideas of God presented in the Bible. I have summarized below some of the key issues that early Christian theologians considered as they hammered out the doctrine of the Trinity.

The Identity of Jesus

Christians faced the challenge of explaining (*a*) their reasons for worshipping Jesus Christ and (*b*) their understandings of God and God's relationship to Jesus of Nazareth, the Christ. As the Bible shows, the earliest followers of Jesus treated him as a "god" by worshipping him. In Paul's letter to the Christians in Philippi, he references the christological ode or hymn that reveals the elevated status Jesus held in the theology and liturgy of the early church. Speaking of Jesus, Paul writes, "Who, being in very nature God, did not consider equality with God something to be grasped, but made himself nothing, taking the very nature of a servant, being made in human likeness" (Phil 2:6–7, NIV). For those early Christians, it was not sufficient to confess that God acted in Jesus Christ, who was a mere messiah. They also believed that Jesus shared God's "form" or nature. Some earliest Christians even went further to state that dishonoring Jesus Christ entails dishonoring God the Father (John 5:22–23). These understandings of Jesus Christ informed the development of the doctrine of the Trinity, particularly its articulation by the Council of Nicaea (325 CE) and the Council of Constantinople (381 CE).

Christians' View of Monotheism

The majority of the earliest followers of Jesus Christ were Jews. Many of them, of course, grew up in families and religious communities where *monotheism* (the idea that only one true God exists) was taught as the major distinguishing factor of Jewish theology. The problem that the earliest Jewish Christians faced was how to worship Jesus Christ as the Messiah who shared God's nature (Phil 3:6–7) and at the same hold the monotheistic view of God (Deut 6:4). This apparent contradiction posed a great threat to the credibility and uniqueness of Christianity. Christians needed to explain their concept of monotheism and its correlation to and difference from Jewish exclusivist monotheism—the view of monotheism that ruled out any idea of plurality. Undoubtedly, Jesus' exalted status signals early Christians' modification of Jewish exclusivist monotheism.[9] While the earliest (Jewish) followers of Jesus Christ were unwilling to abandon the Jewish concept of monotheism, they were ready to construe monotheism in a way that was contrary to exclusivist monotheism.

The Need for Theological Models

Since the second century CE, Christian communities have explored differently ways of speaking about God's relationship with Jesus Christ and the Holy Spirit. Numerous theological models appeared. All were rigorously tested; many were rejected. The Trinitarian metaphors, such as "triune" and "Trinity," survived as the most acceptable. Although the doctrine of the Trinity now enjoys a lasting influence on Christian communities, there were other theological metaphors that had great influence on earlier Christian communities. Some of those theological models continue to appear in contemporary works, albeit in revised and modified forms. I will describe briefly three theological models that appeared in the first three centuries. These models will shed more light on the doctrine of the Trinity.

Modalism: This view is also called *Sabellianism* and is usually associated with two third-century presbyters—Noetus of Smyrna and Sabellius.[10] Modalism teaches that God is numerically one. God has *appeared* in three distinct forms or "costumes," however—namely, Father, Son, and Holy Spirit. They were not concrete beings but rather "the modes by which God has acted in history."[11] God is like an actor in a drama who plays three

9. Hurtado, *Lord Jesus Christ*, 48–53.

10. Kelly, *Early Christian Doctrines*, 119.

11. Zizioulas, *Lectures in Christian Dogmatics*, 47.

characters by wearing three masks or costumes. Terms such as *Father, Son,* and *Holy Spirit* do not represent real distinctions but are merely applicable to one God at different times.[12] One of the implications of the modalistic view of God is *patripassianism*—the belief that God the Father suffered and died on the cross. Modalists aim (*a*) to maintain the identical natures of Jesus, the Holy Spirit, and God the Father, and (*b*) to preserve monotheism and the numerical oneness of God. The weakness of this view is its failure to account for the distinctiveness of the three persons of the Godhead. Jesus Christ (God the Son), for example, was not praying to himself at those times he prayed to God (John 17). Leonardo Boff also argues that modalism "does not advance beyond Judaism and fails to teach the Christian novelty of three divine Persons forming a unity of communion between themselves."[13] Modalism was condemned by the Synod of Braga in the sixth century CE. The official statement of the synod read: "If anyone does not confess that the Father and the Son and the Holy Spirit are three persons of one essence and virtue and power, as the catholic and apostolic church teaches, but says that [they are] a single and solitary person, in such a way that the Father is the same as the Son and this One is also the Paraclete Spirit, as Sabellius and Priscillian have said, let him be anathema."[14] Some theologians continued to hold a revised form of modalism.[15]

Tritheism: According to this view, the Father, Son, and Holy Spirit are three distinct gods whose relationship lies only in the divine nature they share. One way of illustrating this view is to think of three different human beings who are "one" because they share essential properties or characteristics. While modalism aimed to uphold monotheism, tritheism leans heavily towards polytheism. Tritheism intends to restore the distinctiveness of the three divine persons but in the process slips into the error of diminishing the unity of the Godhead. The majority of Christians believe they do not worship three gods but rather one God who exists in three persons. Tritheism seems to stand in direct opposition the Christian idea of monotheism.

Dynamic monarchianism: This view was most likely originated toward the end of the second century CE but exerted little influence on the early church. Dynamic monarchianism is also called *adoptionism*.[16] Like modalism, dynamic monarchianism aims to preserve an exclusivist idea of monotheism and the numerical oneness of God. Unlike modalism, dynamic

---

12. Kelly, *Early Christian Doctrines*, 120.

13. Boff, *Trinity and Society*, 47.

14. Quoted in Pelikan, *Emergence of the Catholic Tradition (100–600)*, 181–82.

15. Trau, "Modalism Revisited," 56–71.

16. Kelly, *Early Christian Doctrines*, 115.

monarchianism denies that God has appeared in three modes or forms. It argues that Jesus Christ was never identical to God and claims that he was an ordinary man whom God adopted as a "Son" and empowered with God's Spirit to do good works. The view can be traced back to Theodotus, a Byzantine leather merchant,[17] who taught that prior to Jesus' baptism, he lived as an ordinary man. During his baptism, however, God's Spirit (or Christ) "descended upon him, and from that moment he worked miracles" without ceasing to be human or becoming divine.[18] This view fails to account for the divinity of Jesus Christ (see John 1:1, 14) and also fails to express the distinctiveness of God the Father, Jesus Christ, and the Holy Spirit.

TABLE 4.1 SUMMARY OF THE THREE THEOLOGICAL MODELS

Views	Description	Strengths	Weaknesses
Modalism	There is one God who appeared in three modes.	It upholds monotheism and the identicalness of the Father, Son, and Holy Spirit.	It fails to account for the distinctiveness of the Father, Son, and Holy Spirit.
Tritheism	The Father, Son (Jesus Christ), and the Holy Spirit are three distinct Gods.	It emphasizes the distinctiveness of the three persons of the Trinity.	It denies monotheism.
Dynamic Monarchianism	There is only one God. The one God empowered Jesus (an ordinary human being) with God's Spirit to do good works.	It upholds monotheism.	It fails to account for the divinity of Jesus Christ. Also, it fails to account for the personhood of the Holy Spirit.

The Trinity and the Bible

The Trinity and the Old Testament

Is there any idea of plurality in the Old Testament (OT) concept of God? Some Christian theologians answer this question in the affirmative. They admit that a Trinitarian idea of God is more developed in the New Testament

17. Ibid., 116.

18. Ibid.

(NT) but insist that the idea was present in some books of the OT. Some argue that the Hebrew word used for God in Genesis 1:1—*Elohim*, which literally means "gods"—indicates an undeveloped idea of plurality. Also, the plural pronouns in the Genesis creation story (Gen 1) are employed by some theologians to support the idea of a plurality of being in the OT. For example, Genesis 1:26 reads, "Let *us* make man in *our* image." Many theologians and biblical scholars, however, have argued that "us" and "our" in the Genesis creation story can be understood as "plurality of majesty" or "royal plurality." Most adherents of Judaism and some Christian theologians also reject the claim that *Elohim* indicates plurality within the Godhead. On the contrary, they argue that *Elohim* describes Yahweh's uniqueness vis-à-vis other gods. Yahweh is unmatched in wisdom, power, and majesty (Isa 41:28–29; 42:17; 43:10–13). The Shema—the Jewish confession of faith—teaches exclusive monotheism and rules out the possibility of a plurality of beings within the Godhead.

For some theologians, God created all things through God's word; God spoke the world into existence. The author of Genesis used the expression "let there be" to describe this divine act. Some theologians contend that the Apostle John picked up this idea when he described Jesus as God's *logos*, a Greek word that can be translated "word" or "reason" (John 1:1, 14). Such theologians contend that *logos* is the equivalent of the Hebrew word *davar* ("word"). Other theologians argue that the Hebrew word *chokmah* ("wisdom"), which is sometimes personified (Prov 8:22–31), may be applied to Jesus Christ.[19] God's wisdom here may be construed as that which later became flesh (cf. John 1:14).

Rûaḥ (Hebrew, "wind" or "spirit"), which is used in the Old Testament to depict God's presence and power, is believed to refer to the Holy Spirit. Although the OT does not teach a Trinitarian God, some theologians continue to argue that the presence of "God," the personification of God's wisdom, and the activity of God's Spirit strongly indicate a Trinitarian idea of God.

The Trinity and the New Testament

Christian Monotheism (2 Cor 13:14)

It is clear from the NT that the followers of Christ worshiped one God—the God of the OT Jews. Yet, the Christ-devotion that permeates the worship of the NT Christians signals a paradoxical theology. If the worship of Jesus

19. McGrath, *Christian Theology*, 320.

does not equate to the worship of an idol, and God is the only one who deserves to be worshipped, it follows that the NT Christians' idea of monotheism differs from the OT idea of monotheism. Larry Hurtado writes, "The Christ-devotion . . . is certainly a novel development. It is equally clearly presented as a religious stance that seeks to be faithful to the concern for the one God, and therefore it must be seen in historical terms as a distinctive variant form of monotheism."[20] Some NT texts (e.g., Rom 15:30; 2 Cor 13:14; Gal 4:4–6) sufficiently indicate that the idea of the Trinity was present in the liturgy and theology of the early church. Alister McGrath has noted that "the foundations of the doctrine of the Trinity are to be found in the pervasive pattern of divine activity to which the New Testament bears witness. The Father is revealed in Christ through the Spirit. There is the closest of connections between the Father, Son, and Spirit in the New Testament writings."[21]

Models of the Doctrine of the Trinity

Many Christians are satisfied with their belief in the Trinity without worrying about how to explain it. They see the task of explaining the concept of the Trinity as one reserved for the theologians. Many theology students, however, are not as excited as some might think when the language of the Trinity is introduced in the lecture hall. Like everyone, they are perplexed by the doctrine many Christians consider to be essential to Christianity's identity. In its simplest form, the doctrine of the Trinity states this: *God is one-in-three* or *there is one God who exists as Father, Son, and Holy Spirit.* The difficulty with the doctrine of the Trinity derives partly from how to understand the "oneness" and the "threeness" of God. There seem to be three possible meanings of "oneness" and two possible meanings of "threeness." God's "oneness" can mean (*a*) *numerical* oneness—of being or person; (*b*) oneness of *substance* or *nature*; or (c) oneness of *purpose* or *relationship*. God's "threeness" can mean (*a*) threeness of *modes of existence* or *being*, or (b) threeness of *modes of operation*. A theologian's view of God or the Trinity will be determined by the combination of oneness and threeness the theologian prefers. For example, if a theologian combines a *numerical* oneness of being and threeness of *modes of operation*, the theologian's view of God will align with modalism.

> FOCUS QUESTION:
> How is the Trinity to be explained?

20. Hurtado, *Lord Jesus Christ*, 50.
21. McGrath, *Christian Theology*, 320.

In the Latin world, from the second to the fifth centuries CE, Trinitarian theologians described God as one *substantia* ("substance") and three *personae* ("persons"). Greek-speaking theologians conveyed a similar idea of God with the following Greeks words: *ousia* ("substance") and *hypostasis* ("nature" or "way of existing"). These are the main operative terms that function as an elastic boundary within which contemporary theologians expound the doctrine of the Trinity. Some theologians may see any attempt to move beyond the boundaries set by these terms as overly ambitious and dangerous. I will discuss some Trinitarian models that have operated within the bounds of the parameters set by these terms. Although some of these models intersect, they are nonetheless different in several ways. I will articulate the models in ways that highlight their understandings of the oneness of God, the threeness of God, and also their unique contribution to the discourses on the doctrine of the Trinity.

Quintus Septimius Florens Tertullianus (c. 160–c. 220 CE)

Many students of theology are unaware that Africa was the home of prominent theologians who shaped the theological conversation during the third, fourth, and fifth centuries CE. Tertullian (Tertullianus) was an African lawyer and theologian. He was born in the province of Roman North Africa in a place that corresponds roughly to the present-day Tunisia. He was trained in the catechetical school of Carthage. Later in his life he is thought to have become a Montanist.[22] It is most likely that the Montanists' zeal for morality and holy living strongly appealed to Tertullian. Some theologians believe that his encounter with Montanism helped him move away from a binitarian view of God to a Trinitarian view of God.[23]

Tertullian made some significant contributions to Christian Trinitarian discourse. For example, although the idea of the Trinity appeared in the writings of other early theologians, such as Justin Martyr (died in c. 165 CE), Tertullian was the first theologian to use the Latin words *trinitas* ("trinity"), *personae*, and *substantia* to describe the relationship that exists between Father, Son, and Holy Spirit. He developed these concepts in his book *Against Praxeas*. He most probably coined the Latin phrase *una substantia, tres personae* ("one substance, three persons"). Gregg Allison notes that "Tertullian's wording became the foundation for the church's definition of the Trinity: God is one essence or substance yet three in persons."[24]

22. For further discussion of Montanism, see chapter 6.
23. Pelikan, "Montanism and Its Trinitarian Significance," 109.
24. Allison, *Historical Theology*, 237.

Tertullian's view of the Trinity was an attack on modalism and dynamic monarchianism. He followed the Trinitarian interpretation that construes God as *one divine nature, three distinct and graded persons*. For him, the Father, Son, and Holy Spirit are a unity because they share the same divine substance (*substantia*). He used the word *trinitas* to describe both the plurality and unity within the Godhead. It is not readily clear how he intended *personae* to be understood in the context of the Trinity. For Tertullian, the Father (the source of divine being), the Son, and the Holy Spirit participate in and share the same divine nature or substance. Some contemporary interpreters have categorized Tertullian and some other Western theologians of the patristic era as those who explained the unity of the Godhead in terms of substance or substance ontology and not relational ontology.

In the ancient Greek world, *prosopon* ("person") originally meant "face" or "the part of the head that is 'below the cranium.'"[25] It later took on other meanings, such as "the mask held up before the face of Greek actors," a character in a drama or plan and also "the bearer of that character, the particular individual concerned."[26] The ancient Latin word *persona* ("person") has the capacity for several meanings. Most commonly, it refers both to a mask worn by an actor in a play and the actual character itself.[27] In the English language, the word *person* can be used in several senses, including a human being, a character in a play, and one recognized by law as the subject of rights and duties (which could be a corporation or a human being).[28] Theologians continue to debate the actual meaning of *person* in Trinitarian thought. Some have suggested that the term be replaced with another that has a more limited meaning.

In *Against Praxeas*, Tertullian employed the word *persona* to accomplish two interrelated theological purposes: to preserve the individuality of the Father, Son, and Holy Spirit, and to highlight the nature of their relationship and oneness. He used *persons* to distinguish Jesus Christ (God the Son) from God the Father and the Holy Spirit. For him, the words *Father*, *Son*, and *Holy Spirit* are not merely names for different appearances of God. It is most likely that he intended *persons*, in this context, to be understood as the individual characters that play active roles in the drama of salvation. These three divine characters share one divine *substantia*. The Father, Son, and Holy Spirit are real "individuals" who are numerically distinct, with different roles in the economy of salvation. He writes, "This economy arranges

25. Zizioulas, *Being as Communion*, 31.

26. Brown, "Trinitarian Personhood and Individuality," 51.

27. Porter, "On Keeping 'Persons' in the Trinity," 531.

28. *Webster's Ninth New Collegiate Dictionary*, s.v. "person."

unity in trinity, regulating three, Father, Son and Spirit—three, however, not in unchangeable condition, but in rank; not in substance, but in attitude; not in office, but in appearance;—but of one nature [*substantia*] and of one reality and of one power, because there is one God from whom these ranks and attitudes and appearances are derived in the name of the Father and Son and Holy Spirit."[29] Tertullian sees Father, Son, and Holy Spirit as three distinct expressions, grades, and manifestations of one divine substance or God-nature. They are divine because they derive from one divine nature. To paraphrase Franz Dünzl, as a spring, a river, and a canal are distinct, yet share one nature—namely, water—so the Father, Son, and Holy Spirit are three distinct and interrelated divine entities that possess one divine nature.

For Tertullian, the Father is the source from whom the Son and the Holy Spirit derive. This does not mean that the Son and the Holy Spirit are by nature inferior to God. He writes that "we . . . 'believe' indeed 'in one God,' but subject to this arrangement, which we call economy, that to the one God there should also belong a Son, His own Word, who has come from Him . . . ; that it was He [the Son] who was put by the Father into 'the virgin,' and 'born from' her, both man and God . . . who afterwards, according to His promise, sent from the Father the Holy 'Spirit, Paraclete,' the sanctifier of the faith of them who believe in the Father and the Son and the Holy Spirit."[30] In the *economy* (the ordered roles) of salvation, the three divine persons who are manifestations of a single indivisible power or divine nature perform different functions in restoring humanity and the whole of God's creation to divine fellowship. As Dünzl puts it, "Like the spring, the Father is the inexhaustible origin of the deity; and just as the river rises from the spring, so the Son comes forth from the Father and brings salvation to human beings; and just as the water is distributed over the fields by canals, so the Holy Spirit is distributed to believers in baptism and makes them fruitful."[31] Tertullian's theology of the Trinity can be summarized thus: the *self-existent divine nature* first expressed the divine self in the person of the Father from whom the Son and the Holy Spirit derive their existence.

Critics of Tertullian's view of the Trinity point out that it could lead to the idea of a fourth "thing" or "character" in the Trinity. If the the self-existent divine nature constitutes the ontological unity and oneness of the three persons of the Trinity, and we are not to accept tritheism, it follows that the self-existent divine nature can be distinguished from *its* three "graded"

29. Tertullian, *Against Praxeas*, 30.
30. Ibid., 28.
31. Dünzl, *Brief History of the Doctrine of the Trinity in the Early Church*, 32.

modes of being—the Father, Son, and Holy Spirit. The self-existent divine nature seems to constitute the fourth "thing" in the Trinity.

The following excerpt captures Tertullian's understanding of the ontology, relationship, and roles of the three persons of the Trinity.

> But amongst us it is only the "Son that knows the Father," and He Himself "has revealed the bosom of the Father" and "He has heard" and "seen" all things with the Father and "what things He was commanded by the Father, these He also speaks"; and it was "not His own will, but" the Father's that He accomplished, that will which He knew at close quarters, nay from His inmost soul. "For who knows what is in God but the Spirit who is in Himself?" The word, moreover, is equipped with the spirit, and if I may say so, the word's body is spirit. The word, therefore, was both always in the Father, even as He says: "I in the Father," and always with God, as it is written: "And the Word was with God," and never separated from the Father or different from the Father, because: "I and the Father are one." This will be the projection of truth, the guardian of unity, by which we say that the Son was brought forth from the Father, but not separated. For God brought forth the Word, even as the Paraclete also teaches, as the root does the shrub, the source the river, and the sun the ray. For these forms too are projections of the natures from which they proceed. Nor should I hesitate to call the Son both the shrub of the root and the river of the source and the ray of the sun, because every origin is a parent, and all that is brought forth from the origin is offspring, much more the Word of God, which also in a real sense received the name of Son. And yet the shrub is not distinguished from the root, nor the river from the source, nor the ray from the sun, even as the Word is not distinguished from God either. Therefore according to the pattern of these examples I declare that I speak of two, God and His Word, the Father and His Son. . . . Where, however, there is a second, there are two, and where there is a third, there are three. The Spirit is third with respect to God and the Son, even as the fruit from the shrub is third from the root, and the channel from the river is third from the source, and the point where the ray strikes something is third from the sun. Yet in no respect is it banished from the original source from which it derives it special qualities. Thus the Trinity running down from the Father through stages linked and united together, offers no obstacle to monarchy and conserves the established position of the economy.
>
> Everywhere remember that I have mentioned that Father and Son and Spirit are unseparated from one another, and thus you will recognize what is meant and how it is meant. Understand then; I say that the Father is one, the Son is another and the Spirit another—every untrained or perverse person

takes this saying wrongly, as if it expressed difference, and as the result of difference meant a separation of the Father, Son, and Holy Spirit; but it is of necessity that I say this, when they contend that Father, Son, and Spirit are the same person, fawning on monarchy at the expense of economy—but that it is not by difference that the Son is other than the Father, but by distribution, and it not by division that He is other, but by distinction, because the Father and Son are not the same, being different one form the other even in measure. For the Father is all being, but the Son is a tributary of the whole and a portion, as He Himself declares, "Because the Father is greater than I."[32]

Question: In what ways does Tertullian explain the unity and individuality of the Father, Son, and Holy Spirit?

John Zizioulas

No theologian since the late twentieth century has given better expression to Eastern Orthodox views on the doctrine of the Trinity than Bishop John Zizioulas. His vast knowledge of both the Western and Eastern traditions sets him apart from other Greek theologians. Following the Cappadocian Fathers—Basil of Caesarea, Gregory of Nazianzus, and Gregory of Nyssa— Zizioulas aimed to reposition *personal relationship* as the most adequate way of conceiving of the being of God. He writes, "The substance of God, 'God,' has no ontological content, no true being, apart from communion."[33] This means that God's "threeness is just as primary as oneness; diversity is constitutive of unity."[34]

Zizioulas' concerns in *Being as Communion* were the communal and relational mode of existence of God and the church. He rejects Tertullian's view of *person* for its lack of ontological content. For him, Tertullian's view moved in the direction of Sabellianism or modalism.[35] He contends that Christianity, particularly its expression in the ancient Greek-speaking church, developed the concept of person in a way that united the *person* with the *being* of an individual human being. In other words, the *hypostasis* ("essence") of a human being was identified with the *prosopon* ("person").[36]

---

32 Tertullian, *Against Praxeas*, 43–46.

33. Zizioulas, *Being as Communion*, 17.

34. Zizioulas, "Relational Ontology," 148.

35. Zizioulas, *Being as Communion*, 37.

36. Ibid., 35–36.

This revolutionary understanding of the person moved away from seeing a *person* as "an adjunct to a being (a kind of mask)" to conceiving of the *person* as that which "becomes the being itself and is simultaneously—a most significant point—the constitutive element (the 'principle' or 'cause') of beings."[37] For Zizioulas, Western (Latin-speaking) theologians located the oneness of God or the unity of the Trinity "in one divine substance, the one divinity." In contrast, Eastern (Greek-speaking) theologians located "the unity of God, the one God, and the ontological 'principle' or 'cause' of the being and life of God" in "*hypostasis*, that is, *the person of the Father*. The one God is not the one substance but the Father, who is the 'cause' both of the generation of the Son and of the procession of the Spirit."[38] How does the Cappadocian Fathers' theology of the Trinity avert tritheism—the existence of three distinct and separate gods who are one because they share a common substance? Zizioulas answers thus: "The Cappadocian Fathers said that the analogy of one human nature exemplified by a multitude of distinct persons could indeed be applied to God, provided that we do not include time and space, and therefore separatedness and mortality, in the analogy. With this condition the question of three different gods disappears."[39]

Zizioulas founds his view of the Trinity on *the ontology of communion*. For him, "there is no being without communion"; this communion derives from the *hypostasis*, which he defines as "a concrete and free person."[40] He identifies the *being* of an individual with the *person* of the individual. He writes, "The person cannot exist without communion; but every form of communion which denies or suppresses the person, is inadmissible."[41] God is a being in communion of three *hypostases* ("persons"). To him, "The being of God is a relational being: without the concept of communion it would not be possible to speak of the being of God. . . . It would be unthinkable to speak of the 'one God' before speaking of the God who is 'communion,' that is to say, of the Holy Trinity."[42] The ground of God's ontology does not lie simply in God's *ousia* ("nature"—that is, uncreated being), but rather in *hypostasis* or personal existence.[43] He distinguishes *ousia* ("nature") from *hypostasis* (essence) and also identifies *hypostasis* with *person* (concrete existence).

37. Ibid., 39.
38. Ibid., 40–41.
39. Zizioulas, *Lectures in Christian Dogmatics*, 51.
40. Zizioulas, *Being as Communion*, 18.
41. Ibid.
42. Ibid., 17.
43. Ibid., 44.

Zizioulas' understanding of the Trinity may be summarized as follows: God (the person of the Father) exists; the Father out of love "freely begets the Son and brings forth the Spirit."[44] It is the Father who wills the Trinitarian communion.[45] Love, Zizioulas argues, is the only exercise of freedom in an ontological manner. This ontological freedom is rooted in God's being or mode of existence: "God is love" (1 John 4:16).[46] Understanding God in terms of love, according to Kallistos Ware, is to say that God exists not for self but for the other. Ware argues that "love," as a theological analogy, presents God as an interpersonal being who exists in communion.[47] But Zizioulas and Ware, following the Cappadocian Fathers, imagine the unity of God or oneness of the Trinity in personalist terms, that is, "a unity established through the interrelationship or *koinonia* of the three divine subjects."[48] Both theologians ground the unity of God in terms of relational ontology and not metaphysical or substance ontology.

In his critique of relational ontology, particularly Zizioulas' version, Lewis Ayres rejects the claim that "'relationship' can function as a useful general descriptor of being—divine, human, and non-human."[49] On the contrary, Ayres argues that "the Father as divine person eternally gives rise to the unique divine being that cannot be reduced to 'person' as a category more basic than the union of the three."[50]

The excerpt below captures Zizioulas' understanding of the oneness and threeness of God.

In God...it is not divine nature that is the origin of the divine persons. It is the person of the Father that "causes" God to exist as Trinity. However, "Father" has no meaning outside a relationship with the Son and the Spirit, for he is the Father *of* someone. This plurality and interdependence of the persons is the basis of a new ontology. The one essence is not the origin or cause of the being of God. It is the person of the Father that is the ultimate agent, but since "Father" implies communion he cannot be understood as a being in isolation. Personal communion lies at the very heart of divine being.

44. Ibid., 41.
45. Ibid., 44.
46. Ibid., 46.
47. Ware, "Holy Trinity," 113–14.
48. Ibid., 114.
49. Ayres, "(Mis)Adventures in Trinitarian Ontology," 132.
50. Ibid., 133.

Now we are in a better position to understand the expression "God is love." Christianity did not invent the notion that God is love. Plato believed that God is love, in the sense that love is a flow of the divine nature, a flow as involuntary as the overflowing of a cup or a crater. The Church rejected this conception of love as involuntary emotion or passion, and insisted instead that the phrase "God is love" means that God is constituted by these personal relationships. God is communion: love is fundamental to his being, not an addition to it. Because it is directly related to the doctrine of the Trinity, this point has to be given a great deal of clarification.

It is perhaps our usual assumption that we exist first, and then that we love. However, let us imagine that our existence depends on our relationship with those we love. Our being derives from our relationship with those we love, and if they cease to love us, we disappear. Love is this communion of relationships which give us our existence. Only love can continue to sustain us when all the material threads of life are broken and we are without any other support. If these threads are not reconnected we cease to exist; death is the snapping of the last thread. Love, or communion with other persons, is stronger than death and is the source of our existence. That "God is love" means that God is the communion of this Holy Trinity. God the Father would lose his identity and being if he did not have the Son, and the same applies to the Son and to the Spirit. If we took away the communion of the Trinity to make God a unit, God would not be communion and therefore would not be love.

It is easy to assume that God is love because he loves the world, but the world did not always exist. God did not *become* love because he loves the world, for this would imply that he became love when the world came into existence. But God is absolutely transcendent, his existence is utterly independent of the world. God is love in his being. It is not however himself that he loves, so this is not self-love. The Father loves the Son and the Spirit, the Son loves the Father and the Spirit, the Spirit loves the Father and the Son: it is another person that each loves. It is the person, not the nature or essence, who loves, and the one he loves is also a person. Because this divine love is a matter of personal communion, this love is free: each person loved is free to respond to this love with love.

Our question was whether it is the substance or the person that is most fundamental, in God. We have seen that, in God, essence and person are co-fundamental, neither is prior to the other.[51]

Question: How does Zizioulas define the oneness and threeness of God, and how does his view differ from Tertullian's view of the Trinity?

---

51. Zizioulas, *Lectures in Christian Dogmatics*, 53–54.

Catherine Mowry LaCugna

On the doctrine of the Trinity, Catherine LaCugna (1952–1997), a Roman Catholic theologian, stands very close to the Cappadocian Fathers and John Zizioulas. According to LaCugna, "the acts of God *in history* (and not ontology) were the original subject matter of Trinitarian theology."[52] She moves away from a speculative theology that aims to describe God apart from God's salvific action in the work and activity of Jesus Christ and the Holy Spirit. She argues that the doctrine of the Trinity should not be construed as "a new way to explain 'God's inner life,' that is, the relationship of Father, Son and Holy Spirit to one another (what tradition refers to as the immanent Trinity)."[53] Rather, the doctrine of the Trinity should be seen as "a way to explain the place of Christ in our salvation, the place of the Spirit in our sanctification or deification, and in so doing to say something about the mystery of God's eternal being."[54] LaCugna is hesitant to discuss the doctrine of the Trinity from the perspective of the *immanent Trinity* (God's inner life) in exclusion from or prior to the *economic Trinity* (the activities of the three persons of the Trinity in salvation history).[55] For her, immanent Trinity cannot be separated from economic Trinity—God's way of existing and relating to the world through the work of Jesus Christ and the activity of the Holy Spirit. God is "who and what God is by having a history, both 'internally' [immanent Trinity] and 'externally' [economic Trinity]."[56]

LaCugna argues that Christian theology ought not to concern itself with "predicating attributes (wisdom, or even love) indifferently of 'deity in general.'"[57] On the contrary, Christian theology should ask "who this God is, who acts in this history, with these people."[58] LaCugna applauds Augustine and other theologians (who argued that the Father, Son, and Holy Spirit share a single, previously existing divine essence or substance) for destroying *Arianism*—the view that argued that Jesus Christ did not have the same substance as God the Father.[59] However, she claims that the price of the victory over Arianism was that the doctrine of the Trinity "came to

---

52. LaCugna, "Philosophers and Theologians on the Trinity," 173. Emphasis LaCugna's.

53. LaCugna, "Practical Trinity," 678.

54. Ibid.

55. LaCugna, *God for Us*, 6–7.

56. LaCugna, "Philosophers and Theologians on the Trinity," 173.

57. Ibid.

58. Ibid.

59. Ibid., 174.

be viewed only as a speculative and purely formal doctrine" and as a result "was detached from ordinary Christian life (liturgy, prayer)."[60]

One of LaCugna's major contributions to the doctrine of the Trinity is the rediscovery of its relation to the rest of Christian doctrine, particularly the Christian life. In *God for Us: The Trinity and Christian Life*, LaCugna argues that the doctrine of the Trinity should be at the center of, and also the source for, reflection on all aspects of Christian doctrine. To her, the Trinity should not be about the esoteric "inner life" of God.[61] She proposes an approach to the doctrine of the Trinity that will "root all speculation about the triune nature of God in the economy of salvation (*oikonomia*), in the self-communication of God in the person of Christ and the activity of the Holy Spirit."[62] This approach is grounded on her understanding of the relationship between *theologia*—the mystery of God's inner life—and *oikonomia*—God's providential will manifested in the Incarnation of Jesus Christ and the activity of the Holy Spirit for the purpose of human salvation.[63] In this approach, as she sees it, *oikonomia* is the most appropriate way of entering into the mystery of God's inner life. In other words, our only access to God's inner being and life is through God's manifestations of God's self as triune. She writes, "We can make true statements about God—particularly when the assertions are about the triune nature of God—only on the basis of the economy [*oikonomia*], corroborated by God's self-revelation in Christ and the Spirit. *Theological* statements are possible not because we have some independent insights into God, or can speak from the standpoint of God, but because God has freely revealed and communicated God's self, God's personal existence, God's infinite mystery."[64]

For LaCugna, "God exists eternally as Father, Son, Spirit," and therefore God is in God's being communal.[65] Like Zizioulas, LaCugna argues that the essence of God is relational: "God exists as diverse persons united in a communion of freedom, love, and knowledge."[66] The personhood (*hypostasis*) of God is not an addition to God's being (*ousia*).[67] Therefore, God's nature and being cannot be successfully imagined and described in isolation from God's personhood. As LaCugna puts it, "God exists always

60. Ibid.
61. LaCugna, *God for Us*, 2.
62. Ibid.
63. LaCugna, *God for Us*, 3–4.
64. Ibid., 2–3.
65. Ibid., 23.
66. Ibid., 243.
67. Ibid., 244.

concretely, existentially, in persons. No substance, especially the divine substance, is self-contained or exists without reference to another."[68] As should be expected, she favors *relational ontology* (the understanding of "being" as being-in-relation or being-in-personhood), considering it the only viable way to "avert the separation of *theologia* and *oikonomia*."[69]

To LaCugna, the Trinity, "which is the specifically Christian way of speaking about God," is ultimately a "practical doctrine with radical consequences for Christian life."[70] The doctrine of the Trinity is the Christian explanation of the encounter between "divine and human persons in the economy of redemption."[71] In God's revelation of God's self as triune, God invites humanity into divine fellowship, making human beings "intimate partakers of the living God."[72] The divine and human personhood intersects in the economy that proceeds from God the Father "through Christ in the unity of the Holy Spirit."[73] The doctrine of the Trinity, properly understood, is the Christian way of articulating both God's self-revelation as a being-in-relation and God's invitation of humanity into the divine life of fellowship, which impacts the relationship of human beings to God and to one another. She writes, "The heart of Christian faith is the encounter with the God of Jesus Christ who makes possible both our union with God and communion with each other. In this encounter, God invites people to share in divine life and grace through Jesus Christ by the power of the Holy Spirit; at the same time, we are called to live in new relationship with one other, as we are gathered together by the Spirit into the body of Christ."[74] For her, God does not exist as triune merely for God's sake or God's self but rather for us. She contends that a doctrine of the Trinity ought to be soteriological—that is, it should be concerned with God's providential care and salvation for God's creation.

Some theologians have criticized LaCugna for emphasizing the economic Trinity at the expense of the immanent Trinity.[75] The primary issue here is God's freedom to exist and also God's capacity for relationship independent of God's relationship and mode of existence in the world. LaCugna is aware of this issue and seeks to resolve it by arguing that "salvation his-

68. Ibid., 246.
69. Ibid.
70. LaCugna, *God for Us*, 1.
71. Ibid., 243.
72. Ibid., 3.
73. Ibid., 246.
74. LaCugna, "Practical Trinity," 679.
75. Grenz, *Rediscovering the Triune God*, 158–62; Kärkkäinen, *Trinity*, 187–93.

tory is one mode of the divine self-communication."[76] She continues, "The incomprehensible and ineffable mystery of God is not diminished by God's self-expression in the history of salvation. Nonetheless, because of the unity of *theologia* and *oikonomia*, the specific details of God's self-revelation in Christ and the Spirit reveal God's nature [and inner life]."[77] Some theologians find her resolution unsatisfactory because she does not make a clear distinction between the immanent Trinity and the economic Trinity. Her understanding of the unity of *theologia* and *oikonomia* appears to collapse "God into the economy of salvation."[78]

Current discussions in trinitarian theology usually are structured by the distinction between the "economic" Trinity and the "immanent" Trinity. There is wide agreement in [Roman] Catholic and Protestant theology with [Karl] Rahner's principle that "The 'economic' Trinity *is* the 'immanent' Trinity, and vice versa."

The terms "economic Trinity" and "immanent Trinity" are ways of speaking about the life and work of God. The phrase "economic Trinity" refers to the three "faces" or manifestations of God's activity in the world, correlated with the names, Father, Son, and Spirit. In particular, economic Trinity denotes the missions, the being sent by God, of Son and Spirit in the work of redemption and deification. These missions bring about communion between God and humankind.

The phrase "immanent Trinity," also called the "essential" Trinity, points to the life and work of God in the economy, but from an "immanent" point of view. The word "immanent" has at least two meanings. First, "immanent" means *near* or *present*, as in "God is immanent to the world." In this first sense it is used as the opposite of "transcendent," which means that God is unrestricted by the conditions of finite existence. Second, immanent means *interior* or *inherent*, as in, "the immanent activities of knowing and loving." The latter is the meaning intended by the phrase "immanent Trinity." Thus, "immanent Trinity" refers to the reciprocal relationships of Father, Son, and Spirit *to each other*, considered apart from God's activity in the world. In Rahner's theology, which presupposes that God is by nature *self*-communicating, the immanent Trinity is the "intradivine" self-communication: Father to Son and Spirit. The economic Trinity is the historical manifestation of that eternal self-communication in the missions of Jesus Christ and the Spirit. The identity

76. LaCugna, *God for Us*, 221.

77. Ibid.

78. Grenz, *Rediscovering the Triune God*, 160. See also Leslie, "Does God Have a Life?," 391–98. Leslie argues that this is an error in LaCugna's doctrine of the Trinity.

of the economic and immanent Trinity therefore means that what God has revealed and given in Christ and the Spirit is the reality of God as God is from all eternity. What is given in the economy of salvation, in other words, is the mystery of God which exists from all eternity as triune. But the distinction between economic and immanent Trinity is strictly conceptual, not ontological. There are not two trinities, the Trinity of experience and transeconomic. There is one God, one divine self-communication, manifested in the one economy of creation, redemption, and consummation....

The doctrine of the Trinity is ultimately a practical doctrine with radical consequences for Christian life. Because of the essential unity of *theologia* and *oikonomia*, the subject matter of the doctrine of the Trinity is the shared life between God and creature....

According to the doctrine of the Trinity, God lives as the mystery of love among persons. If we are created in the image of this God, and if our destiny is to live forever with this God and with God's beloved creatures, then what forms of life best enable us to live as Christ lived, to show forth the Spirit of God, and ultimately to be deified? These questions are best answered in light of what is revealed of God's life in Jesus Christ.[79]

Question: How does LaCugna's doctrine of the Trinity explain the relationship between immanent Trinity and economic Trinity?

Theological Implications of the Doctrine of the Trinity

It is one thing to explain what Christians mean when they confess that God is Trinity. It is another thing to draw out what the doctrine of the Trinity means for Christians. The doctrine of the Trinity should not be seen as a theological idea that has no direct bearing on how Christians ought to speak about God and humanity, and also how they ought to live. Despite the difficulty associated with the doctrine of the Trinity, it remains the unique Christian way of interpreting and appropriating God's acts in enacting and sustaining a relationship with God's creation. The theological consequences of confessing that God is triune are enormous. I will highlight only two.

God's Transcendence and Immanence

Confessing that God is Trinity entails that God is *different from* humanity, on the one hand, and is *one with* humanity, on the other hand (Jer 23:24; Isa

---

79. LaCugna, *God for Us*, 211–12, 377–78.

55:8–9; Acts 17:27–28; 1 Cor 2:10–16). The words *transcendence* and *immanence* are used in theology to convey this understanding of God. To say that God is transcendent is to acknowledge God's *otherness*—God is not bound by or limited to what God has created. God must be distinguished from the world. As a result, God "goes beyond our categories of understanding."[80] Human beings, given their finitude, may know God only when God reveals God's self to them. Christianity, as we saw in chapter 2, teaches that God has revealed God's self in a manner that human beings can know. Regarding God's immanence, to say that God is immanent is to acknowledge that God has revealed God's self to humanity, acts "within nature, human nature, and history," and sustains the world.[81] Even though God has revealed God's self in human history, human talk about God cannot encapsulate the totality of God's acts. Such talk about God (theology) will always fall short of the mystery and transcendence of God. This does not mean that human beings cannot come to adequate and sufficient knowledge of God—they can do so because of God's self-revelation. It is rather that no theology can exhaust the mystery of God.

God's transcendence in some ways presupposes God's life within God's self prior to God's act of creating or bringing the world into existence. Theologians call this life of God *ontological Trinity* (or *immanent Trinity*). God's immanence presupposes God's self-disclosure to humanity, particularly for the purpose of salvation. Some theologians have dubbed this activity of God the *economic Trinity*. The Bible does not give extensive details about the kind of life and fellowship the Trinitarian God enjoyed prior to creating the world. While some theologians contend it is possible to distinguish "God-in-eternity" (ontological or immanent Trinity) and "God-in-revelation" (economic Trinity),[82] others argue that such distinction is unattainable and contend that "the reality of God which encounters us in His revelation is His reality in all the depths of eternity."[83]

The closest the Bible comes to saying something about the inner life of God is 1 John 4:7–21. In verses 8 and 16 John tells us that "God is love." He goes on to say that God has demonstrated this life of love by becoming a human being, Jesus of Nazareth. The purpose of this divine act is so that human beings can relate to God in and through God's son, Jesus Christ (1 John 4:9–21). In this text, God's relational nature is the focal point. John Zizioulas has noted that John's words, "God is love," signify that God exists as "person

---

80. Erickson, *Christian Theology*, 273.

81. Ibid., 329.

82. Grenz, *Rediscovering the Trune God*, 55.

83. Barth, *CD* 1/1, 479.

not substance. Love is not an emanation or 'property' of the substance of God. . . . [I]t is that which makes God what He is, the one God."[84]

Karl Rahner's rule—"The 'economic Trinity' *is* the 'immanent Trinity' and the 'immanent Trinity' is the 'economic Trinity'"—is highly informative.[85] Rahner's aim is to show that God's self-revelation occurs only in a salvific context—God's act of reconciling fallen creation to God's self. Catherine LaCugna concurs: "Both immanence and transcendence must be predicated not just of *theologia* [theology or the mystery of God] but *oikonomia* [economy or fellowship]: God's mystery is grasped as transcendent precisely in the economy of salvation. Vice versa, the economic self-revelation of God in Christ is grasped, albeit obliquely, as the mystery of *theologia* itself."[86] Love—the nature of God—is the grounds of both God's existence as a community of three persons and also God's self-disclosure. Therefore, any distinction made between the ontological or immanent Trinity and the economic Trinity is unhelpful and misleading.

Discussing God's transcendence and immanence in the context of the doctrine of the Trinity also points to God's self-disclosure. While it is possible that upon reflection the created order may lead us to ponder the existence of God and God's power and sovereignty, it is only in the event of Jesus Christ that we encounter God's self-revelation. Jesus Christ, in an unprecedented way, bridges the gulf between God's transcendence and immanence. His divinity and humanity allow him to accomplish this enormous task.[87] Revelation is *personal*. As I said in chapter 2, this is the pinnacle of God's self-disclosure in human history. It takes one to reveal oneself. For example, a dad may be able to know something about his son that people who are not close to his son do not know. But it is still possible for the dad, however close he is to his son, not to know some things that his son has not disclosed to him. It takes God to reveal God's self. Many Christians believe that God has revealed God's self in Jesus Christ. Since Jesus Christ is God (as expressed in the doctrine of the Trinity), it makes sense to posit that he effectively reveals God to humanity (John 14:9–14; Col 2:9; Heb 1:3).

God's Relational Nature and Human Personhood

Doing theology from a Trinitarian outlook, argues Paul Louis Metzger, is not a "restatement" of the doctrine of the Trinity. Rather, "Trinitarian

84. Zizioulas, *Being as Communion*, 46.

85. Rahner, *Trinity*, 22.

86. LaCugna, *God for Us*, 322.

87. For discussion of the divinity and humanity of Jesus Christ, see chapter 5.

theology frames consideration of divine and human being in interpersonal, communal terms, and views this interpersonal God as first in the order of being and knowing, with all this shift implies for human concepts, language and culture."[88] However, the relational approach to the Trinity does not sit well with some theologians who want to retain the metaphysical (or substance) ontology that has been the standard way of understanding the unity of God in the Western tradition.[89] Others have pointed out that it is misleading to assume that all Western theologians, particularly in the patristic era, focused on the primacy of substance and undermined the relational nature of God.[90]

Not only does the Trinity tell us something about the nature of God, but it also tells us something about the nature of human beings. Individualism and the pull toward self-love or isolation is a grave threat to human personhood. The doctrine of the Trinity can rescue us from this predicament. To be a person is to be an "other" in relation to "others." Analogically, as no person of the Trinity exists in fullness in isolation, no single individual human being can achieve his or her full potential in isolation. This mutual relationship among the persons of the Trinity is expressed with the word *perichoresis*. Jürgen Moltmann defines *perichoresis* as "a reciprocal indwelling."[91] He writes, "If we understand the divine life perichoretically, it cannot be realized by a single subject alone, and cannot be thought without the three divine Persons. Their shared nature, their shared consciousness and their shared will is formed intersubjectively through their specific personhood in each case, by their specific consciousness in each case, and by their own will in each case. The Father becomes conscious of himself by being conscious of the Son, and so forth."[92]

Carol Barry has noted that "the Trinity is the ultimate paradigm of all our personal relationships: in the sincere gift of ourselves to and for the other we discover our true selves. God is not solitary; hence we are not created to be solitary. We are called to communion with ourselves, others and God."[93] Contemporary European and North American forms of Christianity need to listen to the communitarian voices sounding from Africa, Asia, and Latin America. Several Western theologians have already heeded to this call. But individualism continues to impede the acceptance of community as

88. Metzger, "Introduction," 7.

89. Ayres, "(Mis)Adventures in Trinitarian Ontology," 130.

90. Ibid., 134–35.

91. Moltmann, *Experiences in Theology*, 322.

92. Ibid., 322.

93. Barry, "Trinity," 116.

what ought to precede and shape the individual. In the indigenous culture of sub-Saharan Africa, an individual exists and derives his or her meaning and relevance only in relation to his or her community. This African notion of community is helpful for reimagining both the doctrines of the Trinity and church.

The greatest challenge of the present-day church (the community of all believers who confess the lordship of Jesus Christ) is not coming to terms with the global face of Christianity, but rather *living globally*—that is, coming to a full recognition that no single Christian community can achieve its full potential (morally, theologically, intellectually, or otherwise) in isolation from other Christians communities around the world. In order for the church to make any meaningful progress in achieving its goal as the "body of Christ," each local Christian community must be willing to learn from other communities; each community must learn to participate in the pain, suffering, joy, theological reflection, and worship of other Christian communities.

Concluding Reflections

In spite of the difficulty of conceptualizing the doctrine of the Trinity, it remains the distinctive concept of God that Christianity offers to the world. Rather than dwelling on its difficulty, it would be wise to concentrate on the unique things the doctrine of the Trinity tells us about God, ourselves, and the world at large. Perhaps in no other Christian doctrine does human finitude and limitation come face to face with the mystery of God. But it is precisely the mystery of God that brings us to our human condition—as creatures of God whose existence and meaning depend entirely on God. Given this condition, "we must expect that our frail, sinful, and limited human capacity to reason will be severely tested when trying to accommodate itself to the divine reality."[94]

In the end, the Trinity only approximately expresses the identity and work of God. The Trinity ought not to be the last "name" Christians give to God or the only way they describe the mystery of God's life and work. There are several reasons for this claim. I will state only two. First, our changing experience and contexts should reflect our understanding, imagination, and description of God. The feminist critique of the traditional description of the Trinity and the insistence on renaming the persons of the Trinity—calling them Creator, Liberator, and Advocate, for example, instead of Father, Son, and Spirit—is a reminder that the use of masculine language for God

94. McGrath, "Doctrine of the Trinity," 19.

cannot be countenanced.[95] If masculine language for God continues to be at the root of women's exclusion and oppression, then such language has fallen short of the glory of God and should be dropped or revised. Second, theologians face the challenge of describing God in ways that Christians with no formal theological training can easily identify and use in preaching and living out the good news of God's work in the world in and through Jesus Christ and the Holy Spirit. Anyone who truly understands the doctrine of the Trinity will witness to its immense difficulty and complexity. The unique and most meaningful name Christians give to God need not be too difficult to comprehend. The name should not be left only to professional theologians and people with formal theological training to describe.

Key Terms

Dynamic Monarchianism: the view that construes God as a king who adopted Jesus as a "Son" and endowed him with God's Spirit to do good works.

Economic Trinity: the "ordered" roles of the three persons of the Trinity in salvation history.

Immanence: when used for God, refers to God's interaction with and actions within God's creation.

Immanent Trinity: the "inner" life of fellowship of the three persons of the Trinity.

Modalism: the view that construes God as a single actor who appeared in three different "masks," namely, "Father," "Son," and "Holy Spirit."

Perichoresis: a term used to express the mutual sharing in the life and acts of the three persons of the Trinity.

Transcendence: when used for God, refers to the *otherness* of God or the belief that God is ontologically different from God's creation.

Tritheism: the view that construes God the Father, Jesus Christ, and the Holy Spirit as three distinct Gods.

95. Johnson, *She Who Is*, 210.

Review Questions

1. What are the "economic Trinity" and the "immanent Trinity"? How do they relate and how do they differ?

2. What are the theological implications of the doctrine of the Trinity?

3. What are the differences in the doctrine of the Trinity articulated by Tertullian, Zizioulas, and LaCugna?

Suggestion for Further Reading

Boff, Leonardo. *Trinity and Society.* Translated by Paul Burns. Maryknoll, NY: Orbis, 1988.

Grenz, Stanley J. *Rediscovering the Triune God: The Trinity in Contemporary Theology.* Minneapolis: Augsburg Fortress, 2004.

LaCugna, Catherine Mowry. *God for Us: The Trinity and Christian Life.* San Francisco: HarperSanFrancisco, 1973.

Ogbonnaya, A. Okechukwu. *On Communitarian Divinity: An African Interpretation of the Trinity.* New York: Paragon House, 1994.

Panikkar, Raimundo. *The Trinity and the Religious Experience of Man: Icon-Person-Mystery.* Maryknoll, NY: Orbis, 1973.

Rahner, Karl. *The Trinity.* Translated by Joseph Donceel. New York: Crossroad, 1997.

5

Jesus Christ

This chapter concerns the ways in which Christian communities from the earliest times have understood and expressed the identity and significance of Jesus Christ. It discuses and highlights some of the christological models that shape the conversation on Jesus Christ in contemporary global Christianity.

On a hot summer afternoon in 2006, a deaconess in the Presbyterian Church of Nigeria who resided in Aba (a city in southeastern Nigeria) told me she sometimes called Jesus Christ "the believers' amulet" (*ọ tụ mọ kpọ ndị kwere-ekwe* in Igbo). This was her response to the question, "Who is Jesus to you?" A little context will help us see her reasons for describing Jesus in this way. Many residents of Aba suffered immense pain and loss at the hands of armed bandits who terrorized the city and other nearby towns in 2006. The bandits fearlessly robbed banks, assassinated many helpless victims, and raped several women in the presence of their children, siblings, and husbands. The residents bemoaned the inability of law enforcement agents to bring the bandits to justice. In response, many police officers claimed the bandits had *ọ tụ mọ kpọ* ("amulet" or "charm") that helped them elude law enforcement agents. Many people believed *ọ tụ mọ kpọ* served as a *spiritual* bulletproof for the bandits, making them fearless terrorists. People lost faith in the police and the military, and as a result, they sought an alternative source of protection. Some consulted witch doctors or native doctors for amulets and spiritual protection. A few formed vigilante groups. Many Christians rekindled their trust in Jesus Christ, describing him as the most powerful ọ tụ mọ kpọ. This was part of their answer to Jesus' question, "Who do you say I am?" (Mark 8:27–29). When these Christians call Jesus the savior, they expect that he will not only restore them to divine fellowship but also rescue or deliver them from physical danger, suffering, and pain.

By asking the question, "Who do you say that I am?" Jesus invites his followers of all times to imagine and describe his identity (his person and work) and his significance (what he means to them) on the basis of their experience of him. They are to accomplish these two interrelated tasks with the words and thought forms that resonate with their culture and experience.

Defining Christology

Christology is the discourse about the person, work, and significance of Jesus Christ. A "Christian" Christology should begin with the question Jesus asked his disciples at Caesarea Philippi: "Who do you say that I am?" In the field of Christian theology, Christology is a response to Jesus' invitation to all people to explore his person, work, and significance in the world. This response involves *interpretation* and *appropriation*. If Christology is the "answer" or "response" of an individual or a community to the invitation that Jesus makes in Mark, then we should seek to understand and explain Jesus' significance and meaning to our communities. When understood in this way, Christology is an ongoing inquiry into the person and work of Jesus Christ. Christology, however, can become obsolete and irrelevant if it is not properly appropriated to a given context. Mark 8:28–29 anticipated that those who would respond to Jesus' invitation would do so from their own experience and context—social location, culture, religious affiliation, and language. For the earliest Christians, God chose to reconcile the world in and through Jesus Christ (2 Cor 5:19). Also, God chose to communicate and interact with humanity through Jesus' work (Heb 1:1–4). The task of subsequent Christians, who share these earliest christological confessions, is to explore and describe them intelligibly and relevantly.

The importance of the Bible, particularly the New Testament (NT), in gaining knowledge about the person and work of Jesus Christ is of

> FOCUS QUESTION:
> What is Christology?

paramount importance. Although the books of the NT were not intended to serve primarily as historical texts, they are the extant texts that contain relevant information about the life and ministry of Jesus Christ. Apart from the NT, all that we have are occasional references to Jesus Christ in non-biblical texts.[1] Richard Longenecker has noted that the NT scholars agree on four key assumptions about the NT books: "(1) that there existed among early believers in Jesus various oral and written christological materials, (2) that these materials were first formed and used in the contexts of worship, preaching, and teaching, (3) that these materials gave guidance to the authors of the New Testament in their presentations and arguments, and (4) that it is possible to identify some of these early materials and to describe some of their essential features.[2] According to Longenecker, the Gospels are the products of "personal remembrance, eyewitness reports, the communal memory of the early church and the work of the Holy Spirit in the retention and interpretation of all the recollections of Jesus of Nazareth."[3]

Centrality of Christology

If theology is human discourse about God, the unique contribution of Christianity to theological discourse hinges on what it says about the identity of Jesus Christ and his rela-

> FOCUS QUESTION:
> How does Christology affect and relate to Christian theology?

tion to God. As Paul Tillich writes, "Theology expresses the faith of the church. It restates the paradoxical statement, Jesus is the Christ, and considers all its presuppositions and implications."[4] Christology is central to Christian theology. John Macquarrie has rightly noted that "Christianity, as the name implies, has Jesus Christ at its very center, so that if Christology is concentrated on the study of Jesus Christ, it is not so much a branch of Christian theology as its central theme; or at least, it shares the center with the equally fundamental doctrine of God."[5]

In practice, what does the understanding of the centrality of Christology mean for theology? It does not mean that Christology replaces all Christian theological themes such as theological anthropology, Holy Spirit,

---

1. Longenecker, "Christological Materials in the Early Christian Communities," 47

2. Ibid., 47–48.

3. Ibid., 48.

4. Tillich, *Shaking of the Foundations*, 124.

5. Macquarrie, *Jesus Christ in Modern Thought*, 3.

Christian life, etc. It does mean, however, that none of these doctrines can be successfully discussed in isolation from Jesus Christ. He ought to function as the revealer of divinity and humanity: the one who conveys divinity and humanity and at the same time reshapes our preconceived views of God and humanity. Our views of humanity, divinity, God's righteousness, and sin, for example, will be incomplete if they are not examined in the light of Jesus Christ. It must be noted that it is Jesus Christ himself, and not Christology, that must become a parameter for testing the theologies that qualify as *Christian*. This is because Christologies are susceptible to distortion of Jesus' identity and significance.

Christological Approaches

Traditionally, theologians approach discussions on Jesus Christ from two perspectives: high Christology (or Christology from above) and low Christology (or Christology from below). These two approaches are highly misleading. They have the potential to widen the gap between divinity and humanity. Although not mutually exclusive, they are significantly different.

High Christology

High Christology begins with the divinity or preexistence of Jesus Christ.[6] It begins with "the confession of faith in the deity of Christ as expressed in the New Testament."[7] Theologians who adopt this approach draw insights from New Testament writers such as Paul and John. For example, John presents the picture of an exalted Christ in chapter 1 of his Gospel (1:1–14). John's contribution to Christology is significant because he establishes that "Jesus is fully and truly divine in a way that does not compromise Jewish monotheism—for he is included within the unique divine identity as understood in Jewish monotheism."[8] Justin Martyr and Emil Brunner are examples of theologians who adopted the high Christology approach. In *The Mediator*, Brunner wrote, "But the Christ who is set forth by the chronicler, by the author of a report, or by the historian who is most

> FOCUS QUESTION:
> How should we do Christology?

6. Richard Bauckham prefers the expression "Christology of divine identity" to "High Christology." See Bauckham, "Monotheism and Christology in the Gospel of John," 148.

7. Kärkkäinen, *Christology*, 12.

8. Bauckham, "Monotheism and Christology in the Gospel of John," 149.

profoundly prepared by all his previous training to understand the great and truly human history, or by the man who in all reverence watches and listens for the voice of God within history, is the 'Christ after the flesh.' The believer alone sees more than the 'Christ after the flesh' in the 'Christ in the flesh.'"[9] As a thinker deeply influenced by the Enlightenment, Brunner's aim was partly to refute the idea that "Christian faith springs out of historical observation, out of the historical picture of Jesus of Nazareth."[10]

Although Justin Martyr and Emil Brunner employed the high Christology approach, they used this approach differently. Brunner adopted a high Christology approach because he believed that "our knowledge of Jesus' deity is not grounded in any historical provable facts about his earthly life. It is a faith based upon the faith of the apostles as enunciated in the kerygma."[11] Justin Martyr, a second-century CE theologian, was not concerned with the relationship between the historical Jesus and the rise of Christianity. On the contrary, his aim (as an apologist writing primarily for his Christian and non-Christian audiences who were influenced by Hellenism and Judaism) was to articulate and defend Christian teaching, especially Jesus' relationship with God "the Father."[12] As an eclectic philosopher and theologian, Justin drew upon different philosophies and religions such as Judaism, Christianity, Platonism, and Stoicism.[13] These philosophical and religious traditions influenced his understanding of Jesus Christ. For him, Jesus Christ—the historical figure who lived on earth—was the incarnation of God's *Logos* ("word" or "reason"). According to Justin, "Jesus Christ alone has been begotten as the unique Son of God, being already his Word [*Logos*], his first-begotten, and his power. By the will of God he became man, and gave us this teaching for the conversion and restoration of mankind."[14]

Low Christology

Low Christology, unlike high Christology, begins with and emphasizes the humanity of Jesus. Many theologians who use this approach adopt the historical-critical method that informs the quests for the historical Jesus. Wolfhart Pannenberg is one example. In *Jesus—God and Man*, he argues that the high Christology approach is inadequate because (*a*) it presupposes

9. Brunner, *Mediator*, 157.

10. Ibid., 158.

11. Erickson, *Christian Theology*, 690.

12. See, for example, Justin, *Dialogue with Trypho*.

13. Hurtado, *Lord Jesus Christ*, 643.

14. Justin, *Apologia*, I.23.

Jesus' divinity rather than seeking to rationally demonstrate it, and (*b*) it leads to a neglect of the historical Jesus.[15] Under this approach, the Gospels and other New Testament books are no longer to be taken at face value. They are to be treated with great suspicion. Pannenberg's goal was to begin with the Jesus of history produced by the scholars of form criticism and work his way up to the divinity of Jesus.

Many adherents of the low Christology approach distinguish the "Jesus of history" (the historical figure Jesus of Nazareth) from the "Christ of faith" (the earliest Christians' interpretations of Jesus, which were rooted in their experience and confession of him as the Messiah). Some of these theologians desire to provide a theological response to form criticism. Rudolf Bultmann (1884–1976) was a key figure in the development of *form history* or *form criticism* (the study of the form and genre of biblical texts). Bultmann argued that the understandings of Jesus presented in the Gospels say more about the life situation of the early Christian communities than about the real, historical Jesus. For him, the Gospels are the records of the earliest Christian communities' theological interpretations of the life and ministry of Jesus Christ. The Gospels, therefore, do not present a complete historical account of Jesus' life. He writes: "One may designate the final motive by which the gospels were produced as the *cultic* (that is, the needs of common worship), if one considers that the high point of Christian life was the gathering of the community for worship, when the figure of Jesus, his teaching as well as his life, was set forth before the eyes of the faithful, and when accordingly the gospels served for public reading."[16]

Bultmann employed the word *myth* to describe the events that are presented in the New Testament as having a supernatural origin. The miracles of Jesus, for him, did not happen in real life. Rather, they are myths intended to communicate spiritual lessons or the ways the early church honored Jesus Christ. Myth, for Bultmann, is the "category for talking about things that cannot be dealt with in the confines of the language of history and scientific observations."[17] The fellows of the Jesus Seminar have also made a similar argument about NT representations of Jesus Christ.[18]

Bultmann developed the idea of demythologization (the stripping of myths) as a process to move beyond the myths that have concealed the real Jesus of history. But unlike the liberals of his day who dismissed all myths as irrelevant to modern people, Bultmann believed that the myths contained

---

15. Pannenberg, *Jesus—God and Man*, 34–35.

16. Bultmann and Kundsin, *Form Criticism*, 64.

17. Kärkkäinen, *Christology*, 123.

18. Funk and Hoover, *Five Gospels*, 7.

in the NT are useful for Christian worship and proclamation (*kerygma*) of faith in Jesus Christ.[19]

Since all quests to establish a radical discontinuity between the "Jesus of history" and the "Christ of faith" ended in fiasco, as Albert Schweitzer argued,[20] some scholars who previously advocated a dichotomous understanding of the "Jesus of history" and the "Christ of faith" are now moving toward a synthesis, identifying "the humiliated Jesus of Nazareth with the exalted *Kyrios*."[21]

Critique of Low and High Christology Approaches

Studying the person of Jesus Christ either "from below" or "from above" is unhelpful. Here we see faith and reason in tension, as Millard Erickson has noted: "Since the Jesus of history is approached through reason and the kerygmatic Christ is seized by faith, we are apparently dealing with a case of the classic faith-reason dichotomy."[22] When either one of these two approaches is used in isolation from the other, it usually undercuts the unique achievement of the Christ-event—God's radical identification with humanity in the form of a true human being. A Christology that hopes to remain faithful to the Jesus of the Gospels and the earliest ecumenical conciliar Christologies should see him as simultaneously divine and human; one that exalts Jesus to the point that his humanity is no longer recognizable, or that presents him as merely human and thus denies his divinity, betrays God's act of Incarnation. Christologies that focus on the person of Jesus Christ (ontological Christology) and ignore his work (functional Christology), or vice versa, are equally misleading and inadequate. This is because who Jesus is and his role in God's salvific activity in the world cannot be neatly separated.

Portraits of Jesus Christ in the New Testament

The adoration of Jesus by his earliest followers is not surprising given that in Jesus' day it was not unusual for disciples to honor their masters. What is astonishing, however, as Larry Hurtado has noted, is that "within the first couple decades of the Christian movement (i.e., ca. 30–50 CE)

---

19. Grillmeier, *Christ in Christian Tradition*, 1:3–4.

20. Schweitzer, *Quest of the Historical Jesus*, 478–87.

21. Grillmeier, *Christ Christian Tradition*, 1:4–5.

22. Erickson, *Christian Theology*, 689.

. . . Jesus was treated as a recipient of religious devotion and was associated with God in striking ways."[23] This unusual form of devotion, Hurtado contends, "amounts to a new and distinctive 'mutation' or variant form of the monotheistic practice that is otherwise characteristic of the Jewish religious matrix out of which the Christian movement sprang."[24] What does such devotion to Jesus tell us about his identity, work, and significance?

Jesus' Self-Estimation

What did Jesus believe about himself? Before the nineteenth century, this question was formulated in terms of *"Jesus' consciousness of divinity*, with the classical two natures [divine and human] doctrine of Christ's person providing the starting point for the debate."[25] James Dunn notes that in the nineteenth

FOCUS QUESTION:
What does the New Testament
say about Jesus Christ?

century, there was a shift in focus. Theologians and biblical scholars reformulated the question in terms of "Jesus' self-consciousness." The defining question was, "could a single personality combine a truly human consciousness with a consciousness of pre-existent divinity?"[26] Varied responses to the question appeared, as one could expect. While some theologians, such as F. D. E. Schleiermacher, argued that the answer must be no, H. P. Liddon contended, based on his reading of the Gospel of John, that Jesus demonstrated consciousness of divinity.[27] As theologians and biblical scholars explored the issues regarding Jesus' self-consciousness, attention was gradually turned to Jesus' *messianic consciousness.*

For some New Testament scholars and theologians, a question such as "Was Jesus consciously aware of his divinity?" is fraught with problems. They argue that such a question assumes it is possible to gain access to what Jesus actually taught and believed about himself. But since Jesus did not write any books, it is difficult to know what he really thought about himself. The Gospels, for these theologians and biblical scholars, contain fragments and distorted sayings of Jesus Christ and thus cannot serve as an authentic source for Jesus' self-understanding. *The Five Gospels*, a project of the Jesus

23. Hurtado, *Lord Jesus Christ*, 2.
24. Ibid.
25. Dunn, *Christology in the Making*, 23.
26. Ibid.
27. Ibid.

Seminar, construes the canonical Gospels in this way.[28] The goal of *The Five Gospels* was to answer the question, "What did Jesus really say?"[29] The conclusion presented in the book is stunning: "Eighty-two percent of the words ascribed to Jesus in the gospels were not actually spoken by him."[30]

J. Harold Ellens has argued that while the Jesus Seminar and the quests for the historical Jesus "are worthy undertakings and will . . . continue to produce some useful data," they are "doomed to fail as efforts to ground the Christian faith or movement in history, precisely because there is no adequate historical data in these sources."[31] Ellens contends that the earliest followers of Jesus Christ adopted the mythic narratives and confession as a strategy to advance their new religion.[32]

Like the fellows of the Jesus Seminar, Ellens has failed to convincingly account for two important issues. First, that the earliest Christians understood Jesus in the context of their religious experiences and hopes does not entail that their faith in him as God's Messiah was grounded in events that are not historically true. On the contrary, it was their experience of the miraculous work in Jesus' ministry that partly propelled them to preach him as God's gospel even when their lives were under threat. Second, even though it is logically possible for those Christians to use mythic confession to win converts or to advance the gospel, it does not mean that was actually the case.

In Stephen Davis' assessment, the project of the Jesus Seminar is "a good example of biblical scholarship that has lost its way."[33] There is no convincing evidence that the sayings and words attributed to Jesus Christ by the Gospel writers are so distorted they can no longer be authentically Jesus'. The vast majority of Christian biblical scholars and theologians reject the conclusions and coding of the Jesus Seminar. One way to gain access to what Jesus believed about himself is to examine Jesus' words reported by the New Testament writers. People exhibit certain characteristics and make utterances and comments that can provide clues to their self-understanding. My focus will be on the sayings of Jesus that indicate his understanding about himself. The major problem that underlies this

---

28. Funk and Hoover, *Five Gospels*. When this work was published there were seventy-four members of the Jesus Seminar.

29. Funk and Hoover, *Five Gospels*, ix.

30. Ibid., 5.

31. Ellens, "Jesus Quest," 435–40.

32. Ibid.

33. Davis, *Disputed Issues*, 7.

task is that Jesus did not write anything—"only sayings passed down to us at best second or third hand" are available to us.[34]

"I Am" Sayings (John 6:35–48; 8:12; 10:7–14; 11:25; 14:6; 15:1)

Richard Bauckham has noted that "the Gospel of John contains two series of sayings of Jesus that include the words 'I am' (*egō eimi*—with the pronoun *ego*, which is not always necessary in Greek, used for emphasis along with the verb *eimi*)."[35] There are "I am" sayings with predicates and the absolute "I am" sayings—those that stand alone without a predicate. Bauckham argues that "I am" sayings with predicates (such as "the bread of life" or "the light of the world") are metaphors Jesus used to describe himself as the one who gives salvation.[36] The theological implications of these sayings are their connection with divine prerogatives. For the Old Testament Jews and the earliest Christians, God alone had sovereignty over life and death. This explains why the Jewish audience in John 5 became angry with Jesus and charged him with blasphemy when he healed a sick man on the Sabbath. Jesus' decision to heal on the Sabbath and to defend his actions before the Jewish audience by "claiming God's unique prerogative of working on the Sabbath: 'My Father is still working and I am working' (John 5:17)" suggest that he believed he had the power to exercise divine prerogatives.[37]

Bauckham sees the absolute "I am" sayings (e.g., John 8:58) as the sayings that indicate a "claim to divine identity."[38] However, he concedes the obscurity that is associated with some of the absolute "I am" sayings. For example, in John 8:24 Jesus said to the Jewish leaders, "I told you that you would die in your sins; if you do not believe that I am [*egō eimi*], you will indeed die in your sins." For Bauckham, when the leaders responded with the question, "Who are you?" (8:25), they were essentially expressing their confusion about what Jesus meant by "I am."[39] In his explanation of how the "I am" sayings express divine identity, Bauckham rejects the idea that Exodus 3:14 is the background of the absolute "I am" sayings.[40] He argues that "a difficulty with understanding this as the background to the absolute 'I am' sayings in John's Gospel is that neither the Septuagint nor any other

34. Dunn, *Christology in the Making*, 25.

35. Bauckham, "Monotheism and Christology in the Gospel of John," 153.

36. Ibid.

37. Ibid., 152.

38. Ibid., 155.

39. Ibid., 156. Bauckham has the Jewish leaders saying, "In other words, what do you mean, 'I am'? 'I am' *who*?"

40. Ibid., 157. See Exod 3:14.

Greek translation of Exodus 3:14 translates 'I am' as *egō eimi*, which is the Greek phrase in John's Gospel. The Septuagint has *egō eimi ho on* ('I am the one who is') and *ho on apestalke me* ('the one who has sent me').[41] It is important to note, however, that the Hebrew word *'eheyeh* ("I am") in Exodus 3:14 and Hosea 1:9 is probably the most electrifying expression of divine identity.

Bauckham sees the Septuagint's translation of the Hebrew *'anîhû* ("I am he"—Deut 32:39; Isa 41:4; 43:10; 46:4) as *egō eimi* as the most plausible explanation for how the absolute "I am" sayings express divine identity. He concludes that *'anîhû* is "a divine self-declaration, which encapsulates Yahweh's claim to unique and exclusive divinity." He goes on to postulate that the "I am he" declarations of Deuteronomy 32 and the Isaiah texts "are among the most emphatically monotheistic assertions of the Hebrew Bible. If Jesus in the Fourth Gospel repeats them with application to himself, he must be seen as unambiguously identifying himself with the one and only God, Yahweh, the God of Israel."[42]

The angry reaction of the Jewish audience to Jesus' using the absolute "I am" sayings in John 8 demonstrates that some individuals in the crowd— who knew Exodus 3:14, Hosea 1:9, Deuteronomy 32:39, and a host of other similar Old Testaments passages in which Yahweh simply introduces Yahweh's self as "I am"—felt strongly that Jesus was making a claim that only Yahweh could make.

Abba Prayers and Son-Father Language

In the Gospels, Jesus' use of *abba* (an Aramaic word for father that expresses an intimate relationship within a family context) suggests that he claims to enjoy a unique relationship with God. Since *abba* was not a commonly used word outside of the family context, Dunn concludes that "Jesus' use of it was not merely a formal convention, but expressed *a sense of sonship*, indeed, on the basis particularly of Mark 14:36, of intimate sonship."[43] Jesus' use of this word for God distinguished him from prophets and other religious figures within Judaism. Paul uses the same word to describe the relationship Christians have with God through the Holy Spirit.[44] There is sufficient evidence in the New Testament to suggest that the earliest Christians understood Jesus' sonship in relation to God in a rather unusual way.

41. Bauckham, "Monotheism and Christology in the Gospel of John," 157.
42. Ibid., 159.
43. Dunn, *Christology in the Making*, 28.
44. Fee, *Pauline Christology*, 37–38.

It is striking that the New Testament writers who used the expression "son of God" for Jesus were consciously monotheistic in their theologies. The earliest use of the title "son of God" for Jesus in the New Testament is recorded in Paul's first letter to the Christians in Thessalonica (1 Thess 1:9–10).

The Doctrine of the Incarnation

Description of the Incarnation

Christianity will lose its uniqueness if the doctrine of the Incarnation is dropped. The doctrine of the Incarnation drives all other doctrines of Christianity. It defines Christianity's understanding of God's self-revelation, salvation, and providence. In its basic form, the doctrine of the Incarnation states that God's "Word" (*logos*) became Jesus of Nazareth, the Christ.

> FOCUS QUESTION:
> What does Christianity teach about the identity of Jesus Christ?

John 1:1 and 1:14 stand out among the many biblical passages Christian theologians reference when discussing the doctrine of the Incarnation.[45] In these passages, the Apostle John writes, "In the beginning was the Word, and the Word was with God, and the Word was God. . . . And the Word became flesh and dwelt among us, and we have seen his glory, glory as of the only Son from the Father, full of grace and truth" (ESV). Verse 14 describes the change God's Word underwent: the Word that "was God" (v. 1) "became flesh" (v. 14), and the Word that "was with God" (v. 1) "dwelt among us" (v. 14). Biblical passages such as these bring to our view the content of some of the earliest Christians' devotion to Jesus Christ.

The doctrine of the Incarnation is the Christian confession that God's self-disclosure has taken place in a human being, namely, Jesus of Nazareth. This is a remarkable confession because it requires the confessor to explain (*a*) how Jesus Christ can ontologically be divine or God, and (*b*) how Jesus Christ can successfully be divine and human. In what follows, I will describe and assess the major views of the Incarnation.

---

45. Other biblical passages are John 7, Rom 8:3, Gal 4:4–6, Phil 2:5–11, 1 John 4:2, and 2 John 7.

Interpreting the Doctrine of the Incarnation

More than any other Christian doctrine, the doctrine of the Incarnation has caused major theological disputes. The doctrine assumes that one encounters both divinity and humanity (in an ontological sense) in the historical figure Jesus Christ of Nazareth. In other words, Jesus Christ possessed both human and divine properties. The "strangeness" of this assumption is mind-boggling to many people, including Christians. The consequence of this is the myriad of interpretations of the doctrine of the Incarnation.

Ebionism

Ebionism, a second-century Christology, was one of the major interpretations of Jesus in the earliest Jewish-Christian communities. Its solution to the "strangeness" of the confession that Jesus was divine and human was the denial of Jesus' divinity. Ebionites understood the person and significance of Jesus from the Jewish concept of a messiah and therefore placed him in the category of individuals, such as prophets, whom God used to accomplish certain tasks in the world. The consequence of this understanding of Jesus is the perception of him as an ordinary human being who could be described as "divine" only in a *functional* sense—God accomplished certain tasks through him in an extraordinary way. Ebionites described Jesus as "a man normally born from Joseph and Mary" who was the "predestined Messiah."[46] They denied the virgin birth and also the doctrine of the preexistence of Jesus. They taught that Jesus was ontologically a human being and not a divine being.

The origin of Ebionism remains unknown. Many scholars today associate Ebionism with the Hebrew word for "poor," *ebion*. Theologians and historians have understood the association of Ebionism with "poor" or "poverty" in various ways. While some describe Ebionites as people who chose a life of poverty, others argue they were called Ebionites because of "the poverty of their intelligence" or because they were "poor in understanding, hope and deeds."[47] Ebionism is today regarded as heretical because of its denial of Jesus' divinity. Christologies that deny Jesus' divinity make Christians who worship him idolaters, since God alone is to be worshipped. Such Christologies also shatter the hope of salvation for Christians who see Jesus as the Savior, since only God can save.

---

46. Kelly, *Early Christian Doctrines*, 139.

47. Grillmeier, *Christ in Christian Tradition*, 1:76.

Docetism

Another Christology that became popular in the second century was Docetism. This Christology stood in direct opposition to Ebionism. Unlike Ebionism, which denied the divinity of Jesus in an ontological sense, Docetism upheld the ontological divinity of Jesus but denied he was a real human being. Docetism derives its name from the Greek verb *dokein* ("to seem"). For Docetists, Jesus only "seemed" or "appeared" to be human; in fact, he was a divine being.

The origin of this Christology is unknown. However, it is possible that it (or at least a similar view) was present during the New Testament era. The Apostle John might have been criticizing a form of docetic Christology when he remarked, "This is how you can recognize the Spirit of God: Every spirit that acknowledges that Jesus Christ has come in the flesh is from God, but every spirit that does not acknowledge Jesus is not from God" (1 John 4:2–3, NIV; see also 2 John 7).

The earliest Christians lived in the Hellenistic world, which was saturated with Platonism and Gnosticism. Docetists were most probably influenced by Gnosticism, which viewed the human body as inherently evil, impure, and a kind of prison in which the spirit is entrapped. Such an understanding of the human body explains why some early Christians found it difficult to believe that God, who is spirit, could be willing to become a human being with a real human body. Salvation, for Docetists, is not a holistic act that includes "healing the whole person, body and spirit, but [is] about escaping from the body."[48] Salvation for all who accept Gnostic dualism is knowledge that frees "divine elements, fragment of spirit, in fallen humanity."[49] Docetists believed that all of the human characteristics Jesus seemed to exhibit, such as hunger and suffering, were unreal.

Like Ebionism, Docetism has been considered by most Christians to be heretical. Jesus of Nazareth was a historical figure who grew in knowledge and stature (Luke 2:41–52), suffered real pain, and died on the cross. Docetism distorts the Old Testament understanding of the Messiah as a real human being. It also distorts the Christian belief in God's act of identifying with humanity as a human being (Heb 4:14–16).

48. Sweet, "Docetism," 26.
49. Kelly, *Early Christian Doctrines*, 141.

Arianism

Arianism, which reached its high point in the fourth century CE, consisted of a number of complex ideas of God and Jesus Christ. Arianism is traditionally associated with the theology and Christology of Arius (c. 260–336), a Libyan theologian and priest. Some scholars of Arianism have argued that many of the supporters of Arius were called "Arian" because, like him, they opposed the teaching of Bishop Alexander, and not because they had access to or understood the teaching of Arius.[50] Therefore, *Arianism* may be a misleading term when it is employed to describe the teaching of Arius and his supporters.

In his letter to Eusebius of Nicomedia, Arius described himself as *sulloukianista* (a "fellow Lucianist"), which may suggest he studied in Antioch and most probably under Lucian of Antioch.[51] He was ordained in Alexandria (Egypt) by Bishop Achillas and served under Bishop Alexander of Alexandria, who gave him "authority to 'expound the Scriptures in church.'"[52] Our knowledge of Arius' teaching comes from his few letters and *Thalia* that are preserved in patches and fragments in the writings of his chief opponent, Athanasius. Arius most probably began to publicly expound his theology and Christology around 318 CE.[53]

Unlike Bishop Alexander, who taught that God's *logos* (rational capacity) became Jesus Christ, who was always with God, thus implying the eternal status of Jesus Christ, Arius argued that Jesus Christ was created by God (the Father) and therefore was ontologically different from God. For Alexander, as the *logos* of God, Jesus shared the same nature as God and therefore is the "true God." Arius, however, was unwilling to describe Jesus Christ as the "true God." In arguing that God created Jesus Christ, Arius maintained that God was not always the Father and also that *there was time when the Son of God did not exist.* Arius' goal was to be faithful to those biblical passages that present God as being one (Deut 6:4) and also as being "before all things" (see Col 1:16–17).

Here are three of the theological implications of Arius' Christology: (*a*) God alone is unbegotten and self-existent. God is monad (one) and indivisible and without any plurality. Therefore, God cannot communicate or share God's essence. To do so entails divisibility. (*b*) As a creature of God, albeit a special kind, Jesus Christ does not have the exact nature of God. (*c*)

---

50. Ayres, *Nicaea and Its Legacy*, 13–14.

51. Williams, *Arius*, 97.

52. Ibid., 32.

53. Ayres, *Nicaea and Its Legacy*, 15; Young, *From Nicaea to Chalcedon*, 42.

Given that Jesus was created, he could not know God exhaustively. Arius wrote, "For the Son does not know his own substance, since being a son, he came into actual subsistence by a father's will. What scheme of thought, then, could admit the idea that he who has his being from the Father should know by comprehension the one who gave birth to him?"[54]

Bishop Alexander vehemently opposed the teaching of Arius and excommunicated him. Alexander also opposed Emperor Constantine for demanding the readmission of Arius to the church of Egypt. But Arius found support in bishops such as Eusebius of Caesarea (Palestine) and Eusebius of Nicomedia (a city near Constantinople), who were sympathetic with his teaching. The theological feud between Alexander and Arius would continue despite the attempt of several non-ecumenical councils or synods in Bithynia, Palestine, Alexandria, and Antioch to resolve the matter.

The dispute between Bishop Alexander and Arius would take a notable twist when it caught the attention of Emperor Constantine, who wrote to them demanding a decisive resolution of the matter. In 325 CE, Emperor Constantine summoned an ecumenical council that met from May to July to deal with the mater. I have described below the christological themes in the official statement of the Council of Nicaea.

The Christology of the Council of Nicaea (325 CE)

In the early part of 325 CE, a synod was convened at Antioch under the leadership of Ossius, the confidant of Emperor Constantine.[55] The synod condemned and pronounced anathemas on Arius' theology and Christology. It also placed Eusebius of Caesarea, one of the key supporters of Arius, "under provisional excommunication."[56] The anathemas of the synod of Antioch did not stop the already developing disunity in the church caused by the teaching of Arius. Emperor Constantine was unwilling to turn a deaf ear to it because he feared that the theological dispute posed a serious threat to the peace of his empire. Under Constantine's direction, the first ecumenical church council met at Nicaea, a city that was close to the state capital (Constantine most probably favored Nicaea because it was nearby). Nicaea was an appropriate location because it afforded easier travel access for the bishops from the western hemisphere of the empire. There were over two hundred bishops and church leaders in attendance. It is most likely that

54. Arius, *Thalia*, quoted in Williams, *Arius*, 62.
55. Kelly, *Early Christian Doctrines*, 231.
56. Ibid.

Arius was not present at the council. It is unclear who presided over the council, but many scholars favor the aforementioned Ossius of Cordova.

The extent of Constantine's influence on the outcome of the council remains ambiguous. What is clear, however, is that he supported the decision of the council. If we accept Eusebius of Caesarea's account of the council, we can conclude that Constantine had enormous influence on its decision. Eusebius' reported, as Pier Franco Beatrice writes, that "the word *homoousios* (same substance) was inserted in the Nicene Creed solely by the personal order of Constantine."[57] But whether Constantine desired or demanded the insertion of *homoousios* into the Nicene Creed remains largely unknown. *Homoousios*, however, became an operative word that defined the council's understanding of Jesus' identity and also his relationship to God (the Father). In the theology of the council, as expressed in the Nicene Creed, Jesus Christ was begotten and not created by God the Father. He shared the exact nature of God the Father. The council rejected Arius' teaching, excommunicated him, and pronounced anathemas on all that uphold his teaching: "But as for those who say, There was when He was not, and, Before being born He was not, and that He came into existence out of nothing, or who assert that the Son of God is from a different hypostasis or substance, or is created, or is subject to alteration or change—these the Catholic Church anathematizes."[58]

NICENE CREED

We believe in one God, the Father almighty, maker of all things, visible and invisible;

And in one Lord Jesus Christ, the Son of God, begotten from the Father, only-begotten, that is, from the substance of the Father, God from God, light from light, true God from true God, begotten not made, of one substance [*homoousios*] with the Father, through Whom all things came into being, things in heaven and things on earth, Who because of us men and because of our salvation came down and became incarnate, becoming man, suffered and rose again on the third day, ascended to the heavens, and will come to judge the living and the dead . . .

(quoted in Kelly, *Early Christian Doctrines*, 232)

---

57. Beatrice, "Word 'Homoousios' from Hellenism to Christianity," 243.

58. Quoted in Kelly, *Early Christian Doctrines*, 232.

Theologians disagree on the origins of the Greek word *homoousios*. They also disagree on how the attendees of the council who signed the official theological/christological statement intended it to be understood. Regarding its origin, *homoousios* seems to have appeared in the second century in some Gnostic writings and was used to describe "the relationship between beings compounded of kindred substance."[59] *Homoousios* was "used alongside notions of emanation and derived being which described the ontological links between the highest deity, lower deities, and that within the human being which enabled union with those deities."[60] Origen of Alexandria (c. 185–c. 251 CE) used the term in the sense of a "community of substance." For him, the Son is the effluence of the Father.[61]

Since the Council of Nicaea did not explain how the term was to be understood, it was open to different interpretations. For example, Eusebius of Caesarea, in his letter to the Church of Caesarea in which he set out to justify why he subscribed to the Nicene Creed, argued that *homoousios* did not mean the Son was part of the substance of the Father.[62] The ambiguity of the meaning of *homoousios* might have been what made it attractive to people who wanted to see Christians in the empire coexist in peace. They were willing to "hide some of their idiosyncrasies in order to provide a common front and to achieve wider consensus at the council."[63]

Homoousios could be used to describe the "relationships between realities that [are] hierarchically distinct in other ways."[64] It is noteworthy that the Nicene Creed did not say that the Son was eternally begotten. Lewis Ayres suggests that the absence of the expression "eternally begotten" reflects the "impossibility of getting agreement" on the term *homoousios* and its christological implications.[65] *Homoousios* may have been used to qualify the preceding expression in the creed—"from the substance [*ousia*] of the Father." If this is true, it was used in a generic sense to indicate that "the Son was truly from the Father."[66] The Greek term *ousia* could be used either in a "generic" sense or in a "numerical identity of substance" sense.[67] When understood in the generic sense, God's *logos* (which became Jesus Christ)

---

59. Ibid., 235.
60. Ayres, *Nicaea and Its Legacy*, 93.
61. Kelly, *Early Christians Doctrines*, 130.
62. Ayres, *Nicaea and Its Legacy*, 91.
63. Ibid., 99.
64. Ibid., 95.
65. Ibid., 91.
66. Ibid., 96.
67. Kelly, *Early Christian Doctrines*, 234.

shares the *ousia* of God only by derivation or emanation. If used in the sense of numerical identity of substance, then God's *logos* eternally shares an identical substance with God the Father.

How did the attendees of the Council of Nicaea intend *homoousios* to be understood? We do not really know. Theologians with opposing Christologies, such as Athanasius of Alexandria and Eusebius of Caesarea, claimed to be pro-Nicene Christology. Many theologians now see Athanasius' Christology as a faithful representation of Nicene Christology. After the death of Bishop Alexander, Athanasius became the chief opponent of Arius' Christology and Arius' supporters, such as Marcellus of Ancyra and Asterius. He articulated his Christology in a series of polemical works, notably his *Orations against the Arians*, written between c. 339 and 343 while he was in exile in Rome. Before succeeding Bishop Alexander in 328 CE, Athanasius was a deacon and secretary to Alexander. He attended the Council of Nicaea in this capacity. In what follows I summarize Athanasius' Christology and his polemics against Arius.

"Arians" are not "Christians": Athanasius argued that those who follow the teaching of anyone excommunicated by the church are no longer "Christians"—that is, followers of Jesus Christ, the head of the church. Instead, they must be named "Arians"—an appropriate name, he argued, for those who followed the teaching of Arius, who was excommunicated by Bishop Alexander and some of whose teachings were condemned by the ecumenical council of Nicaea. He encouraged Christians to refuse the hand of fellowship from Arians. He writes, "Wherefore have no fellowship with the most impious Arians. For there is no communion between light and darkness. For you are good Christians, but they, when they say that the Son of the Father, the Word of God, is a created being, differ in nought from the heathen, since they worship that which is created, rather than God the creator."[68]

The Son's eternal generation from the Father: For Athanasius, Jesus Christ, the incarnate *logos* of God, derived from God the Father. As God's wisdom, Jesus was intrinsic to the being of God the Father. Although in the *Orations against the Arians* Athanasius used the word *homoousios* only once, he employed "proper to" or "own" (*idios* in Greek) most often in connection with "from the substance of," which is a key phrase in the Nicene Creed.[69] Athanasius' aim was to refute the claim that Jesus Christ was not truly God and that his divinity was inferior to the divinity of God the Father as Arius

68. Athanasius, *Life of Anthony of Egypt*, 69.
69. Ayres, *Nicaea and Its Legacy*, 114–15.

taught. Athanasius referenced and interpreted several passages of the Bible (such as John 1:14; 14:10; Phil 2:6) to substantiate his arguments. He argued that Jesus did not attain his divinity by God's favor but rather that he was equal with God the Father in substance.[70] To him, the biblical passages that describe Jesus as being "created," "formed," and "appointed" by God do not "indicate the beginning of his being" or suggest that "his essence is created." Rather, they refer to the "renewal that came to be for our sake through his bounty."[71]

Athanasius argued that Arius' rejection of Jesus' consubstantiality with God had serious theological consequences. First, such denial entailed that Christians who are devoted to Jesus and worship him are idolaters, since only the true God is to be worshipped. Second, Athanasius reasoned that the salvation Christians hope for, which is anchored in the person and work of Jesus Christ, was unsecure if he was not truly God. If Jesus Christ was not divine, Athanasius argued, then he was incapable of saving humanity from sin and death.[72]

The Christology of the Council of Chalcedon (451 CE)

Although the Nicene Creed, which was rectified and developed by the Council of Constantinople (381 CE), dominated the history of theological interpretation of Jesus Christ in the fourth century CE, the teaching of Arius survived. The attacks of the Council of Nicaea and the polemics of Athanasius did not eradicate Arius' Christology. It continued to exist in different forms in the works of some of his supporters. However, what the Council of Nicaea achieved, at least in the minds of those who accepted its creed, was the depiction of Jesus Christ as "very God of very God" who had the same divine substance as God the Father.

For several years, theologians struggled to explain in precise terms how Jesus of Nazareth could be "very God" and at the same time truly human. Several councils met between 339 and 451 CE to resolve this christological matter. By the fourth century, two major trends shaped christological discourse. The first trend focused on the unity of the person of Christ; the second emphasized the distinctiveness of his divine and human natures. While the christological views proposed by several theologians between 381 and 451 CE need not delay us, I will highlight some of them.

70. Anatolios, *Athanasius*, 19.

71. Athanasius, *Orations Against the Arians*, 3.53.

72. Ibid., 3.67.

Apollinarianism: This view is associated with Apollinarius (c. 310– c. 390 CE), the bishop of Laodicea in Syria. Following the Nicene Creed, Apollinarius taught that Jesus was consubstantial with God the Father. Like Athanasius, Apollinarius argued for a Trinitarian theology that maintained the divinity of the Father, the Son, and the Holy Spirit.[73] He opposed ontological duality with reference to the person of Jesus Christ. He argued against dualistic Christologies such as *dyoprosopic* Christology—the view that construed Jesus as consisting in two independent personalities (divine and human), and *dyophysite* Christology—the view that construed Jesus as consisting in two distinct natures.[74] To avoid these two dualistic Christologies, Apollinarius proposed a Christology that imagined Jesus Christ within the boundary of the Trinity. His Christology aimed to avoid introducing a "fourth" person into the Trinity. In his *Detailed Confession of the Faith*, Apollinarius wrote, "For we do not say we worship four persons, God and Son of God and man and Holy Spirit."[75] For Apollinarius, dualistic Christologies have disastrous theological consequences. Following Athanasius, he argued that if Jesus' divinity was separated from his humanity, he could not successfully redeem sinful humanity. Also, he argued that Christians are in danger of idolatry since they do not distinguish between Jesus' divinity and humanity during worship.[76]

> "The one without flesh, who was manifested in flesh, is true God, perfect by virtue of the true and divine perfection, and is neither two persons nor two natures. For we do not say we worship four persons, *God* and Son of God and man and Holy Spirit. Consequently we also anathematize those who are so impious that they place a man in the divine doxology. For we say that the Word of God has become man for our salvation, so that we might receive the likeness of the heavenly man and be divinized in the semblance of the true Son of God according to nature, and of the Son of Man our Lord Jesus Christ according to the flesh."
>
> —Apollinarius, *Detailed Confession of the Faith*

For Apollinarius, the unity of the person of Jesus Christ must be maintained. His aim to maintain this unity led him to conclude that in the Incarnation God's *logos* united with flesh or a human body. God's Word (*logos*) fulfilled the roles of the soul and human mind of Jesus of Nazareth.[77] This

---

73. Spoerl, "Liturgical Argument in Apollinarius," 130–32.

74. Ibid., 135.

75. Quoted in Spoerl, "Liturgical Argument in Apollinarius," 135.

76. Kelly, *Early Christian Doctrines*, 291.

77. Ibid., 291.

implied that Jesus had a human body but did not have a human soul. He utilized the theological concept of *communicatio idiomatum* (a Latin phrase that means "sharing of properties or attributes") to develop his understanding of the union of God's word with humanity in Jesus Christ.

The theological implications of *communuicatio idiomatum* were that God became man in order to liberate human beings from sin (redemption), and God became man in order that human beings might become "God" (deification). Apollinarius contended that Jesus was God-man and therefore was worthy of worship. Jesus Christ, he argued, was one person, with one incarnate nature, and one single personality.

Apollinarius' Christology was declared heretical by the synod of Alexandria (378 CE), the synod of Antioch (379 CE), and the Council of Constantinople (381 CE).[78] He was accused of failing to account properly for the humanity of Jesus Christ. Also, his Christology was perceived to have come very close to Docetism, for he denied that Jesus had a human soul.

Nestorianism

This was another Christology that was prominent in the fourth century CE. It was associated with the teaching of Nestorius (d. c. 450 CE), the patriarch of Constantinople. Nestorius contended that *Theotokos* (a Greek word that means "God-bearer" or "the one who gave birth to God") was an inappropriate honorific title for Mary, the mother of Jesus Christ.[79] On Christmas Day, 428 CE, in Constantinople, Nestorius preached a sermon that condemned the use of *Theotokos* as a title for the Virgin Mary.[80] He argued that Mary could not have carried God in her womb or given birth to God. Although the use of *Theotokos* as a title for Mary was present in the fourth century CE, it is unclear when the title *Theotokos* became part of the liturgy and confession of the early Christians. In the sixth century, the Feast of the Entrance of Theotokos was cemented in the liturgy of the Eastern Roman Empire when a basilica in Jerusalem (Church of St. Mary the New) was dedicated to the Virgin Mary.[81]

Nestorianism understood Jesus to have consisted of two distinct natures and two distinct persons. Nestorius, however, distanced himself from this christological position.[82] Some scholars have argued that Nestorius was

78. Ibid., 296.

79. Pelikan, *Mary Through the Centuries*, 55.

80. Olson, *Story of Christian Theology*, 213.

81. Carlton, "Temple that Held God," 103.

82. Kelly, *Early Christian Doctrines*, 312.

not a Nestorian. In *The Bazaar of Heracleides*, Nestorius argued in favor of the unity of the humanity and divinity of Jesus Christ and in favor of "Christ-bearer" (*Christotokos*) as an adequate replacement for "God-bearer."[83] Also, he argued that Mary only gave birth to the humanity of Jesus Christ and that even after the Incarnation the divine and human natures of Jesus Christ were unaltered and distinct. This distinction was important for Nestorius because he insisted that God was impassible and as such could not undergo any change such as dying and suffering. Also, he feared that the title *Theotokos* could lead to the worship and divinization of Mary. He opposed vehemently Cyril of Alexandria's ideas of *communicatio idiomatum* and *hypostatic union* (union of substance or nature), arguing that it suggested a confusion or mixture of the two natures of Jesus Christ.

Nestorius preferred the word *conjunction* to *union* when speaking of the relationship of the divine and human natures of Jesus Christ. These two natures dwelled in a single person—Jesus Christ. Nestorius also described the two natures of Jesus Christ as two *prosopa* ("persons"). These two "persons" were united in a common *prosopon* or common person. He used the word *prosopa* for the two natures in order to convey the idea that each nature had its own concrete character.[84] His view can be summarized as follows: in the Incarnation, two natures (divine and human), which had their own independent and concrete characters, united in a common person, namely, Jesus Christ.

Some theologians contend that Nestorius failed to successfully demonstrate the unity of the person of Jesus Christ in his Christology. As Roger Olson has remarked, "In the end, in spite of his valiant attempt to explain how a conjunction of two persons could count as one person (*prosopon*), his Christ turns out to be two individuals and not one."[85]

Eutychianism

This christological position was linked to the teaching of Eutyches (c. 378–c. 454 CE), an abbot of a monastery in Constantinople. He was uncomfortable with Nestorius' position on the relationship of the two natures of Jesus Christ. To Eutyches, in the union of the two natures in the Incarnation, the divinity of Jesus Christ absorbed his humanity. Given this union, he was reluctant to say that Jesus Christ shared this same substance or nature with

---

83. Nestorius, *The Bazaar of Heracleides*.

84. Kelly, *Early Christian Doctrines*, 313.

85. Olson, *Story of Christian Theology*, 218.

the rest of humanity.[86] He contended that Christologies that spoke of the two natures of Christ (after the Incarnation) were biblically unwarranted.

Pope Leo I, in his famous *Tome* (a letter he wrote in 499 CE to patriarch Flavian of Constantinople), condemned the Christology of Eutyches. In this document, Leo I argued that Jesus was one person with two natures. Although the two natures did not mix together in the Incarnation, they coexisted in Jesus Christ. Leo's *Tome* was instrumental in the condemnation of Eutyches' Christology by the synod of Constantinople in 450 CE.[87]

Two major interpretations of Eutyches' Christology have survived. The first interpretation argues that Eutyches' view of the union of the two natures in the Incarnation implied that Jesus was a hybrid person, resulting from a mixture or fusion of divine and human natures. The second interpretation associates his Christology with a form of Docetism. According to this interpretation, Eutyches' Christology implied that the divinity of Jesus swallowed up his humanity. This meant that the "one nature" of Jesus was divine and as such Jesus could no longer be truly human.[88]

In 451 CE, the newly enthroned Emperor Marcian called for an ecumenical council to deal with several christological disputes. His goal for calling the council was to establish a single faith throughout his empire. With more than five hundred attendees, the Council of Chalcedon sought to maintain the unity of Jesus' personhood. It also distinguished Jesus' two natures. The Council of Chalcedon produced a document that is known today in theological literature as the Chalcedonian Definition.

The achievements and failures of the Council of Chalcedon are noteworthy. In its christological definition, it used phrases that created and enforced the parameter for interpreting the person and work of Jesus within the empire. For example, it stated that Jesus was "at once complete in Godhead and complete in manhood" and also that he was "truly God and truly man." The contents of these christological phrases are dense and can only be fully appreciated when they are understood within the context of a compromise. The Chalcedonian Definition skillfully weeded out the extremes of the Christologies that failed to maintain the unity of the person of Jesus and those that did not preserve this distinctiveness of his divine and human natures.

The Council of Chalcedon, however, failed to achieve an ecumenical or theological unity. Some attendees who accepted Cyril of Alexandria's view of hypostatic union and doctrine of one incarnate nature refused to sign the

---

86. Kelly, *Early Christian Doctrines*, 333.

87. Grillmeier, *Christ in Christian Tradition*, 1:529.

88. Kelly, *Early Christian Doctrines*, 333.

Chalcedonian Definition. Those who argued that Jesus had one incarnate nature were labeled *Monophysites*. The Monophysite position continues to exist today in Coptic and Armenian Orthodox Churches.[89]

Theological Implications of the Doctrine of the Incarnation

What are the theological implications of the confession "Jesus is God incarnate"? More specifically, what does the doctrine of the Incarnation signify or mean for God, Jesus Christ, and humanity? Since the Council of Nicaea and the Council of Constantinople, the majority of Christians see Jesus Christ as God *incarnate* (God's Word in flesh). In the theological statements and creed of these councils, the honorific phrases "God of God," "Light of Light," "very God of very God," and "of the same substance with the Father" were ascribed to Jesus Christ.[90] Given the frequency of the usage of these terms during Christian worship, some may think they are used in the Bible. These honorific phrases now serve as lenses through which many Christians interpret the person and significance of Jesus Christ. The phrases, for example, informed the christological definition of the Council of Chalcedon, which construed Jesus as "complete in Godhead and complete in manhood," or to put it differently, "fully God and fully man." The Christologies of these three earliest councils have become the foundation of the majority of contemporary Christologies. Pope Benedict XVI, for instance, in his *Credo for Today*, writes, "Jesus is a man and possesses human nature in the fullest sense. At the same time, he is one with God, not simply by reason of his conscious dedication to the Lord, but by reason of his very being. As Son of God he is just as truly God as he is truly man."[91]

God and the Doctrine of the Incarnation

The Christian confession that Jesus Christ is God incarnate entails that God's *logos* or Son did not simply dwell in a human being; he *became* human. This entails a radical change in God's mode of being and mode of operation. The Incarnation has an ontological consequence. Since God is ontologically different from humans, it follows that in becoming human, God's Son or *logos* experiences a change in his mode of existence. The doctrine of the Incarnation attests to God's relational mode of being.

---

89. See Baker, "Chalcedonian Definition," 77–97.

90. See the Nicene Creed (also known as the Niceno-Constantinopalitan Creed).

91. Ratzinger, *Credo for Today*, 51.

Christological questions paved the way for the robust discussions on the Trinity in the early church. Before the birth of Jesus Christ in c. 4 CE, God showed God's self in history in various ways, as many Christians believe. God created all things; God conversed with people in dreams, visions, and events; and God spoke through individuals such as prophets (Rom 1 and 2; Heb 1:1–2). God has never remained completely hidden from humanity. Since creation, God has continued to communion with humanity. But if God has interacted with God's creation from the beginning, why did God become human? Were the other forms of God's mode of operation insufficient? What does the Incarnation say about God's character and identity? Theologians answer these questions in different ways. Some, focusing on the relationality of God, see the Incarnation as God's intimate and uttermost expression of God's self as love (1 John 4:8).

Thomas F. Torrance saw God's self-disclosure in Jesus Christ in this way: "In Christian theology, personal participation in knowledge is understandably accentuated through the self-communication of God to us in Jesus Christ, which is personalizing as well as a personal activity."[92] Torrance continued, "However, we have to take into account here something more than the establishing of personal reciprocity between God and man, for since it is God as Communion of personal Being who communicates himself to us through Christ and in his Spirit, it is a community of persons in reciprocity both with God and with one another that is set up."[93]

Some theologians may answer the question, "Why did God become a human being?" from the perspective of salvation. For them, the purpose of the Incarnation is to deal with humanity's sin (Heb 9:26; 1 Pet 1:18–21; 1 John 4:10). Anselm of Canterbury, in *Cur Deus Homo* (Why God Became Man), puts it in this way: "For when death entered into the human race through man's disobedience, it was fitting that life should be restored through the obedience of man. When the sin which was the cause of our condemnation had its beginning from a woman, it was fitting for the author of justice and salvation to be born of a woman. Since the devil, when he tempted man, conquered him by the tasting of a tree, it was fitting for him to be conquered by man's bearing of suffering on a tree."[94]

92. Torrance, *Reality and Evangelical Theology*, 46.
93. Ibid., 46.
94. Anselm, *Cur Deus Homo*, I.3.

The Divinity of Jesus Christ and the Doctrine of the Incarnation

The doctrine of the Incarnation presupposes Jesus' divinity. The belief in the divinity of Jesus Christ is one the major Christian confessions of faith. It is no surprise that many Christians today readily talk about the divinity of Jesus and not his humanity. One question that might lead us to the heart of the issue is this: Should we understand Jesus' divinity functionally or ontologically? To put it differently, is Jesus Christ "God" because God accomplished certain special tasks through him (functionally), or is Jesus God because he shares God's nature (ontologically)? The majority of Christians lean more toward the ontological understanding of Jesus' divinity. There are some theologians who have argued that Jesus is divine because he is the *locus* of God's salvfic act.[95] This, of course, implies that Jesus was ontologically a human being and not a divine being or God. To say that Jesus the Christ is divine in an ontological sense implies he has a divine nature (John 1:1; 1:18; 20:28; Rom 9:5; Titus 2:13; Heb 1:8; 2 Peter 1:1). To paraphrase the language of Nicene Christology, God's eternal *logos* became a human being, that is, became Jesus of Nazareth.

As God (in the ontological sense), Jesus' divinity preexists his humanity. In Christian theology, this belief is known as the *preexistence of Jesus Christ*. In the Bible, the expression "word of God" connotes God in action. In Genesis 1:1–24 (cf. Ps. 33:6), God's word brought things into existence. When the word of God is personified, it becomes God's creative agent or messenger (Ps 107:20). In John 1:1, the word of God is identical with God: "the Word was God" (*theos ēn ho logos*). This same word of God, at a certain time in human history, assumed a human nature and became Jesus Christ (John 1:14; Gal 4:4–5). In the words of Karl Barth, "the Word, and therefore the Jesus Christ who is identified with the Word according to John 1:1–18, is 'very God.' And 'very God' means the one, only, true, eternal God."[96]

As truly divine, Jesus Christ discloses or unveils God. If we accept the words of Hebrews 1:1–2, we can conclude that "the final revelation has taken place" in Jesus Christ. John Webster observes that "God has spoken in his Son, and in so doing has inaugurated a new era of fulfillment, in which the divine Word is present with unambiguous clarity, definition and completeness."[97] Hebrews 1:1–2, however, ought to be read in light of John 1:18: "No one has ever seen God, but God the One and Only, who is at the Father's side, has made him known" (NIV). Here we might ask, does Jesus

---

95. Baillie, *God Was in Christ*.

96. Barth, *CD* 1/2, 132.

97. Webster, "One Who Is Son," 71.

reveal God because he is God incarnate? Or does Jesus reveal God because, *in and through him*, God has made God's self known in human history? These questions highlight the issues I have already identified as the ontological and functional senses in which the expression "Jesus is God," or in the words of the Nicene Creed "very God of very God," can be understood.

God's self-revelation to humanity needs to meet two requirements. First, it needs to unveil God's identity (character, nature, vision, mission, action, and so on). And given that God is ontologically different from human beings, it is only God or one who is identical to God who can truly unveil God's identity. Second, God's self-revelation needs to be recognizable by human beings. The Incarnation meets these two requirements. F. F. Bruce's commentary on John 1:18 highlights how Jesus Christ meets the first requirement. He writes, "Only one who fully knows him can make him fully known."[98] Since Jesus is truly human, he can also identify with us as humans and also at the same time reveal how human beings can *become truly human* in the way that God wills and desires for them.

The Humanity of Jesus Christ and the Doctrine of the Incarnation

The doctrine of the Incarnation also teaches Jesus' humanity. Christians sometimes are guilty of deemphasizing his humanity. This is a serious theological problem. The doctrine of the Incarnation teaches that God was not restricted to speaking to humanity from where human beings could not have any direct access. Also, God was not satisfied with relating to human beings as a phantasm. In a radical act, the triune God moved God's relational nature in a surprising direction by allowing God's *logos* to become a human being—a boy who grew up within the Jewish and Greco-Roman cultures.

The humanity of Jesus Christ cannot be taken for granted. Doing so is tantamount to ignoring the miracle of *God with us* in the person of Jesus Christ. Karl Barth remarks, "What makes revelation revelation and miracle miracle is that the Word of God did actually become a real man and that therefore the life of this real man was the object and theatre of the acts of God, the light of revelation entering the world."[99]

The New Testament teaches that Jesus was a real human being. He was born Jewish and exhibited his humanness by crying and by getting angry and hungry. He lived among other people. He died and experienced pain, but was raised from the dead by God. He developed physically, mentally,

98. Bruce, *Gospel of John*, 45.
99. Barth, *CD* 1/2, 147.

and socially (Luke 2:52). Writing about the meaning of "flesh" in John 1:18, Thomas F. Torrance states:

> John means that the Word fully participates in human nature and existence, for he became man in becoming flesh, true man and real man. He was so truly man in the midst of mankind that it was not easy to recognize him as other than man or to distinguish him from other men. He came to his own and his own received him not. He became a particular man, Jesus, who stands among other men unsurpassed but unrecognized. That is the way he became flesh, by becoming one particular man. And yet this is the creator of all mankind, now himself become a man.[100]

What kind of human being was Jesus? Was he like all human beings in every way? Was he unlike human beings in any way? The answers we give to these questions will have a significant impact on our understanding of God's sovereignty, God-human relations, the doctrine of sin, the doctrine of salvation, Christian life, and so on. Augustine's theology of original sin, in which he argued that because of the disobedience of Adam and Eve human beings are born with sin natures, has had a significant impact on Christology. Did Jesus inherit a sin nature? Karl Barth answers the question in the affirmative. He writes,

> God Himself in person is the Subject of a real human being and acting. And just because God is the Subject of it, this being and acting are real. They are a genuinely and truly human being and acting. Jesus Christ is not a demigod. He is not an angel. Nor is He an Ideal man. He is a man as we are, equal to us as a creature, as a human individual, but also equal to us in the state and condition into which our disobedience has brought us. And in being what we are He is God's Word. Thus as one of us, yet the one of us who is Himself God's Word in person, He represents God to us and He represents us to God. In this way He is God's revelation to us and our reconciliation with God.[101]

Barth understands the word *flesh* in John 1:14 to mean "human nature and existence." He argues that the *logos'* becoming flesh "cannot be real except in the concrete reality of one man"; therefore, it must be said that the *logos* became a man.[102] The *logos* did not adopt a generic humanity

---

100. Torrance, *Incarnation*, 61.

101. Barth, *CD* 1/2, 151.

102. Ibid., 149.

or a preexisting human body. Rather, the *logos* became Jesus Christ. "In so doing," writes Barth, the *logos* "did not cease to be what He was before, but He became what He was not before, a man, this man."[103] If Jesus did not have a fallen nature, for Barth, he could not concretely identify with the rest of sinful humanity. "But there must be no weakening or obscuring of the saving truth that the nature which God assumed in Christ is identical with our nature as we see it in the light of the Fall. If it were otherwise, how could Christ be really like us?"[104]

On the contrary, some theologians argue it is possible for a human being to be truly human without being sinful or possessing a sin nature. For these theologians, sin nature is not an essential attribute of human beings. Consequently, they argue that although Jesus was truly human, he did not have a sin nature. As truly human, Jesus is like all human beings in some concrete ways. However, he is different from the rest of humanity in other ways—and this is not only because he was divine but also because he had a different human nature, a non-creaturely human nature. As Thomas Morris argues, "The many properties of metaphysical limitation and dependence that characterize you and me do so, then, not because they are essential elements in our common human nature. They may characterize you and me necessarily. Presumably, they do. But it is not in virtue of our being human; rather, it is in virtue of our being the humans we are."[105] For Morris, Jesus was *fully* human but not *merely* human. His human nature differs from our human nature in that he did not have a creaturely, sinful nature. "Thus, God the Son," Morris writes, "through whom all things are created, need not have taken on any of those limitation properties distinctive of our creatureliness in order to take on a human nature. He could have become fully human without being merely human."[106]

Examples of the Interpretation and Appropriation of the Person and Significance of Jesus in the Twenty-First Century

The goal of this section is to highlight some of the major Christologies of the twenty-first century. In the Western world, theologians have continued to search for a "rational faith." Many are preoccupied with the desire to explain Christian doctrines in a manner that is rational and logically justifiable. Two Christologies in particular—kenotic Christology and two-minds

103. Ibid.
104. Ibid., 153.
105. Morris, *Our Idea of God*, 165.
106. Ibid.

Christology—exemplify the search for a rational faith within Western Christianity. The focus of these two Christologies is to answer the question, how is it logically possible for one person (Jesus Christ) to have two distinct natures? But in the non-Western world, many theologians focus on God's active involvement in human affairs in their interpretations of Jesus Christ. They explore God's acts of healing, protection, and provision in the person and work of Jesus. For these theologians, the primary question of Christology should be this: What does Jesus Christ mean for people who are searching for spiritual and physical healing and who also desire to know God experientially? This question informs and shapes the ancestor Christologies of sub-Saharan African theologians and the liberation Christologies of Latin American theologians. Instead of searching for a "rational faith," these Christologies focus on the significance of Jesus Christ for women who are victims of gender, racial, and class warfare and are desperately in need of healing.

Kenotic Christology

Kenotic Christology became popular in Europe in the sixteenth century. Some German theologians, following in the footsteps of Martin Luther (1483–1546), imagined the question of Jesus' humanity and divinity from the perspective of the doctrine of "the communication of attributes" (*communicatio idiomatum*). This doctrine teaches that the divinity and humanity of Jesus mutually shared their properties and experiences. Questions such as "Did Jesus need to abandon any of his divine attributes in order to be genuinely human?" and "Did Jesus make use of any of his divine attributes during his earthly life?" shaped the christological discourse of this era. Two responses emerged.

First, some theologians believed that Jesus did not empty himself or divest himself of any of his divine attributes. They argued that if in the hypostatic union the human nature of Jesus participated or shared in his divine nature, it follows that Jesus' divinity experienced things appropriate to his humanity, such as death and pain; and consequently, his humanity experienced things appropriate to his divinity, such as omnipresence and omnipotence. However, theologians who shared this view of *communicatio idiomatum* differed in their understanding of Jesus' use or nonuse of his divine attributes during his earthly life. While some argued that Jesus Christ used his divine attributes secretly (*krypsis* theory), others argued that Jesus abandoned the use of his divine attributes (*kenotic* theory).

The second response, while kenotic in vision, moved radically in a different direction. According to this view, as God-man, Jesus did not use his nonessential divine attributes (that is, those attributes he could divest himself of without ceasing to be God) during his earthly life because he did not posses them. Theologians who adopted this kenotic view argued that the pre-incarnate divine *logos* (God's Son) willingly divested himself of some of his divine attributes in order to be truly human in his incarnate state. I will only focus on the kenotic theory.

The German theologian Gottfried Thomasius (1802–1875) championed the view of divine emptying. Thomasius' kenotic Christology was deeply informed by *soteriology* (the doctrine of salvation). He reasoned that "human sinfulness made the incarnation necessary, and only someone who shares natures with both God and human beings can work to correct what has gone wrong."[107] Operating with a two-nature Christology, Thomasius argued that God's Word (or God's Son) willingly emptied himself of his nonessential attributes in order to become truly human.[108] This kenotic model understands literally the verb "empty" (*kenoo* in Greek) in Philippians 2:7. Thomasius argued that kenosis or self-limitation was required in order for Jesus to be a real human being. He taught that the self-limitation or kenosis of the Son of God involved the abandonment of his relative or nonessential divine attributes only, such as omniscience, omnipotence, and omnipresence. God's Son retained his essential or "immanent" divine attributes—those attributes "which God 'has' in and for himself without respect to the existence of the world, things like truth, holiness and love."[109] Since God's Son did not relinquish or divest himself of his essential divine attributes, he remained fully God in his incarnate state. Also, since he emptied himself of his nonessential divine attributes, he was fully human. Thus, he relied on the Holy Spirit to know and accomplish what human beings are incapable of knowing and accomplishing.[110] At the completion of his work on earth, Thomasius argued, God's Son regained the relative or nonessential attributes he had abandoned for the purpose of becoming a genuine human being.

There are four main criticisms against Thomasius' kenotic Christology. First, some theologians have argued that it is impossible to differentiate God's essential from God's nonessential attributes. Second, some theologians claim that omniscience, omnipotence, and omnipresence are in fact

107. Brown, *Divine Humanity*, 44.

108. Thomasius, "Christ's Person and Work," 44–46.

109. McCormack, "Karl Barth's Christology," 246.

110. Thomasius, "Christ's Person and Work," 65–67.

God's essential attributes. So if Jesus divested himself of any of these attributes he was not truly God. Third, some theologians question Thomasius' construal of the temporality of the divestment of the nonessential divine attributes. Oliver Crisp has articulated this problem. He writes, "If the Word relinquished certain divine attributes for the duration of Christ's life and ministry, what are we to make of the ongoing life and ministry of Christ after the ascension? For, traditionally, theologians have taught that after his ascension Christ sits at the right hand of the Father, interceding for his saints, and will come again in glory to judge the living and the dead. What is more, Christ will remain fully human as well as fully divine beyond the last judgment, into eternity."[111] Fourth, some biblical theologians have argued that *kenoo* in Philippians 2:7 should be understood metaphorically. When thus understood, *kenoo* does not refer to Jesus' emptying or divesting himself, but rather to his acts of humility and self-giving, which resulted in his death on the cross.[112]

In the excerpt below, Thomasius describes his version of kenotic Christology, which states that God's eternal Word set aside temporarily his nonessential divine attributes in order to become a true human being.

Gottfried Thomasius: Self-Limitation of the Eternal Son of God

This divine-human person can only have originated through God's determining of himself to actual participation in the human mode of being, *i.e.*, in the human form of life and consciousness, and indeed in that form which is peculiar to the present state of our race. And thus we shall have to posit the incarnation itself precisely in the fact that he, the eternal Son of God, the second person of the deity, gave himself over into the form of human limitation, and thereby to the limits of a spatio-temporal existence, under the conditions of a human development, in the bounds of an historical concrete being, in order to live in and through our nature the life of our race in the fullest sense of the word, without on that account ceasing to be God. Only so does there occur an actual entrance into humanity, an actual becoming-one with it, a becoming-man of God; and only so does there result that historical person of the mediator which we know to be the God-man.

The transition into this condition is manifestly a self-limitation for the eternal Son of God. It is certainly not a divesting of that which is essential to deity in order to be God, but it is divesting of the divine mode of being in favor of the humanly creaturely form of existence, and *eo ipso* a renunciation of the

111. Crisp, *Divinity and Humanity*, 135.
112. Fee, "New Testament and Kenosis Christology," 32.

divine glory which he had from the beginning with the Father and exercised vis-à-vis the world, governing and ruling throughout.

In the unity of the two the incarnation is itself the deepest mystery of self-denying love, a deed of love in which the eternal Son of the Father becomes like unto us, in suffering and dying to reconcile us with God and to make us hereafter participant in his glory—the wonder of the love whose praise reverberates from every believing heart, and of which the church sings in adoration: "In our poor flesh and blood is veiled the highest good; he who bears all things alone, has become a little child" . . .

[T]he Holy Spirit first governs formatively in the depth of his natural and personal life and then imparts himself to [the incarnate one] in peculiar fullness for his vocation; the Spirit shows him the temporal moments of the divine will of salvation and mediates to his human nature the ability to carry out that will. Thus the Spirit is here too shown to be the objective unity of the two, common to both the Father and the incarnate Son, but in such a way as corresponds to that relationship of the two to each other which came into being by the incarnation, and to the purpose for which that relationship came to be. How early would this influence of the Holy Spirit on Jesus have begun? It will have been linked directly with the conception, and consequently will never have stopped; it will have ruled over the life of the holy child like a silent, secret stirring and wafting; it will have shed its light even in the condition of relative unconsciousness, and will have opened that still inchoate consciousness early to the light of self-consciousness.[113]

Questions: How does Thomasius establish the humanity of Jesus Christ? What are your responses to the criticism against Thomasius' kenotic Christology?

Not all kenotic theologians consider a metaphysical self-emptying of divine attributes a precondition for the Incarnation. These theologians insist that the pre-incarnate divine *logos* need not, and in fact did not, empty himself of any of his divine attributes in order to be truly human (like all human beings in their limitations) in his incarnate state. Gordon Fee presents a clear account of this version of kenotic Christology. Fee asks whether the Greek word *ekenōsen* in Philippians 2:7 "is best understood literally or metaphorically as a way of expressing what Christ did 'as God'. Did he literally 'empty himself of *something*' when he took the form of a slave? Or did he metaphorically 'make himself nothing' by assuming the form of a slave, in becoming human?"[114] Fee's response is that the idea of Christ emptying

113. Thomasius, "Christ's Person and Work," 47–49, 66.
114. Fee, "New Testament and Kenosis Christology," 33.

himself of something (e.g., divine attributes) is foreign to Paul, and therefore *kenoo* in Philippians 2:7 should not be taken literally. Fee writes, "The real issue for Paul is the selflessness of God, expressed by the pre-existent divine Christ, whereby in his 'becoming human' he took the *morphe* [form] of a slave—one who expressed his humanity in lowly service to others."[115] Paul chose the word *morphe*, according to Fee, because it is "the one word available in Greek that would fit the two participial expressions on either side of the main verb (*ekenōsen*); thus here it does not carry the sense of 'image' (which it never carries in any case), but refers rather to the essential godlikeness, on the one hand, and of servanthood, on the other."[116] Fee concludes that God's Son deliberately chose "by the very nature of his assuming a truly human life, to limit certain divine prerogatives that in the end seem incompatible with his being truly human, most notably his omnipresence, omnipotence, and omniscience. Thus, without ever 'setting aside' or 'emptying himself of' anything essential to his being truly God, he chose in becoming incarnate to live out a truly human life on our planet, in which he would be totally dependent on the Father through the work of the Holy Spirit."[117] Thus Jesus performed miracles and accomplished extraordinary tasks by the power of the Holy Spirit (Luke 4:14–21; Acts 10:38).

The criticisms against both Thomasius' kenotic Christology and Fee's kenotic Christology are articulated in two-minds Christology.

Two-Minds Christology

No version of kenotic Christology has gained universal acceptance. Some theologians have insisted that the Son of God need not empty himself of or suspend the use of any of his divine attributes in order to be genuinely human. Thomas Morris, an American philosophical theologian, is a key exponent of this claim. He espoused the two-minds asymmetric Christology, arguing that Jesus Christ "retained all of the resources and prerogatives of divinity in the most robust sense" while living out a human life on earth.[118] Morris's aim is to demonstrate that it is logically possible for God's Son to be fully divine and fully human without relinquishing any of his divine attributes. Morris contends that Jesus did not possess two abstract natures. Instead, he had two different consciousnesses or mentalities.[119]

115. Ibid., 34.
116. Ibid., 32.
117. Ibid., 34.
118. Morris, *Our Idea of God*, 169.
119. Ibid.

For Morris, Jesus had both a divine mind and a human mind. Rather than using "natures," Morris employs the word *mind* to describe the divinity and humanity of Jesus Christ. To Morris, Jesus Christ had the "eternal mind of God the Son" and an "earthly mind." The eternal mind of God the Son was by nature divine, possessing divine consciousness. The eternal mind was all-knowing and was "empowered by the resources of omnipotence."[120] The "earthly mind" was human in nature. According to Morris, the consciousness of the earthly mind "came into existence and developed with the conception, human birth and growth of Christ's earthly form of existence."[121]

On the relationship of the two minds, Morris proposes that they enjoyed a somewhat asymmetric fellowship. He writes, "The two minds of Christ should be thought of as standing in something like an asymmetric accessing relation: The human mind was contained by, but did not itself contain, the divine mind; or, to portray it from the other side, the divine mind contained, but was not contained by, the human mind. Everything present to the human mind of Christ was thereby present to the divine mind as well, but not vice versa."[122]

Morris also argues that Jesus drew resources mostly from his earthly mind as he lived out his life as a Palestinian Jew.[123] However, at the same time, "in his properly divine form of existence," Jesus Christ continued to "exercise his omnipotence, with the wisdom of his omniscience, in his omnipresent activities throughout creation."[124] To illustrate how it is logically possible for Jesus to have had two minds or consciousnesses, Morris draws some insights from human experience to provide what he calls "partial analogies." He writes, "There seems to exist, for example, cases of dreams in which the dreamer both plays a role within the environs of the dream story, operating with a consciousness formed from within the dream, and yet at the same time, *as* dreamer, retains an overarching consciousness that the drama of the dream is just that—only a dream."[125]

So, did Jesus have "erroneous beliefs"? Morris argues that the answer must be yes and no since he had a limited human mind and a divine, all-knowing mind.[126] Morris also warns that it is important when answering this sort of question to be mindful of the risk of destroying the unity of the

120. Ibid.
121. Ibid.
122. Ibid., 169–70.
123. Ibid., 173.
124. Ibid., 170.
125. Ibid.
126. Ibid., 172.

person of Jesus.[127] What about sin? Did Jesus sin? Morris responds to these questions by stating that Jesus, using his "earthly mind," "freely, of his own accord, decided not to succumb to temptation. It was a choice for which, as matter of fact, he was responsible."[128] But could Jesus have sinned, even though he did not actually sin? According to Morris, Jesus could not have sinned because his "divine nature would have prevented it."[129] Morris adds, however, that since Jesus was "unaware in his earthly consciousness that he was necessarily good," and also since he willingly chose not to sin, we must conclude that the divine mind did not force him to remain sinless.[130]

If Morris' two-minds Christology is taken too far, it can introduce a division that can destroy the unity of the person of Jesus. His two-minds Christology comes very close to Nestorianism, the fifth-century christological heresy that construed Jesus as two distinct persons. It can also render Jesus as a person with a personality disorder or a schizophrenic.

John Hick has pointed out that Morris's two-minds Christology reduces Jesus to a being with a single will. Hick argues that Morris's effort to demonstrate that Jesus had both a human will and a divine will is unsuccessful. Hick argues that the two-minds Christology does not show convincingly that Jesus was God incarnate as taught by the classical councils. He writes,

> I suggest that the resulting picture does not amount to divine incarnation in the Chalcedonian sense that Morris is trying to make intelligible and believable. We are left with the human Jesus, to whose mind God the Son has full cognitive access; and if, or whenever, the human mind began to make a wrong decision, God the Son prevented him from proceeding with it. That is to say, Jesus is God incarnate in the sense that God singled the human Jesus out for a special role—namely by not allowing him to go wrong.
>
> It follows that if God, in addition to being omnisciently aware of the full contents of someone else's mind, were to prevent her from making any wrong choices, that person would be another instance of God incarnate. But has not the heart of the Chalcedonian conception now been missed out—namely the unique personal presence of God in a human life, so that those who talked with the human Jesus were talking with God the Son? The nearest that Morris' theory comes to this is that those

127. Ibid., 173.

128. Morris, *Logic of God Incarnate*, 153.

129. Ibid., 150.

130. Ibid., 152.

who talked with Jesus were talking to a man whom God the Son was invisibly monitoring and preventing from going astray.[131]

The excerpt below is taken from Thomas Morris' *The Logic of God Incarnate*. The excerpt highlights the major arguments of Morris' two-minds Christology.

Thomas Morris: One Person with Two Minds

In the case of Jesus, God Incarnate, the full relation between the earthly mind and the divine mind is in important ways different from the totality of the relation which holds between the mind of any merely human being (such as you and me) and the mind of God. The completeness of epistemic access which God enjoys may be no different. But in Jesus' case, the earthly mind is contained in the divine mind in a distinctive way. Jesus was a being who was fully human, but he was not a created human being. He was not a being endowed with a set of personal cognitive and causal powers distinct from the cognitive and causal powers of God the Son. For Jesus was the same person as God the Son. Thus, the personal cognitive and causal powers operative in the case of Jesus' earthly mind were just none other than the cognitive and causal powers of God the Son. The results of their operation through the human body, under the constraints proper to the conditions of a fully human existence, were just such as to give rise to a human mind, an earthly noetic structure distinct from the properly divine noetic structure involved with the unconstrained exercise of divine powers. Thus there came to be two minds, the earthly mind of God Incarnate and his distinctively divine mind, but two minds of one person, one center of causal and cognitive powers. The asymmetric accessing relation holding between the two minds, if it were thought to involve no more than mere epistemic access of one mind to the other with respect to information, would indeed not suffice for single ownership, for both minds being minds of one and the same person. However, the precise relation the two-minds view can claim to hold in the case of Christ, involving as it does a unity of cognitive and causal powers productive of the contents of each mind, is sufficient to distinguish the case of Christ from any merely human being. In the two-minds view ... we thus appear to have what can rationally be seen as a partial explication and modeling of the doctrine of the Incarnation.[132]

Questions: What does this text reveal about the humanity of Jesus? How does Morris reconcile the difficulty of the doctrine of the Incarnation?

---

131. Hick, *Metaphor of God Incarnate*, 57–58.
132. Morris, Logic of God Incarnate, 161–62.

Ancestor Christology

With the rise of serious theological reflection in sub-Saharan Africa, Asia, and Latin America since the 1950s, it is unsatisfactory to describe Christian theology without considering the unique contribution of non-Western theologians. Sub-Saharan African theologians have made significant progress in the area of Christology. They have developed important images that capture the experience of African people and also highlight their understanding of the person and significance of Jesus Christ.[133] One such model is ancestor Christology. Although many versions of ancestor Christology exist in sub-Saharan African Christianity, what most of these Christologies share in common is the conscious attempt not to discuss the person and work of Jesus Christ in abstract and speculative terms.

Three issues formed the context in which African Christologies, including ancestor Christology, were developed in the 1980s. The first issue was a change of theological vision in African scholarship. Earlier theologians, beginning from the 1950s, produced works that provided guidance on how to proceed in the construction of a theological identity for sub-Saharan African Christianity. For several decades, however, sub-Saharan African Christianity depended largely on foreign theologies and liturgies imported from the Western world for its existence. Not until the 1980s did sub-Saharan African Christianity witness a surge of theological works, particularly in the area of Christology, written by theologians who did not want to please their Western professors or answer the questions their friends in the West were asking. On the contrary, they constructed Christologies that aimed to answer the questions that African Christians were asking.

The demographic shift in Christianity's center of gravity from the Western to the non-Western world was the second issue. Although this shift was not entirely unexpected, many African theologians found that merely adopting foreign theological models imported from Europe and North America was increasingly unappealing to African intellectuals. Theologians were being challenged to produce theologies that touched the core of the religious and socioeconomic experiences of Africans. They were also expected to construct theologies that benefited Christianity globally.

The third issue concerned the relationship between Christianity and the pre-Christian religions of Africa. From the late 1980s onward, many theologians began to construct Christologies that advocated mutual interaction between African indigenous religions and Christianity. Many believed that Christianity can only be relevant in Africa if it is perceived

---

133. See Ezigbo, *Re-imagining African Christologies.*

as the fulfillment of the socioreligious aspirations of Africans, which must include the indigenous. Some theologians argued that African vernaculars and thought forms are capable of expressing the mystery of Jesus Christ. It was in this context that ancestor Christologies were born.

Despite a rising suspicion from some theologians in Africa, the use of African indigenous beliefs about ancestors to explain the person and work of Jesus Christ has remained largely appealing to many African theologians. Some argue that ancestor Christology is one of the most unique contributions of Africans to Christology. For them, the cult of ancestors provides a culturally familiar framework in which to interpret the significance of Jesus' work for humanity.

Ancestor Christology is the christological model that equates the mediatory work of Jesus Christ with the work of ancestors. In the indigenous (traditional) religions and cultures of Africa, ancestors are the class of people who attained great positions in society (such as kings and warriors) while living on earth. Ancestors are people whose deaths did not result from the violations of the customs of their communities. Upon the completion of the burial ceremony and rituals, they join the community of ancestors of the families and clans. They are called the "living dead" because they are believed to be actively involved in human affairs. According to Hans Visser and Gillian Bediako, "In African life the ancestors play important roles. They are the living dead who are present in people's lives. Ancestors provide identity and protection."[134]

In indigenous African thought, ancestors can bring fortune or misfortune to members of the clan. Their wrath is incurred when the customs of the land are ignored or violated. Ancestors mediate between human beings and the spirit beings—the Supreme Being and lesser gods. In ancestor Christologies, Jesus is presented as the chief ancestor or proto-ancestor, the one who not only mediates between God and human beings but also restores humanity to divine fellowship.

The key contribution of these christological models to the discussion of the person and work of Jesus Christ in African Christianity is the attempt to make Jesus Christ an "African." Unlike the Christologies of classical Western missionaries, which made Jesus a stranger to Africans, ancestor Christologies present Jesus as a "clansman" or a "brother" of Africans. The Ghanaian theologian Kwame Bediako has remarked, "Our Savior is our Elder Brother who has shared in our African experience in every respect, except our sin and alienation from God, an alienation with which our myths of origins make us only too familiar. Being our true Elder Brother [ancestor]

---

134. Visser and Bediako, "Introduction," xiv.

now in the presence of his Father and our Father, he displaces the mediatorial function of our natural 'spirit-fathers' [ancestors]."[135]

A major criticism of ancestor Christologies is that they seem to endorse the worship or veneration of the dead. Some Roman Catholic theologians have responded to this criticism by comparing the cult of ancestors to the communion of the saints. Bediako, who is a Protestant, deals with the criticism by labeling the cult of ancestors a myth. He writes, "Once the meaning of the cult of ancestors as myth is granted and its 'function' is understood within the overall religious life of traditional society, it becomes clear how Jesus Christ fulfills our aspirations in relation to ancestral function too."[136]

As the following excerpt shows, Bediako favors an ancestor Christology model. His ancestor Christology is grounded in the belief that Jesus Christ fulfills the religious aspirations that many Africans seek through the ancestor cult.

It is also important to realize that since ancestors do not originate from the transcendent realm, it is the myth-making imagination of the community itself that sacralizes them, conferring upon them the sacred authority that they exercise through those in the community, like kings, who also expect to become ancestors. The potency of the cult of ancestors is not the potency of ancestors themselves; the potency of the cult is the potency of myth.

Once the meaning of the cult of ancestors as myth is granted and its "function" is understood within the overall religious life of traditional society, it becomes clear how Jesus Christ fulfills our aspirations in relation to ancestral function too. Ancestors are considered worthy of honor for having "lived among us" and for having brought benefits to us; Jesus Christ has done infinitely more. They, originating from among us, had no choice but to live among us. But he, reflecting the brightness of God's glory and the exact likeness of God's own being (Hebrews 1:3), took our flesh and blood, shared our human nature and underwent death for us to set us free from the fear of death (Hebrews 2:14–15). He who has every reason to abandon sinful humans to their just deserts is not ashamed to call us his brethren (Hebrews 2:11). Our natural ancestors had no barriers to cross to live among us and share our experience. His incarnation implies that he has achieved a far more profound identification with us in our humanity than the mere ethnic solidarity of lineage ancestors can ever do. Jesus Christ surpasses our natural ancestors also by virtue of who he is in himself. Ancestors, even described as "ancestral spirits," remain essentially human spirits; whatever benefit they may be said to bestow

135. Bediako, *Jesus and the Gospel in Africa*, 26.
136. Ibid., 30.

is effectively contained by the fact of their being human. Jesus Christ, on the other hand, took on human nature without loss to his divine nature. Belonging in the eternal realm as Son of the Father (Hebrews 1:1, 48; 9:14), he has taken human nature into himself (Hebrews 10:19) and so, as God-man, he ensures an infinitely more effective ministry to human beings (Hebrews 7:25) than can be said of merely human ancestral spirits.

The writer of Hebrews, confronted by the reality of the eternal nature of Jesus Christ, falls back on the enigmatic Melchizedek of Genesis 14:17–20 for analogy; without father or mother, without beginning or end, he (Melchizedek) is like the Son of God (Jesus Christ). The likeness is only in thought. For Jesus has actually demonstrated, through his resurrection from the dead, the possession of an indestructible life (Hebrews 7:16). This can never be said of ancestors. The persistence of the cult of ancestors is owed, not to their demonstrable power to act, but to the power of the myth that sustains them in the corporate mind of the community. The presumption that ancestors actually function for the benefit of the community can be seen as part of the same myth-making imagination that projects departed human beings into the transcendent realm. While not denying that spiritual forces do operate in the traditional realm, we can maintain that ancestral spirits, as human spirits that have not demonstrated any power over death, the final enemy, cannot be presumed to act in the way tradition ascribes to them.[137]

Question: What does this text tell us about Bediako's approach to the problem of the incarnation of Jesus Christ in an African context?

Womanist Christology

Womanist Christology arose in the mid-1980s in the United States as a critique of the earliest forms of feminist Christology or theology that failed to take seriously the unique experience of African American women. Alice Walker's *In Search of Our Mother's Garden* was monumental in inspiring African American women to exert their selfhood and to incorporate race in their gender talk. The works of earlier African American women who were highly critical of racism and classism, such as Sojourner Truth (c. 1797–1883), remain inspirational to many womanist theologians.

Womanist Christology brings the particular experience of black women, particularly African American women, to the forefront in feminist theological discourse. Womanist theologians distinguish the experience of

137. Ibid., 30–31.

white American women from the experience of African American women. The contrast between the experiences of these classes of women in North America is striking, as evidenced in Jacquelyn Grant's assessment:

> what is often unmentioned is that feminist theologians' sources for women's experience refer almost exclusively to White women's experience. White women's experience and Black women's experience are not the same. Indeed all experiences are unique to some degree. But in this case the difference is so radical that it may be said that White women and Black women are in completely different realms. Slavery and segregation have created such a gulf between these women, that White feminists' common assumption that all women are in the same situation with respect to sexism is difficult to understand when history so clearly tells us a different story.[138]

Like feminist Christology, womanist Christology is highly critical of the entanglements of the maleness of God incarnate (Jesus Christ) and patriarchy. Both feminist and womanist Christologies focus on gender analysis and the experience of women in patriarchal societies. Both locate the salvific significance of the Incarnation in God's act of becoming a *human being*. For them, the maleness of Jesus has no soteriological value in God's self-disclosure to humanity. The gender of Jesus Christ does not exclude women from benefiting from his salvific work, and therefore his gender ought not to be used as an ally of patriarchal Christologies. As Rosemary Ruether has argued, "Theologically speaking, then, we might say that the maleness of Jesus has no ultimate significance. It has social symbolic significance in the framework of societies of patriarchal privilege. In this sense Jesus as the Christ, the representative of liberated humanity and the liberating Word of God, manifests the kenosis of patriarchy, the announcement of the new humanity through a lifestyle that discards hierarchical caste privilege and speaks on behalf of the lowly."[139]

Unlike feminist Christology, womanist Christology draws upon the race and class of African American women in their theological works. Many were dissatisfied with the word *feminism* because it captures the experience of white American women and conceals the struggles of African American women. To say "womanist" in theological discussions, for African American women theologians, is to show that the African American women's liberation movement is not a white middle-class women's project. Jacquelyn Grant writes, "A womanist is one who has developed survival strategies in

138. Grant, *White Women's Christ and Black Women's Jesus*, 195–96.
139. Ruether, *Sexism and God-Talk*, 137.

spite of the oppression of her race and sex in order to save her family and her people."[140] Womanist theologians also refer to themselves as "women" in order to assert the womanhood that was denied them by white American women.

Womanist Christology uses the experience of African American women, which derives from their struggles to counter racism, classism, and sexism, as an interpretative framework to read and interpret classical and contemporary Christologies. Womanist theologians listen attentively to how African American women whose lives have been impacted by racism, classism, and sexism answer Jesus' question "Who do you say that I am?"

In womanist Christology, the structures, systems, and theologies that have contributed to the oppression of African American women in the church and society at large are exposed. Jesus is presented as the great liberator who inspires African American women to pursue liberation from all that subjugates them. Also, Jesus is construed as "the divine co-sufferer, who empowers them in situations of oppression."[141] For womanist theologians, Jesus does not sit on the fence; he takes sides. He identifies with the experience of African American women. Grant writes, "For Christian Black women in the past, Jesus was their central frame of reference. They identified with him. As Jesus was persecuted and made to suffer undeservedly, so were they. His suffering culminated in the crucifixion. Their crucifixion included rape, and babies being sold."[142]

The suffering and oppression experienced globally have received attention in the works of some womanist theologians.[143] However, some have accused womanist theologians of erring by not drawing on the struggles of white American women as sources of their theology. Also, some have argued that adopting the term *womanist* instead of *feminist* inhibits African American women from entering into the "larger streams of feminist thought."[144]

140. Grant, "Womanist Theology," 343.

141. Grant, *White Women's Christ and Black Women's Jesus*, 212.

142. Ibid.

143. See Crawford, "Womanist Christology and the Wesleyan Tradition," 217.

144. Mitchem, "Finding Questions and Answers," 67.

Jacquelyn Grant: Womanist Theology and Christology

Womanist theology begins with the experiences of Black women as its point of departure. This experience includes not only Black women's activities in the larger society but also in the churches, and reveals that Black women have often rejected the oppressive structure in the church as well.

The experiences provide a context which is significant for doing theology. Those experiences had been and continue to be defined by racism, sexism and classism and therefore offer a unique opportunity and a new challenge for developing a relevant perspective in the theological enterprise. This perspective in theology which I am calling womanist theology draws upon the life and experiences of some Black women who have created meaningful interpretations of the Christian faith.

Black women must do theology out of their tri-dimensional experience of racism/sexism/classism. To ignore any aspect of this experience is to deny the holistic and integrated reality of Black womanhood. When Black women say that God is on the side of the oppressed, we mean that God is in solidarity with the struggles of those on the underside of humanity, those whose lives are bent and broken from the many levels of assault perpetrated against them.

Theological investigation into the experience of Christian Black women reveals that Black women considered the Bible to be a major source of religious validation in their lives. Though Black women's relationship with God preceded their introduction to the Bible, this Bible gave some content to their God-consciousness. The source for Black women's understanding of God has been twofold: first, God's revelation directly to them, and secondly, God's revelation as witnessed in the Bible and as read and heard in the context of their experience. The understanding of God as creator, sustainer, comforter, and liberator took on life as they agonized over their pain and celebrated the hope that, as God delivered the Israelites, they would be delivered as well.[145]

Question: What impact does the experience of African American women have on womanist Christology and theology?

Liberation Christology

Although the idea of liberation is present in many theological works by theologians outside of Latin America, liberation theology is usually associated with the works of Latin American theologians such as Gustavo Gutiérrez

145. Grant, "Womanist Theology," 341, 344–45.

and Jon Sobrino. The distinguishing mark of Latin American liberation theology is the construal of the liberation of the oppressed as the primary motif of the Christian message and as the primary hermeneutical framework for understanding and expressing the Christian message. This understanding of the relationship between the Christian message and liberation entails the confrontation of the injustices perpetrated against the marginalized in Latin America. A liberation theologian participates in the struggles of the poor and the oppressed. According to Leonardo and Clodovis Boff, "Before we can do theology we have to 'do' liberation. The first step for liberation theology is pre-theological. It is a matter of trying to live the commitment of faith: in our case, to participate in some ways in the process of liberation, to be committed to the oppressed."[146] Latin American liberation theologians imagined the "people of God" in a radical way: they are the poor and the marginalized who may or may not identify with Christianity.

Prior to the 1968 conferences of the Latin American Catholic bishops held at Chimbote (Peru) and Medellín (Colombia), lay members of the Roman Catholic Church in Latin America led a series of movements in the 1930s and 1940s that took a stand against social injustice.[147] These movements were the forerunners of liberation theology. Following the call for socially committed Christian communities issued by the Second Vatican Council (1962–1965), the Latin American Catholic bishops met in 1968 to discuss practical ways in which to implement the council's demand. The Medellín conference condemned the misery and institutionalized violence committed against people in Latin American countries. The attendees of this conference described poverty as "an outrage in terms of the message of the Bible" and as a situation "wholly contrary to the will of God."[148]

In 1979, some Latin American bishops also met in Puebla, Mexico, to assess the condition of the poor in Latin America and to discuss some strategies for sustaining the work already being done to correct social injustice. The Puebla conference highlighted the condition of women, declaring them to be the most oppressed class of people in Latin America. Also, the idea of a *preferential option for the poor* as an essential theological concept that would help Christians in Latin America confront the causes and effects of poverty was adopted.

The Peruvian theologian Gustavo Gutiérrez is among those Latin American theologians who have brought the issue of poverty to the forefront of Christian theology. Gutiérrez argues that one of the most effective

---

146. C. Boff and L. Boff, *Introducing Liberation Theology*, 22.

147. Gutiérrez, *Theology of Liberation*, xvii–xviii.

148. See Gutiérrez, "Task and Content of Liberation Theology," 25.

ways to deal with poverty is to be in solidarity with the poor. He contends that Jesus Christ models this approach. According to him, Jesus "assumes the sins of humanity in this way, both out of love for the sinner and in rejection of sin."[149] Gutiérrez agrees with the idea of the preferential option of the poor advocated by both the Medellín conference and the Puebla conference:

> The poor, the oppressed, are the members of one social class that is being subtly (or not so subtly) exploited by another social class. The exploited class, especially, in its most clear-sighted segment, the proletariat, is an active one. Hence, an option for the poor is an option for one social class against another. An option for the poor means a new awareness of class confrontation. It means taking sides with the dispossessed. It means entering into the world of the exploited social class, with its values, its categories. It means entering into solidarity with its interests and its struggles.[150]

Latin American theologians have been criticized for making the liberation of the poor and marginalized the primary focus of theology. The problem with this view of liberation theology, as some critics have pointed out, is that "objective focus of theology should be the gospel vision of liberation and not the context of oppression."[151] For some critics, focusing on the changing human condition rather than on the unchanging and objective gospel message of Jesus risks identifying Christianity with socialism. Some critics argue that liberation theology encourages a preferential option for socialism. Peter Burns has remarked that "one major factor in generating the heat surrounding the liberation debate has been the tendency, common to both its proponents and critics, to regard liberation theology as bound up with an unmistakably left-wing political stance."[152] It is misleading, however, to mistake the call for social justice as a call for socialism. This of course does not mean that some Latin American liberation theologians have not found Marxism helpful in the articulation of their theologies.

The liberation Christology developed in Latin America focused on the theological consequences of poverty and human misery. It arose in the context of marginalization, exploitation, and concentration of wealth in Latin America. It is a political Christology grounded in the experience and teaching of Jesus Christ. Leonardo Boff makes this clear in his reflection on the official document produced by the bishops who met at Puebla, Mexico,

149. Ibid., 26.

150. Gutiérrez, *Power of the Poor in History*, 45.

151. Osborn, "Some Problems of Liberation Theology," 86.

152. Burns, "Problem of Socialism in Liberation Theology," 493.

in 1979: "Politics is understood in the context of the lordship of Jesus Christ. He is not only the Lord of small places like the heart, the soul, the Church; he is the cosmic Lord, of large spaces like that of politics." Boff goes on to state, "Politics has to do with the Kingdom of God because it has to do with justice, a messianic good. Primitive Christians professing 'Jesus is Lord' were making a political statement."[153] Boff's work on liberation Christology has inspired several theologians around the world. The excerpt below is taken from his *Jesus Christ Liberator*.

The advent of the eschatological kingdom as the full embodiment of liberation has been delayed. In this context human life possesses a paschal structure. This translates into following the crucified and risen Jesus Christ.

The first and primary aspect of following Jesus is proclaiming the utopia of the kingdom as the real and complete meaning of the world that is offered to all by God.

Second, the following of Jesus means translating that utopia into practice. We must try to change the world on the personal, social, and cosmic level. This utopia is not an ideology, but it does give rise to functional ideologies that will guide liberative practices. The following of Jesus is not mere imitation. We must take due account of the differences between Jesus' situation and our own. . . . Hence there must be differences in the way we organize love and justice in society.

To be sure, for both Jesus and us God is the future and his kingdom has not yet fully arrived; but our way of shouldering history will vary from his. Jesus did not prescribe any concrete model. Instead he offered a way of being present in every concrete embodiment of the kingdom, though such embodiments will obviously depend on the details of a given situation. What he offers us by way of example is an option on behalf of those who are treated unjustly, a refusal to succumb to the will for power and domination, and solidarity with everything that suggests greater participation in societal living and fraternal openness to God.

Third, God's liberation translates into a process that will entail conflict and struggle. These conflicts must be taken on and understood in the light of Jesus' own burdensome journey. It is a journey of love that sometimes must sacrifice itself. It is a journey of eschatological hope that must go by way of political hopes. It is a journey of faith that must move ahead gropingly; the fact that we are Christians does not provide us with a key to decipher political and economic problems. Cross and resurrection are paradigms of Christian

153. L. Boff, *Church*, 26.

existence. To follow Jesus means to follow through with his work and attain his fulfillment.

This basic vision, possessing all the limitations of a vision, is meant to be put in the service of the cause of liberation. And here I am referring to the political, social, economic, and religious liberation of our oppressed peoples in Latin America. It is a contradiction on the level of theoretical expression that seeks to illuminate and enrich an already existing praxis of liberative faith.

We live in the dependent Third World. If we seek to ponder and live our christological faith in a truly historical way, then we find that it points us toward the ideological option of liberation, a particular type of analysis, and a very definite commitment. We do not think that we can read the gospel message and follow Jesus in some way that is not liberative. To do so would be to turn our christological faith upside down, or to live it in an ideological way that has bad connotations.

The theology of liberation, of Jesus Christ the Liberator, is the pain-filled cry of oppressed Christians. They are knocking on the door of their affluent brothers and sisters, asking for everything and yet for nothing. Indeed all they ask is to be people, to be accepted as persons. All they ask is that they be allowed to fight to regain their captive freedom.[154]

Question: What does this text reveal about the nature and function of the Christian gospel message and Christian theology?

Key Terms

Arianism: the christological view that denied Jesus was truly God. It also taught that Jesus Christ was a special creature of God.

Apollinarianism: the christological view that denied that Jesus had a human mind even though he had a human body.

Docetism: this christological view taught that Jesus was not truly human and that he only appeared to be a human being.

Eutychianism: the view that argued Jesus was a hybrid persons, which is the consequence of the mixture of divine nature and human nature in the incarnation.

---

154. L. Boff, *Jesus Christ Liberator*, 291–93, 295.

Ebionism: the view that claimed Jesus was a human being and not a divine being.

Homoousios: Greek word that means "of the same substance" and that was used by some theologians to argue that Jesus had the same nature as God the Father and therefore was truly God.

Homoiousios: Greek word that means "of similar substance" and that was used by some theologians to argue that Jesus had a *similar* nature to God the Father, not the same nature, and therefore was not the true God.

Incarnation: the belief that the eternal Son or Word of God assumed a human nature and became Jesus of Nazareth.

Kenotic Christology: some versions of this view teach that the eternal Son of God temporarily abdicated some non-essential attributes in order to become a human being. Others argue that Jesus only suspended the use of his divine attributes.

Kryptic Christology: the view that teaches God's eternal Son did not empty himself of any of his divine attributes in order to become a human being. On the contrary, it teaches that the eternal Son of God secretly used his divine attributes.

Nestorianism: the christological view that claimed Jesus had two different natures and also held that Mary was not *Theotokos* ("God-bearer").

Review Questions

1. How are the Councils of Nicaea and Chalcedon significant for christological discussions today?

2. How do ancestor Christology, liberation Christology, kenotic Christology, and two-minds Christology differ in focus, content, and style?

3. What acts and claims of Jesus support his divinity?

Suggestions for Further Reading

Bediako, Kwame. *Jesus and the Gospel in Africa: History and Experience*. Maryknoll, NY: Orbis, 2004.

Boff, Leonardo. *Jesus Christ Liberator: A Critical Christology for Our Time*. Maryknoll, NY: Orbis, 1978.

Grant, Jacquelyn. *White Women's Christ and Black Women's Jesus: Feminist Christology and Womanist Response*. Atlanta: Scholars, 1989.

Hick, John. *The Metaphor of God Incarnate: Christology in a Pluralistic Age*. Louisville: Westminster John Knox, 1993.

Kärkkäinen, Veli-Matti. *Christology: A Global Introduction*. Grand Rapids: Baker, 2003.

6

Holy Spirit

Who is the Holy Spirit? How did some early theologians come to the conclusion that the Holy Spirit is a distinct divine person? Is the work of the Holy Spirit distinct from the work of the Father and Jesus Christ? These questions will be discussed in this chapter. I will first consider the portraits of the Holy Spirit in the Old and New Testaments. I will proceed to discuss the major theological issues about the person and work of the Holy Spirit. In the chapter on the doctrine of salvation I will discuss the work of the Holy Spirit in the life of Christians.

Many Christians today readily associate the Holy Spirit with the Charismatic and Pentecostal churches. Some Christians assume that the emphasis on the Holy Spirit is a recent phenomenon that is connected with the rise of the Pentecostal and Charismatic movements. This assumption is not entirely accurate. As early as the second century, there were some Christian movements that emphasized the work of the Holy Spirit. Founders of these movements were deeply concerned that "the freedom of the Holy Spirit was dying out in the churches," and they "longed for the 'good old days,' when signs and wonders were regularly performed" and experienced in Christian communities.[1]

---

1. Robeck, "Montanism and Present-Day 'Prophets,'" 418.

Montanism was one such movement. Montanism derives its name from one of its founders, the prophet Montanus. Montanism's prophets, apostles, and prophetesses claimed to be the spokespersons of the Holy Spirit. They equated their prophetic utterances with the words of the Holy Spirit. Montanism laid emphasis on prophecy, ecstasy, the gifts of tongues, vision, self-discipline, and dreams. Although Montanism began in Asia Minor (modern-day Turkey), it spread to North Africa. Some scholars trace the theologies of the Holy Spirit of the Pentecostal and Charismatic movements to Montanism.[2]

The Holy Spirit holds a unique place in Christianity. The work of the Holy Spirit is present in every aspect of God's mission to create, redeem, reconcile, and perfect God's creatures. Christianity's doctrine of the triune God presupposes three divine *persons* who share the same divine nature and enjoy mutual fellowship and relationship. Christians have traditionally named these divine persons "Father," "Son," and "Holy Spirit." But while many Christians think of God the Father and God the Son as distinct persons, some find it extremely difficult to conceptualize and relate to the Holy Spirit as a distinct person. Some see the Holy Spirit as an impersonal divine force or an activity of God. This understanding of the Holy Spirit is in conflict with the Christian doctrine of the Trinity. It is also partly responsible for the marginalization of the Holy Spirit in some Christian communities.

Portraits of the Holy Spirit in the Bible

"The earth was without form and void, and darkness was over the face of the deep. And the Spirit of God was hovering over the face of the waters" (Gen 1:2, ESV). This is the first time we encounter God's Spirit in the Bible. The issue that concerns theologians is whether the "Spirit of God" mentioned here is a divine person distinct from Yahweh.

FOCUS QUESTION:
In what ways did the biblical writers understand the identity and function of the Holy Spirit?

Does this Genesis text indicate "a distinction-in-identity that will eventually allow the Christian church, after the coming of Christ and the Pentecostal outpouring of the 'Holy Spirit,' to elaborate its doctrine" of the Trinity?[3] The answer to this question will have an enormous impact on several Christian doctrines, especially the doctrine of the Trinity. The answer will also have an effect on the Christian understanding of the relationship between the He-

2. See Tabbernee, *Prophets and Gravestones*.
3. Wainwright, "Holy Spirit," 273.

brew Bible (Old Testament) and the New Testament. For example, does Genesis 1:2 have any bearing on Jesus' words in John 14:16–17: "I will ask the Father, and He will give you another Helper, that He may be with you forever; that is the Spirit of truth, whom the world cannot receive, because it does not see Him or know Him, but you know Him because He abides with you and will be in you" (NASB).

The "Spirit of God" in the Old Testament

The Hebrew word in Genesis 1:2 that is translated as "spirit" in some Bible translations is *rûah*. This word has a broad range of meanings that include "storm," "disposition," "wind," "breath," "vitality," and "life." Throughout the Old Testament, *rûah* is frequently associated with Yahweh. What is the identity of this *rûah*? What is the nature of the relationship between *rûah* and Yahweh? The Old Testament uses *rûah* as a metaphor to express the character and acts of God. I have summarized the use of *rûah* under four broad categories.

First, *rûah as a metaphor for God's judgment and restoration*: In the Old Testament, *rûah* may refer to the unpredictable force of nature displayed in wind and storm (1 Kgs 18:45; 2 Kgs 3:17) that is "under the divine and sovereign control of Yahweh."[4] When understood as "wind," *rûah* could refer to God's acts of judgment or restoration. The hot wind and sandstorm from the desert in the east of Israel, known as the "east wind," is "typically associated with the judgment or wrath of Yahweh (Ps 48:7; Jer 18:17; Ezek 17:10; Hos 13:15; Jonah 4:8)."[5] God manifests God's power and justice by destroying or punishing the wicked with the east wind (a force of nature). In contrast, the west wind from the Mediterranean Sea brings moisture in the winter and a cooling wind in the summer. Like the west wind, which restores life to dying crops, God's Spirit brings restoration to the repentant, resulting in the well-being of the sinner as he or she is restored into divine fellowship.[6]

Second, *rûah as a metaphor for God's gift of life and creative agency*: In this context, *rûah* is usually translated as "breath," which is the "essence of life (Gen 6:17; Job 12:10; Isa 38:16; 42:5; Ezek 37:4–14; Mal 2:15–16)."[7] The Old Testament presents God as the giver and sustainer of life. No human life can exist apart from God's act of sustenance (Job 4:9). *Rûah* reminded the

4. Pelt, Kaiser, and Block, "*Rûah*," 1073.

5. Ibid., 1073–74.

6. McGrath, *Theology*, 99.

7. Pelt, Kaiser, and Block, "*Rûah*," 1074.

people of ancient Israel of God's creation and providence. This is illustrated in the story of Adam's creation (Gen 2:7; 8:1; Ps 104:29; Job 33:4) and the vision of the dry bones in which God breathed into empty shells and brought them to life (Ezek 37).[8] The *rûaḥ* of God plays a role in God's continuing work of creation: "When you send your Spirit, they are created, and you renew the face of the earth" (Ps 104:30, NIV).

Third, *rûaḥ as a metaphor for God's gift of wisdom and cognition*: *Rûaḥ* also denotes God's gift of wisdom to certain individuals, such as judges, kings, and prophets (Judg 6:34; Num 11:17, 29; 1 Sam 10:10; Mic 3:8; Hos 9:7). God also gave God's Spirit to people to accomplish some specific tasks, such as the building of the tabernacle (Exod 28:3).[9] This view of the Spirit of God is sometimes expressed in an eschatological sense. The prophets foresaw a time when God will pour out God's Spirit on God's people (Isa 32:15; 44:3–4; Ezek 39:29; Joel 2:28–31). This outpouring of God's Spirit on people will represent God's identification with and presence among God's covenant people and will "amount to the re-creation of the very heart of humankind in obedience."[10] In that *age to come*, all Israel would share in the power and manifestations of God's Spirit (Joel 2:28–29). Peter quotes this passage in his explanation of the event of Pentecost (Acts 2:14–41).

Fourth, *rûaḥ as a metaphor for God's essence*: Grieving the Spirit of God, for the people of the Old Testament, meant grieving God. Isaiah 63:10 illustrates this: "Yet they rebelled and grieved his [Holy] Spirit. So he turned and became their enemy and he himself fought against them" (NIV).[11] The *rûaḥ* of God is "the extension of his own invisible presence."[12] *Rûaḥ* could also refer to "God's own 'mind' or 'will' (Isa 20:1–2; 40:12–14; Wis 7–9)."[13] The *rûaḥ* of God is sometimes described as having God's attributes, such as omniscience (Ps 139:7) and omnipresence (Isa 40:13).

The "Holy Spirit" in the New Testament

In Greek thought, *pneuma* is the primary word for "wind" and "breath." However, unlike in Jewish thought, the Greeks tended not to associate

---

8. McGrath, *Theology*, 100.

9. Pelt, Kaiser, and Block, "*Rûaḥ*," 1075.

10. Turner, *Holy Spirit and Spiritual Gifts*, 5.

11. I have set the word *Holy* in brackets to indicate that the idea of the Holy Spirit as a distinct person from Yahweh is foreign to this text. The expression "Holy Spirit" appears only three times in the Old Testament (Ps 51:11; Isa 63:10, 11).

12. Turner, *Holy Spirit and Spiritual Gifts*, 3.

13. Ibid.

pneuma with God.[14] *Pneuma* was used to describe the force of nature and the organic life of human beings and animals.[15] However, the authors of the Septuagint (the Greek translation of the Old Testament) translated *rûaḥ* with *pneuma*. The authors' tendency to translate *rûaḥ* with *pneuma* added a Jewish flavor to the Greek ideas of *pneuma*.[16]

Like the Old Testament, the New Testament speaks frequently about God's Spirit in the community of God's people. Some New Testament writers drew upon the Old Testament ideas of *rûaḥ* (Acts 2:17–21; 1 Thess 4:8). Unlike the Old Testament, however, the New Testament describes the Spirit of God in a manner that differs significantly from the Old Testament. For example, while the Old Testament does not describe the Spirit of God as a divine person distinct from God, the New Testament moves radically in this direction.

In the New Testament, "spirit" is used in three senses with reference to God. First, God is described as "spirit," albeit on very rare occasions. In this sense, God's immaterial mode of existence is in view. John 4:24 is a clear example: "God is spirit, and his worshippers must worship in spirit and in truth" (NIV). To say that God *is* spirit is to distinguish God's invisible mode of existence from our human visible mode of existence. It is to also to assert that God exists "like a powerful wind, not like a frail creature that is easily pushed around."[17]

Second, *pneuma* is used in the New Testament to describe God's communicative agent and God's mode of expression. Paul highlights this idea of *pneuma* when he writes, "The Spirit searches all things, even the deep things of God. For who among men knows the thoughts of a man except the man's spirit within him? In the same way no one knows the thought of God except the Spirit of God" (1 Cor 2:10–11, NIV). The Spirit of God is "the link between God and humanity" and the agent "from God himself who makes the knowing possible."[18]

Third, *pneuma* is used in a manner that suggests a divine person who is not God (the Father). The Apostle Paul in his letters to the churches in Corinth treats Jesus, God (the Father), and the Holy Spirit as distinct persons. In 2 Corinthians 13:14 Paul writes, "May the grace of the Lord Jesus Christ, and the love of God, and the fellowship of the Holy Spirit be with you all" (NIV). Gordon Fee argues that "this benediction is the most profound

14. Menzies, *Empowered for Witness*, 50.

15. Kleinknecht, "Πνεῦμα, Πνευματικός," 335.

16. Menzies, *Empowered for Witness*, 50.

17. Pinnock, *Flame of Love*, 24.

18. Fee, *God's Empowering Presence*, 99.

theological moment in the Pauline corpus."[19] Paul presents a clearer parallel in 1 Corinthians 12:3–6: "Therefore I tell you that no one who is speaking by the Spirit of God says, 'Jesus be cursed,' and no one can say 'Jesus is Lord,' except by the Holy Spirit. There are different kinds of gifts, but the same Spirit. There are different kinds of service, but the same Lord. There are different kinds of working, but the same God works all of them in all men" (NIV). Paul here emphasizes the importance of diversity to the health of the church. The expressions "different kinds," "same Spirit," "same Lord," and "same God" underscore that "the one Spirit/Lord/God each manifests himself in a wide variety of gifts and ministries. Thus, the unity of God does not imply uniformity in gifts; rather the one and the same God is responsible for the variety itself."[20]

The Relationship between the "Spirit of God" of the Old Testament and the "Holy Spirit" of the New Testament

Is there any relationship between the ideas of the Spirit of God in the Old Testament and the concept of the Holy Spirit in the New Testament? The connection between the Old Testament and New Testament understanding of the Spirit of God is not clearly evident. Theological and exegetical reflections are required to unearth this relationship. The Old Testament concept of the Spirit of God, however, exerted enormous influence on the New Testament writers' discussions on the Holy Spirit.

The Holy Spirit and the Jewish Ideas of the "Spirit of Prophecy"

One of the helpful ways to engage in the discussion on the relationship between the ideas of the Spirit of God in the Old Testament and the concept of the Holy Spirit in the New Testament is to explore the concept of the "Spirit of prophecy" in Judaism. In the Targumim (Aramaic translations of the Old Testament), the Spirit of God is regularly described as "the prophetic Sprit" or "Spirit of prophecy."[21] Max Turner provides a helpful description of the idea of the "Spirit of prophecy" in Jewish religious thought. He writes that "by the term 'Spirit of prophecy' Jews meant something much wider, namely, the Spirit acting as the organ of communication between God and

---

19. Fee, *God's Empowering Presence*, 363.

20. Ibid., 161.

21. Turner, *Holy Spirit and Spiritual Gifts*, 5.

a person, typically inspiring at least four types of gifts."[22] The four types of gifts are the gift of revelation and guidance; the gift of wisdom; the gift of invasively inspired speech, which occurs when the Spirit of God comes upon a person and inspires that person to speak; and the gift of invasively inspired charismatic praise or worship.[23] Turner notes that there is considerable diversity in Judaism on the gifts of the Spirit of God. However, he argues that the diversity "was less at the level of which charismata [gifts] the divine Spirit enabled than in the import of the respective charismata for the life of the individual and of the nation."[24]

The concept of the "Spirit of prophecy" in Judaism and its influence on the New Testament writers is debated among biblical scholars. Eduard Schweizer argues that Luke's view of the Spirit is informed by the Jewish idea of the Spirit of prophecy. Schweizer understands the Spirit of prophecy primarily in the sense of prophetic utterances and preaching. According to Schweizer, "Luke adopts the typically Jewish idea that the Spirit is the Spirit of prophecy. This may be seen in Luke 4:23–27, where the miraculous signs mentioned in the quotation in verse 18 are specifically rejected as a fulfillment of prophecy. Though the miracles are important for Luke, they are never ascribed to the Spirit. Healing power is associated with the name of Jesus, with faith in Jesus, with Jesus himself, with prayer, with bodily contact through the disciple, his shadow or his handkerchief."[25] Robert Menzies holds a similar view. Focusing on Luke-Acts, Menzies argues that "Luke, influenced by the dominant Jewish perception, consistently portrays the gift of the Spirit as a prophetic endowment which enables its recipient to participate effectively in the mission of God."[26] For Menzies, Luke understood the Holy Spirit to be the "source of special insight and inspired speech."[27] Menzies also argues that the Apostle Paul's association of salvation with the gift of the Spirit is foreign to Judaism.

Max Turner disagrees with Menzies on the role of the Spirit of God in salvation. Turner faults Menzies for limiting Judaism' concept of the Spirit of prophecy to inspired speeches and prophetic utterances. Turner contends that although inspired speeches and prophetic utterances were the primary characteristics of Judaism's concept of the Spirit of prophecy, the Jewish people attributed other functions to the Spirit of God.[28]

22. Ibid., 7.
23. Ibid., 7–12.
24. Ibid., 12.
25. Schweizer, "Πνεῦμα," 407.
26. Menzies, *Empowered for Witness*, 45.
27. Ibid.
28. Turner, *Power from on High*, 90.

The Targumim and the Septuagint are the primary sources for judging the development of the idea of the Spirit of prophecy in Judaism. There is sufficient evidence in the Targumim and the Septuagint that the Spirit of God is associated with supernatural power (Judg 14:6; LXX Judg 14:6; *Tg. Neb.* Judg 14:16) and ethical and religious living (Ps 50:11–12; LXX 50:11–12; *Tg. Neb.* Ps 51:13).[29] New Testament writers such as Luke, John, and Paul borrowed and developed Judaism's concept of the Spirit of prophecy in their discussions on the activities and functions of the Holy Spirit.

Theological reflections on the Holy Spirit should seek to uncover the overall teaching of the Scriptures on the identity—the mode of existence and mode of operation—of the Holy Spirit.

The Identity of the Holy Spirit

The Holy Spirit, traditionally called "the third person of the Trinity" in Christian theology, has troubled theologians since the earliest days of Christianity. The major issue in *pneumatology* (the theology of the Holy Spirit) concerns the Holy Spirit's mode of operation. Jesus Christ highlights this issue in John 3:8: "The wind blows wherever it pleases. You hear its sound, but you cannot tell where it comes from or where it is going. So it is with everyone born of the Spirit" (NIV). These words of Jesus should be a reminder to theologians that it may be impossible to assemble their reflections on the Holy Spirit into a neat and coherent whole.

FOCUS QUESTION:
Who is the Holy Spirit?

In the early Christian era, theologians wrestled with the appropriate way in which to address the Holy Spirit. Some addressed the Holy Spirit as "it," whereas others described the Holy Spirit using masculine pronouns (e.g., "him") to indicate the ontological identity of the Holy Spirit. Many of the discussions on the Holy Spirit prior to the sixteenth century focused on the relationship of the Holy Spirit to the other two members of the Trinity. Prior to the Council of Constantinople (381 CE), theologians and some earlier church councils made cursory statements about the Holy Spirit. For example, the Council of Nicaea made the following brief statement in its article on the Holy Spirit: "We believe in the Holy Spirit." In contrast, the council devoted longer paragraphs to describe God (the Father) and Jesus Christ. This attests to the marginalization of the Holy Spirit in the theological discussion of some early Christian communities. The Council of Constantinople expanded the Council of Nicaea's cursory statement on

29. Hui, "Spirit of Prophecy and Pauline Pneumatology," 100–101.

the Holy Spirit. In its creed, which is known in theological literature as the Nicene-Constantinopolitan Creed (or simply the Nicene Creed), the Council of Constantinople affirmed, "We believe in the Holy Spirit, the Lord, the Giver of Life, who proceeds from the Father; with the Father and the Son he is worshipped and glorified; he has spoken through the Prophets."

Since the sixteenth century, the discussion on the Holy Spirit has focused on the work of the Holy Spirit in the lives of both Christians and non-Christians. The emergence of healing centers, Charismatic ministries, and Pentecostal churches since the nineteenth century (e.g., the healing center of Johann Christoph Blumhardt in Bad Boll, Germany, and the church founded by Charles Fox Parham in Topeka, Kansas) has pushed theological discussions on the Holy Spirit to the center of Christian theological reflection in the twenty-first century. The Holy Spirit is no longer an afterthought in Christian theology.

In the wake of the eruption of the theologies of the Holy Spirit in the academy and the church in the twenty-first century, theologians have revisited the issues of the identity and activity of the Holy Spirit. The remainder of this chapter will focus on these issues. As Veli-Matti Kärkkäinen has remarked, "The times are gone when it was commonplace to say that the Holy Spirit is the Cinderella of the Trinity; when the other two 'sisters' [Father and Son] went to the ball, Cinderella was left at home."[30]

The Holy Spirit as Creature or Nondistinct Divine Person

Some of the earliest constructive pnuematologies depicted the Holy Spirit as a nonindependent divine person. While some pnuematologies can be classified as *anhypostatic* (a Greek expression that means "lacking independent subsistence"), other pnuematologies depicted the Holy Spirit as a creature of God. To illustrate these two pnuematologies, I will describe the pneumatology of the *Pneumatomachoi*, which denied the divinity of the Holy Spirit, and the pnuematology of W. H. Lampe, which denied the personhood of the Holy Spirit.

The Pneumatology of the Pneumatomachoi

The ahypostatic view of the Holy Spirit has been expressed in different ways since the early church. Its earliest expression is found in the theology of the *Pneumatomachoi* or Pneumatomachians ("opponents of the Spirit" or "fighters against the spirit," from the Greek words *pneuma*, "spirit," and

---

30. Kärkkäinen, *Pneumatology*, 16.

machomai, "to fight.") The Pneumatomachians were fourth-century (CE) theologians who were both anti-Nicene and anti-Trinitarian and who thought that by "fighting against the doctrine of the Holy Spirit's divinity . . . they would succeed in undermining Nicene orthodoxy."[31] The Pneumatomachians seemed to have flourished, albeit temporarily, under the leadership of a man named Macedonius (hence the *Pneumatomachoi* are also called "Macedonians").[32] They taught that the Holy Spirit was a creature of God. They were binatarians: they upheld the divinity of God the Father and the divinity of God the Son, but denied the divinity of the Holy Spirit. The Council of Constantinople condemned and anathematized the Pneumatomachians for refusing to endorse the divine substance and identity of the Holy Spirit.[33]

Our knowledge of the pnuematology of the Pneumatomachians comes from the works of the great Cappadocian theologians Basil of Caesarea, Gregory of Nazianzus, and Gregory of Nyssa. It is most likely that Basil of Caesarea was referring to the pneumatology of the Pneumatomachians when he wrote, "They say it is not suitable to rank the Holy Spirit with the Father and the Son, because He is different in nature and inferior in dignity from them."[34] A clearer reference to the Pneumatomachians is, however, found in Gregory of Nyssa's theology of the Holy Spirit. The excerpt below is taken from Gregory of Nyssa's *On the Holy Spirit*.

What then is the charge they bring against us? They accuse us of profanity for entertaining lofty conceptions about the Holy Spirit. All that we, in following the teachings of the Fathers, confess as to the Spirit, they take in a sense of their own, and make it a handle against us, to denounce us for profanity. We, for instance, confess that the Holy Spirit is of the same rank as the Father and the Son, so that there is no difference between them in anything, to be thought or named, that devotion can ascribe to a Divine nature. We confess that, save His being contemplated as with peculiar attributes in regard of Person, the Holy Spirit is indeed from God, and of the Christ, according to Scripture, but that, while not to be confounded with the Father in being never originated, nor with the son in being the Only-begotten, and while to be regarded separately in certain distinctive properties, He has in all else, as I have just said, an exact divinity with them. But our opponents aver that He is a stranger to any

31. Anderson, "Introduction," 9.

32. MacCulloch, *Christianity*, 219.

33. Burgess, *Holy Spirit*, 117.

34. Basil, *On the Holy Spirit*, 45.

vital communion with the Father and the Son; that by reason of an essential variation He is inferior to, and less than they in every point; in power, in glory, in dignity, in fine in everything that in word or thought we ascribe to Deity; that, in consequence, in their glory He has no share, to equal honor with them He has no claim; and that, as for power, He possesses only so much of it as is sufficient for the partial activities assigned to Him; that with the creative force He is quite disconnected.

Such is the conception of Him that possesses them; and the logical consequence of it is that the Spirit has in Himself none of those marks which our devotion, in word or thought, ascribes to a Divine nature. What, then, shall be our way of arguing? We shall answer nothing new, nothing of our own invention, though they challenge us to it; we shall fall back upon the testimony in Holy Scripture about the Spirit, whence we learn that the Holy Spirit is Divine, and is to be called so. Now, if they allow this, and will not contradict the words of inspiration, then they, with all their eagerness to fight us, must tell us why they are for contending with us, instead of with Scripture. We say nothing different from that which Scripture says. But in a Divine nature, as such, when once we have believed in it, we can recognize no distinctions suggested either by the Scripture teaching or by our own common sense; distinctions, that is, that would divide that Divine and transcendent nature within itself by any degrees of intensity and remission, so as to be altered from itself by being more or less. Because we firmly believe that it is simple, uniform, incomposite, because we see in it no complicity or composition of dissimilars, therefore it is that, when once our minds have grasped the idea of Deity, we accept by the implication of that very name the perfection in it of every conceivable thing that befits the Deity. . . .

If, then, the Holy Spirit is truly, and not in name only, called Divine both by Scripture and by our Fathers, what ground is left for those who oppose the glory of the Spirit? He is Divine, and absolutely good, and Omnipotent, and wise, and glorious, and eternal; He is everything of this kind that can be named to raise our thoughts to the grandeur of His being.[35]

Question: How does this text argue for the personhood of the Holy Spirit?

G. W. H. Lampe: "Holy Spirit" as Metaphor for God

G. W. H. Lampe's pneumatology construes the Holy Spirit as impersonal divine activity. In his 1976 Bampton Lectures at Oxford University, Lampe

35. Gregory of Nyssa, *On the Holy Spirit* (NPNF² 5:315–16).

argued that the Holy Spirit is neither "an impersonal influence, an energy transmitted by God but distinct from God" nor "a divine entity or hypostasis which is a third person of the Godhead."[36] Lampe argued that Jews and Christians from the earliest times have used several parallel metaphors, such as "wisdom," "logos," "light," and "spirit," to express God's saving work and relationship with humanity. He writes, "Wisdom, Word, Spirit, interchangeable images, stand for the creative mind of God . . ."[37] Lampe, however, argues that the metaphor of "spirit" is the most helpful way to articulate and express Christianity's views of God's relationship with humanity. He also argues that the metaphor of "spirit" is the most preferable model to "express the continuity" of God's "action and self-revelation" because it is less liable to be construed in a hypostatic sense and will save Christians the headache of demonstrating the rationality of the doctrine of the Incarnation.

> The one continuous creative and saving work of God as Spirit begins with the origin and evolution of the cosmos itself, becomes personal communion with created persons when rational human beings come into existence, comes to be defined, so far as God's indwelling in man is concerned, in Christ as the pattern and archetype of personal union between God as Spirit and the spirit of man, and moves forward towards the goal of creation when humanity will be fully formed into the likeness of Christ, the model "Adam." The mark of this continuous presence of God in man is the "fruit of the Spirit" and at every stage in the process of the making of the human personality God's immanent presence is recognizable in the Christlike qualities, and pre-eminently in love.[38]

For Lampe, the Holy Spirit is God's inherent mode of communication and therefore should not be viewed as "a divine hypostasis distinct from God the Father and God the Son."[39] Lampe argues that it is misleading to restrict the term "'Spirit' to the 'Holy Spirit' as a third person of the Trinity."[40] According to Lampe, the idea of the Holy Spirit as a third person of the Trinity emerged as "a result of the hypostatization of the concepts of Wisdom and Logos."[41] "Christ" and "Spirit," for Lampe, are two modes of

36. The lectures were published in 1977 with the title *God as Spirit*. See Lampe, *God as Spirit*, 208.

37. Ibid., 121.

38. Ibid., 115.

39. Ibid., 10.

40. Ibid., 210.

41. Ibid.

God's salvific work in creation. He writes, "We should recognize, not that we experience the presence of Christ 'through' the Spirit, but rather that when we speak of the 'presence of Christ' and the 'indwelling of the Spirit' we are speaking of one and the same experience of God: God as Spirit, who was revealed to men, in his interaction with human personality, at a definite point in the history of man's creation, in Jesus Christ."[42]

Lampe clearly departs from the Trinitarian theology of the Councils of Nicaea, Constantinople, and Chalcedon. His reinterpretation of the Trinitarian theology of these councils reveals his radical departure from orthodoxy.[43] Lampe also fails to account for the New Testament passages that treat the Holy Spirit as person. Some of these passages will he highlighted below.

The Holy Spirit as Divine Person

Following the classical council of Nicaea, many Christians confess that the Holy Spirit is a distinct divine person. What does it mean to be a "person"? The meaning of "person" is highly debated in Christian theology. Many Christian theologians construe "person," when applied to God, as a *being* with capacity for relationship, self-determination, and conscious existence. There are principally two paths theologians follow to demonstrate the divinity of the Holy Spirit.

First, some follow the path of *biblical reflection*: they focus on the personal pronouns used for the Holy Spirit and on the personal qualities attributed to it in the Scriptures. It is noteworthy that the use of masculine pronouns for the Holy Spirit is rare.[44] Grammatically, *rûaḥ* is usually in the feminine gender and *pneuma* is usually in the neuter gender. Exceptions are found in the Gospel of John. For example, John used the neuter pronoun "it" (*ekeino* in Greek) in 14:17 and, interestingly, in the same chapter, the masculine pronoun "he" (*ekeinos* in Greek) in 14:26 (cf. John 15:26; 16:8, 13–14).

"The Spirit is more than God's presence: the Spirit is a Person in fellowship with, but distinct from, Father and Son. Called the Paraclete in John's Gospel, the Spirit is personal agent, teacher and friend."

—Pinnock, *Flame of Love*

The major problem with examining personal pronouns in the discussion of the personhood of the Holy Spirit is that in Hebrew and Greek

42. Ibid., 117–18.

43. Ibid., 228.

44. Pinnock, *Flame of Love*, 15.

grammar, personal pronouns do not necessarily indicate personhood. The Scriptures, however, are replete with instances of personal qualities that are ascribed to the Holy Spirit. These include knowledge (1 Cor 2:10–11), mind (John 14:26; Rom 8:27), emotions and feelings (Rom 8:26; Eph 4:30), and will (Acts 16:7). It is much more promising to explore the qualities of a personal being ascribed to the Holy Spirit than to focus on personal pronouns.

The second path that theologians follow in the discussion of the personhood of the Holy Spirit is *theological reflection*: some theologians draw insights from the Scriptures' testimony about the relationship of the Father, Jesus Christ, and the Holy Spirit. One advantage of this approach is that it encourages a rigorous reflection on the New Testament's teaching on the pattern of relationship between the Father, Son, and Holy Spirit (see Matt 28:19; 1 Cor 12:4–6; 2 Cor 13:14; Titus 3:4–6; Heb 9:14). The works of the following theologians exemplify helpful theological reflections on the personhood of the Holy Spirit.

Basil of Caesarea

Basil of Caesarea (c. 330–379) was one of the famous Cappadocian theologians. His major writing on pneumatology is *De Spiritu Sancto* (On the Holy Spirit), written in 374 CE at the request of his spiritual son, Amphilochius. Nowhere in *De Spiritu Sancto* does Basil say that the "Holy Spirit is God," which is ironic since his goal was to demonstrate the divinity and distinct personhood of the Holy Spirit. But through a rhetorical strategy, Basil leads his readers to conclude that the Holy Spirit is a distinct member of the Trinity. An example of this rhetorical strategy is Basil's reflection on Peter's rebuke of Ananias and Sapphira in which Peter accused them of lying against the Holy Spirit and went on to ask Sapphira, "How could you agree to test the Spirit of the Lord?" (Acts 5:3–11, NIV). In his reflection on Peter's question, Basil wrote, "Peter's words to Sapphira . . . show that sins against the Holy Spirit and against God are the same; and thus you might learn that in every operation the Spirit is closely conjoined with, and inseparable from the Father and Son."[45] Like many theologians in the fourth century CE, Basil was reluctant to call the Holy Spirit "God" because the Scriptures do not explicitly do so. Some theologians have concluded that Basil's reluctance to argue for the divinity of the Holy Spirit explicitly and in strong terms indicates that he was "not altogether clear about the Spirit's nature and divinity."[46]

45. Basil, *On the Holy Spirit*, 16.37.
46. Beeley, "Holy Spirit in the Cappadocians," 95.

Basil's argument for the person and divinity of the Holy Spirit arises from the relationship of the Holy Spirit with the Father and the Son as depicted in the Scriptures. Basil also examines the functions the Scriptures assign to the Holy Spirit. The following excerpt is taken from his *De Spiritu Sancto.*

But we must proceed to attack our opponents, in the endeavor to confute those "oppositions" advanced against us which are derived from "knowledge falsely so-called."

It is not permissible, they assert, for the Holy Spirit to be ranked with the Father and Son, on account of the difference of His nature and the inferiority of His dignity. Against them it is right to reply in the words of the apostles, "We ought to obey God rather than men."

For if our Lord, when enjoining the baptism of salvation, charged His disciples to baptize all nations in the name "of the Father and of the Son and of the Holy Ghost," not disdaining fellowship with Him, and these men allege that we must not rank Him with the Father and the Son, is it not clear that they openly withstand the commandment of God? If they deny that coordination of this kind is declaratory of any fellowship and conjunction, let them tell us why it behoves us to hold this opinion, and what more intimate mode of conjunction they have.

If the Lord did not indeed conjoin the Spirit with the Father and Himself in baptism, do not let them lay the blame of conjunction upon us, for we neither hold nor say anything different. If on the contrary the Spirit is there conjoined with the Father and the Son, and no one is so shameless as to say anything else, then let them not lay blame on us for following the words of Scripture.

But all the apparatus of war has been got ready against us; every intellectual missile is aimed at us; and now blasphemers' tongues shoot and hit and hit again, yet harder than Stephen of old was smitten by the killers of the Christ. And do not let them succeed in concealing the fact that, while an attack on us serves for a pretext for the war, the real aim of these proceedings is higher. It is against us, they say, that they are preparing their engines and their snares; against us that they are shouting to one another, according to each one's strength or cunning, to come on.... We will not cowardly abandon the cause. The Lord has delivered to us as a necessary and saving doctrine that the Holy Spirit is to be ranked with the Father. Our opponents think differently, and see fit to divide and rend asunder, and relegate Him to the nature of a ministering spirit. Is it not then indisputable that they make their own blasphemy more authoritative than the law prescribed by the Lord?

Whence is it that we are Christians? Through our faith, would be the universal answer. And in what way are we saved? Plainly because we were regenerate through the grace given in our baptism. How else could we be? And after recognizing that this salvation is established through the Father and the Son and the Holy Ghost, shall we fling away "that form of doctrine" which we received? Would it not rather be ground for great groaning if we are found now further off from our salvation "than when we first believed," and deny now what we then received? ... Can I then, perverted by these men's seductive words, abandon the tradition which guided me to the light, which bestowed on me the boon of the knowledge of God, whereby I, so long a foe by reason of sin, was made a child of God? But, for myself, I pray that with this confession I may depart hence to the Lord, and them I charge to preserve the faith secure until the day of Christ, and to keep the Spirit undivided from the Father and the Son, preserving, both in the confession of faith and in the doxology, the doctrine taught them at their baptism.[47]

Question: What arguments did Basil use in his defense of the identity of the Holy Spirit?

Caleb Oluremi Oladipo

The Nigerian theologian Caleb Oladipo, like many African theologians who explore the relationship between Christianity and African indigenous religions, developed a pneumatology that answers the question, "How could the understanding of the Holy Spirit . . . provide a connection between Christianity and other living faiths?"[48] Oladipo explores the idea of "ancestors" in African indigenous thought as a theological hermeneutic for expressing the Christian idea of the Trinity. In the indigenous thought of some African communities, the ancestors are called the "living dead" because people see them as the "guardian spirits" that protect the lives of their progeny.[49]

Oladipo argues that the majority of Yoruba (an ethnic group in western Nigeria) Christians relate to God the Father as the "Great Ancestor," Jesus as the "Proto-ancestor," and the Holy Spirit as the "Grand Ancestor."[50] For Oladipo, most Yoruba Christians relate to God the Father as the great ancestor because "God the Father is creator and the beginning and end of

---

47 Basil, *De Spiritu Sancto* (NPNF² 8:16–17).

48. Oladipo, *Development of the Doctrine of the Holy Spirit*, 102.

49. Orobator, *Theology Brewed in an African Pot*, 113.

50. Oladipo, *Development of the Doctrine of the Holy Spirit*, 102.

all reality."[51] They see Jesus Christ, God the Son, as a proto-ancestor because he is "the one in whom they can have a new beginning and a renewed relationship with God the creator."[52] The Holy Spirit is construed as the grand ancestor because the Holy Spirit provides "spiritual guidance" and enables people to direct their own destiny.[53]

Oladipo's pneumatology is unique because of the choice of the ancestral cult as a theological model to express the personhood and function of the Holy Spirit in the African context. Most African theologians who adopt the ancestral theological model focus on the doctrine of the Father and Christology.

The excerpt below is taken from Oladipo's *The Development of the Doctrine of the Holy Spirit in the Yoruba (African) Indigenous Christian Movement*.

Functional Similarities between the Holy Spirit and Ancestors

First, the ancestorship of the living-dead is founded upon a consanguineous relationship with the living relatives. . . . The relationship of the Holy Spirit to the believers can be said to be also consanguineous because following the resurrection and ascension of Christ, the Holy Spirit is sent to believers as comforter, for the purpose of guidance, reminding, witnessing, convicting, leading, speaking, hearing, glorifying, and teaching. Second, the supernatural status of the ancestors endows them with superhuman powers, and they can also perform the function of a mediator between God and their living relatives. Likewise, supernatural status endows the Holy Spirit with supernatural powers and with the roles of being the mediator and intercessor between God the Father and believers in Jesus Christ. Third, the ancestors are models of acceptable conduct as well as the source and teachers of traditional beliefs. The Holy Spirit is also the model of Christian living. He is the teacher of acceptable Christian beliefs and practices. Fourth, a regular communication is maintained between the ancestors and their living relations through prayers and rituals. As a mark of this communication, the ancestors also bestow various benefits such as longevity of life, happiness, and so on. In the same manner, believers see a line of communication between them and the Spirit of God in them. . . . As the ancestor is believed to bestow longevity of life, it is not inconceivable that the presence of the Holy Spirit in the lives of believers is a mark of everlasting life. Fifth, a neglect of regular communication on the part

51. Ibid.
52. Ibid.
53. Ibid.

of the living is regarded as a serious offence against the ancestors. . . . In the same manner, a neglect of communications with God through the Holy Spirit . . . is also regarded as a serious offence against the principle of true Christian discipleship.

Sixth, the Yoruba people believe that their ancestors visit their living relatives through other people who are still living. Occasionally, the Holy Spirit can visit believers through other people who have been chosen to deliver specific messages.

Functional Differences between the Holy Spirit and Ancestors

The first fundamental difference between the Holy Spirit and the ancestors is that the Holy Spirit does not acquire his status after death like the ancestors. The Holy Spirit is related to believers because of his supernatural union with God the Father and God the Son. . . . As such, the Holy Spirit transcends not only family boundaries, but also any consanguineous limitations whatsoever. Second, it can be said that the Holy Spirit is more infinitely perfect as the guidance and source of Christian living than the Yoruba ancestors can ever be. Third, no one can appease God . . . by merely outward rituals [as in the case of ancestors]. Only a sincere expression of sorrow and total conversion of heart towards the Spirit of God is efficacious in appeasing [or amending] a severed relationship with God.[54]

Question: How does Oladipo's pneumatology demonstrate the principle of contextual theological thinking? Also, how does his pneumatology show the personhood of the Holy Spirit?

The Holy Spirit's Relationship with Jesus Christ

Beginning in the sixth century CE, the doctrine of the Holy Spirit once again became a central theological issue in Christianity. But unlike in the late fifth century when the divinity, personhood, and "class" of the Holy Spirit were the focal point in the Trinitarian debate, in the sixth century the focal point was the Holy Spirit's relationship with Jesus Christ. Two

"Where the Spirit is understood as 'applying' the benefits of Christ, then she seems in danger of being reduced to the power of Christ's person."

—Milbank, *The Word Made Strange*

54 Ibid., 108–11.

pneumatological-christological positions appeared. Some theologians argued that the Holy Spirit proceeded *only* from God the Father. These theologians remained faithful to the Nicene-Constantinopolitan Creed (481 CE), which stated that the Holy Spirit "proceeds from the Father." Other theologians proposed an alternative position, arguing that the Holy Spirit proceeded both from the Father and from the Son; they altered the Nicene-Constantinopolitan Creed by adding the Latin word *filioque* ("and from the Son.") These two pneumatological-christological positions formed the backdrop to what theologians now refer to as the *filioque* controversy.

The *Filioque* Controversy

Two versions of the Nicene-Constantinopolitan creeds exist today: the version with the clause "and from the Son" (*filioque*), which is used in the Roman Catholic Church, and the version without the clause, which is used in the Eastern and Greek Orthodox churches. For some theologians, the primary issue in the *filioque* controversy, as John Milbank notes, seems to be how to "emphasize both the agency of the Spirit in the life of Christ and the eschatological giving of the Spirit *by* Christ."[55] Other theologians see the *filioque* controversy as a theological dispute that focused primarily on the nature of the relationship of the three divine persons both in their *immanent* life and *economic* life (see chapter 4 on the Trinity). Some theologians were unwavering in their attempt to preserve God the Father as the sole source of life in the Trinity. For them, to say that the Holy Spirit proceeded both from the Father and the Son was tantamount to a *double procession*—dual sources of life in the Trinity. The *filioque* dispute could well be the consequence of "rival scholasticisms."[56] Yet for other theologians, the real issue in the *filioque* controversy was not theological but political. It was one thing to propound and defend a theology of *filioque*; it was another thing to defend its insertion in the Creed. Some theologians were willing to accept the theology of *filioque* but "refused to sanction any interference with the wording of the Creed."[57]

> "The [Holy] Spirit of both [the Father and the Son] is a kind of consubstantial communion of Father and Son."
> —Augustine, *On the Trinity*

The path of the *filioque* controversy was fraught with several difficulties. An early indication of a theological move in the direction of *filioque*

55. Milbank, *Word Made Strange*, 172.

56. Ibid., 173.

57. Heron, "Filioque Clause," 65.

could be found in the writing of St. Augustine (c. 354–430). In *On the Trinity*, Augustine wrote, "But the Holy Spirit does not proceed from the Father into the Son, and from the Son proceed to sanctify the creature, but proceeds at once from both; although the Father has given this to the Son, that He should proceed, as from Himself, so also from Him."[58] Augustine could be depicted as a major precursor of the doctrine of *filioque*. Augustine's description of the Holy Spirit as the "bond of love" between the Father and Son provided the context for his contention that the Holy Spirit proceeded from both the Father and the Son.

In 589 CE, the Third Council of Toledo (Spain), a non-ecumenical council, approved the insertion of "and from the Son" in the Nicene-Constantinopolitan Creed. The question is whether a non-ecumenical council can unilaterally amend the Creed of an ecumenical council. Since the sixth century CE, the *filioque* controversy has divided the Western Church and the Eastern Church. The churches of the Latin West accepted the insertion of *filioque* in the Nicene-Constantinopolitan Creed, whereas the churches of the Greek East rejected any alteration of the Creed.[59] There was a general belief that the theological decisions of the ecumenical councils were "inspired by the Holy Spirit to guide and express the mind of the universal Church. Consequently, only another council with the same standing and authority could modify or add to what they had defined."[60]

No theological consensus has been reached on the *filioque* controversy between the Eastern Church and the Western Church. All decrees of reunion have been short-lived. There have been several attempts to clarify or resolve the theological divide between the Eastern Church and the Western Church—some unilateral, others bilateral. In the ninth century, Photius of Constantinople argued that the Holy Spirit proceeded *eternally* from the Father alone, but has also in the context of the economy of salvation proceeded *temporarily* from the Son.[61] In other words, for Photius, "any progression of the Spirit by the Son was on the level of the economy only, involving its temporal mission—never its eternal hypostatic derivation."[62] The Council of Lyons (1274), the Council of Blachernae (1285), the Council of Florence (1439), and the North American Orthodox-Catholic Consultation (2003) attempted to clarify the theological significance of the doctrine of *filioque*. The Councils of Lyons and Florence argued that *filioque* did not

---

58. Augustine, *On the Trinity*, XV.27.48.
59. Papadakis, "Beyond the Filioque Divide," 142.
60. Heron, "Filioque Clause," 68–69.
61. Papadakis, "Beyond the Filioque Divide," 144.
62. Ibid., 145.

mean that the Holy Spirit "had two separate and distinct sources in the Father and the Son."[63] The Council of Lyons, despite its reconciliatory efforts, still pronounced an anathema on those who deny the doctrine of *filioque*. The Council of Blachernae explored the possibility of adopting a modification of *filioque*, which stated that the Holy Spirit "proceeds from the Father through the Son." The assumption seemed to be that "through" was the same as "proceeding from." The Council of Florence "made no change in faith, but simply explicated it more clearly."[64]

The *filioque* controversy is usually remembered for its role in the ecclesiastical and theological divide between the Eastern Church and the Western Church. Theologians usually do not explore the contributions of the controversy to pneumatology. The *filioque* controversy is theologically significant because it led to rigorous reflections not only on the relationship of the three divine persons, but also on the person and identity of the Holy Spirit. The controversy also was instrumental in fostering theological reflection on the work of the Holy Spirit in the creation of the church—the community of people whom the Holy Spirit incorporated into Christ and empowered to benefit from the salvific work of God. As the nature of the relationship between the Holy Spirit and the Son was being ironed out, many theologians explored the roles of the Holy Spirit in the economy of salvation.

The Holy Spirit in the Life of Jesus Christ

What is usually ignored in discussions on the *filioque* controversy is the logical and chronological distinction between the work of the Holy Spirit *in the life of Jesus Christ* and the work of the Holy *in the life of the followers of Jesus*. As we will see in the next section, the life and ministry of Jesus Christ depended on the Holy Spirit. The work of the Holy Spirit precedes the work of Jesus of Nazareth. The Holy Spirit is the forerunner of Christ. By the power of the Holy Spirit Jesus was born, and through the enablement of the Holy Spirit Jesus was able to live his earthly life and accomplish his work. The followers of Jesus, however, could experience the Holy Spirit only through Jesus Christ. Paul in Titus depicts Jesus Christ as the agent through which God pours God's Spirit on believers in Christ: "He [God] saved us through the washing of rebirth and renewal by the Holy Spirit, whom he poured out on us generously through Jesus Christ our Savior, so that, having been justified by his grace, we might become heirs having the hope of

63. Heron, "Filioque Clause," 66.
64. Congar, *I Believe in the Holy Spirit*, 204.

eternal life" (3:5-7, NIV). As the *parakletōs* (advocate or witness), the Holy Spirit persuades people that Jesus is God's anointed one (John 15:26).

The emphasis on Christology in certain Christian circles has in some ways blinded many Christians from exploring the scriptural teaching on the Holy Spirit in the life of Jesus Christ. However, any Christology that overlooks pneumatology is unsustainable. The Holy Spirit initiated and sustained the life and ministry of Jesus Christ. The Holy Spirit was actively involved in Jesus' conception, birth, inauguration into ministry, miraculous work, and resurrection (Luke 1:35; 3:22-23; John 15:26; Acts 10:38; Titus 3:4-7; 1 Pet 3:18-19).

One of the areas that has received enormous theological attention is the relationship of the Holy Spirit to the "sonship" of Jesus Christ. When Christians call Jesus the "Son of God," what exactly do they have in mind? Does the expression refer to the eternal loving relationship between Jesus and God the Father? Or does it refer to the position or relationship into which Jesus was adopted? Or does it refer simply to an honorific title given to Jesus by his earliest followers on the basis of what God accomplished through him?

> "I still have many things to say to you, but you cannot bear them now. When the Spirit of truth comes, he will guide you into all the truth, for he will not speak on his own authority, but whatever he hears he will speak, and he will declare to you the things to come. He will glorify me, for he will take what is mine and declare it to you" (John 16:12-14, ESV).

Mark 1:10-11 is central to the attempt to answer these questions. Mark writes, "As Jesus was coming up out of the water, he saw heaven being torn open and the Spirit descending on him like a dove. And a voice came from heaven: 'You are my Son, whom I love; with you I am well pleased'" (NIV). What are the theological implications of this divine declaration? Some theologians argue that, since God declared Jesus to be God's Son only after the pneumatic anointing at the river Jordan, Jesus became something he was not prior to the pneumatic experience. For them, Jesus of Nazareth *became* God's son after God anointed him with God's Spirit. God's Spirit or the Holy Spirit therefore signifies God's adoption of Jesus into divine sonship.[65] Others have argued that although Jesus could be construed as God's son from birth, he only became the Messiah after the pneumatic anointing. For them, it was at the

---

65. For extensive discussion on this view, see Menzies, *Empowered for Witness*, 132-56.

river Jordan that God initiated Jesus Christ into the new age and covenant.[66] By anointing him with the Holy Spirit, God declared Jesus the awaited Messiah who will lead people into the new covenant.

These two positions deny the traditional understanding of Jesus as ontologically divine—God's eternal *logos* that became flesh (John 1:1, 14). Also, in these two positions one encounters a form of *Spirit Christology*—Christology that understands the divinity of Jesus Christ not on the basis of the eternal divine *logos* but rather on the basis of God's Spirit. The form of Spirit Christology that can be associated with these two positions regards Jesus as divine only functionally—that is, God acted in and through Jesus by endowing him with God's Spirit.

Other theologians, including Robert Menzies, have argued that the pneumatic anointing at Jordan does not provide Jesus with "a new awareness of God as Father and/or initiate him into the new age and covenant."[67] Menzies writes, "The divine declaration does not designate Jesus' reception of the Spirit as the beginning, in any sense, of his sonship or messiahship. On the contrary, through his reception of the Spirit Jesus is equipped for his messianic task. We may speak of the Jordan even as signaling the beginning of Jesus' messianic ministry, but not of his messiahship."[68] The divine declaration in Mark 1:11 is most probably derived from Psalm 2:7, in which God declares the king of Israel God's son: "You are my Son, today I have become your Father" (NIV). Mathew, Mark, and Luke all excluded the clause "today I have become your Father" in their accounts of the baptism of Jesus (Matt 3:17; Mark 1:11; Luke 3:22). This exclusion seems to suggest that God's declaration of Jesus' sonship does not "proclaim Jesus' newly established status of sonship consequent upon his installation as Messiah; rather it confirms his already existing filial consciousness" and relationship with God the Father.[69] By declaring Jesus "divine Son," God the Father attests to God's active presence in the life and work of Jesus Christ. It is in this light that Jesus understood his mission. This can be seen in his words to the crowd that followed him to Capernaum: "I have come down from heaven not to do my will, but to do the will of him who sent me" (John 6:38).

I will now highlight some theologians who have reflected and defended the work of the Holy Spirit in the life and ministry of Jesus Christ.

---

66. Ibid., 137.

67. Menzies, *Empowered for Witness*, 137.

68. Ibid.

69. Cranfield, *Gospel According to St. Mark*, 55.

Yves Congar

Yves Congar (1904–1995), a French Dominican priest, was one of the most influential Roman Catholic theologians of the twentieth century. Congar's most influential work on pneumatology is *I Believe in the Holy Spirit*. Congar's pneumatology is significant partly because of its enormous influence on Roman Catholic theologians after the Second Vatican Council. Before the Second Vatican Council, the majority of theological manuals used in Roman Catholic seminaries paid minimal attention to the Holy Spirit.[70] One of the many contributions of Congar was his integration of pneumatology with other Christian doctrines such as Christology, theological anthropology, ecclesiology, and soteriology. The following excerpt highlights only his pneumatological Christology.

> The hypostatic union is a metaphysical fact by means of which a human nature subsists through the person of the Son of God. It clearly requires the man who is thus called into existence to be holy. In Scholastic theology, this is the work of the Holy Spirit, who follows the presence of the Word, and of sanctifying grace, which follows the grace of the union as its consequence.... That grace, which is given in its absolute fullness to Christ, is both his personal grace and his grace as the Head (*gratia capitis*). In the New Testament, the coming and the action of the Spirit made the fruit conceived by Mary "holy," that is, realizing the will of "God" (= the Father) perfectly (see Luke 1:35).
>
> The will of God, which Irenaeus called the "Father's good pleasure," was that the man Jesus should live perfectly in obedience as the Son (Heb 10:5–9). The way that the Father wanted him to follow was the way that led, through the cross, to glory. It was, in other words, not the way of (beatific) vision, but the way of obedience. That obedience consisted in going where God wanted him to go without knowing where it led (see Heb 11:8). It was the way of prayer—for how is it possible not to see Jesus' own life of prayer and the prayer that he himself taught us (see Matt 6:9–11) within the context of his whole "mission" and the history of salvation? It was also the way of *kenōsis* and of the suffering Servant (Phil 2:6–8). It was, then, in this way that Jesus acted as a son.
>
> What consciousness did he have, in his human soul, of his quality of Son of God? This is something that is hidden from us. The hypostatic union left his human soul, which was consubstantial with ours, in his human condition of *kenōsis*, obedience and prayer. The Spirit, who sanctified him in that condition (see Luke 2:40 and 52), however, enabled him to understand more and also

70. Groppe, "Contribution of Yves Congar's Theology of the Holy Spirit," 452.

more deeply than the teachers of the law (2:47) and even than his mother, to whom he replied: "Did you not know that I must be in my Father's house?" (2:49). What consciousness of himself and of the fatherhood of God is concealed within this reply? The "I" is that of the eternal Son, but it is at the level of the "me," the objectively conscious content (or the content that is qualified to be conscious) of his experience, which may be called "personality." Jesus only realized his relationship with the Father in and through the acts of his spiritual life as a son, the Spirit being the source of these in him. These acts include prayer, his clinging in love to the Father's plan for him, and the "works" that the Father gave him to fulfill.

The event in the Jordan [Jesus' baptism] marks the beginning of the messianic era. The period of John the Baptist is over and that of Jesus begins. The fact that Luke has John the Baptist put in prison before Jesus' baptism and the theophany is no doubt intentional—it points to this end and beginning. The Spirit who descended on Jesus anoints him as Messiah or the "Christ" (see Acts 10:38). He [the Holy Spirit] then leads him out into the desert and makes him begin his messianic activity.[71]

Question: How does Congar understand the sonship of Jesus and the role of the Holy Spirit in the life of Jesus?

Rowan Williams

Rowan Williams, the 104th archbishop of Canterbury, developed a pneumatology that aims to address two major theological concerns. First, he is dissatisfied with the tangential treatment of pneumatology in the works of key European theologians such as Karl Barth, Eberhard Jüngel, and Karl Rahner. Second, Williams takes issue with a form of binatarianism—"a trinity of two persons (agents) and a force, or quality, or 'mode of presence'"—in the writing of some English theologians. Third, Williams is also at odds with those pnuematologies that ignore Christology. The excerpt below highlights some of the unique insights Williams brings to the discussion on Christology and pnuematology.

---

71. Congar, *I Believe in the Holy Spirit*, 3:166–67.

If the sonhip of Jesus means the poverty and vulnerability of Jesus in the world, it is indeed both active and contemplative, both the taking of responsibility for one's place in the world and the refusal to interpret and enact this as coercive power. The modern apostles of non-violence are right to deny that non-violence implies indifference or passivity.

How are we to relate all this to the theology of the Spirit? It does at least suggest a way in which pneumatology might be reconnected with central Christological issues so as to bear more directly on the *humanum*; and it also points to the possibility of restating the classical argument that rests the claim for the Spirit's divinity upon his share in the work of salvation or divinization. In this perspective, to see the Spirit in second-century style as a secondary mediator makes no sense: the work of Spirit, like the Son's work, is bound up precisely with the *loss* of mediatorial concepts designed to explain how the transcendent God (who is *elsewhere*) can be communicated *here*. The pivotal image of Jesus as Son radically changes in the simple schema of God-and-the-world. . . . The Spirit's "completion" of Christ's work is no longer to be seen epistemologically, as a supplement or extension to the teaching of Christ, or even as that which makes it possible to hear and receive the Word. It is, rather, a completion in terms of liberation and transformation: it is *gift*, renewal and life. It is not possible to speak of Spirit in abstraction from the Christian form of life as a whole: Spirit is "specified" not with reference to any kind of episodic experience but in relation to the human identity of the Christian. The question "Where, or what, is Holy Spirit?" is not answered (as it might be by Luke) by pointing to prophecy and "charismata" and saying, "Spirit is the agency productive of phenomena like this."

How then is it answered? Perhaps not at all. The theological quest which is preoccupied with identifying the *distinctive* quality or work of the Spirit has so often . . . produced only the most sterile abstractions. And there is at least in eastern Christian thought a sense that the "face" of the Holy Spirit is not there for us to see. If what we are speaking of is the agency which draws us to the Father by constituting us children, we are evidently speaking of an agency not simply identical with "Father" or "Son," or with a sum or amalgam of the two. That perhaps is obvious, or even trivial, but it may be that no more can be said of the Spirit's distinctiveness. The grammar of our talk about the Holy Spirit is not that proper to "God" as source, ground, terminus of vision and prayer, and so forth, nor that proper to "God" as the disturbing presence of grace and vulnerability within the world of human relationships as a particular focal story. It is the grammar of "spirituality" in the fullest sense of that emasculated word, the grammar of the interplay in the human self between the given and the future, between reality as it is and the truth which encompasses it; between Good Friday and Easter.[72]

Question: What is Williams' concept of the work of the Holy Spirit? What are the implications of Williams' pneumatology for Christology and anthropology?

Frank Macchia

Frank Macchia is one of the leading scholars of Pentecostal theology and studies today. His *Baptized in the Spirit: A Global Pentecostal Theology* has won the attention of non-Pentecostal theologians. Macchia has held important positions in the Pentecostal community, such as president of the Society for Pentecostal Studies and editor of *The Journal of the Society for Pentecostal Studies*. Macchia' pneumatology is representative of the ideas of the Holy Spirit in many Pentecostal communities.

Since the Pentecostals do not place much of an accent on the Father or creation, being more oriented toward the eschatological works of new creation in Christ and the Spirit, they generally confront the Trinitarian framework for Spirit baptism through issues surrounding the relationship between Word and Spirit. In this context, all Pentecostals recognize that the Spirit is the agent by which we are incorporated into Christ and born anew. In search of a way to distinguish this Spirit indwelling from charismatic empowerment, some Pentecostals have made a distinction between the Spirit's baptizing us into Christ at regeneration (1 Cor 12:13) and Christ's baptizing us in the Spirit at Spirit baptism as power among believers for witness (Acts 1:8).

This difference becomes metaphorical for how baptism in the Spirit reflects a fullness of spiritual experience allegedly not characteristic of prior existence "in Christ." One is reminded here of the medieval assumption that the mystics or ascetics experienced a greater fullness of the Spirit than ordinary Christians. Pentecostals, however, attached this greater fullness mainly to those caught up in Spirit's drive toward global mission. Though elitist assumptions have no place in the body of Christ, is there not an element of truth to this Pentecostal assumption? Do not Christians (Pentecostal or not) involved in charismatic ministry and mission in the world experience the Spirit in greater fullness than those who merely warm a bench on Sunday?

72. Williams, *On Christian Theology*, 122–24.

But the elitist assumptions of Pentecostal revivalism must still be addressed. Dale Bruner has noted that the difference between Spirit indwelling and baptism calls into question the sufficiency of Christ for the spiritual life.[73] Paul says that all spiritual blessings are in Christ (Eph 1:3). There can thus be no stage of spiritual blessings "beyond" faith in Christ. Pentecostals can counter, however, that Christ is sufficient for the Christian life (Gal 3:1–5) and experience the Spirit in greater and greater fullness. There is thus no necessary contradiction between saying that Christ is all sufficient for the Christian life and maintaining that believers are to seek a greater "fullness" of the Spirit's working through us from and in Christ.

One could argue that Pentecostals generally do not intend to seek for an encounter with the Spirit "beyond Christ," even though their language has given that impression with negative results. . . .[74]

Question: What are the pneumatological and Christological issues that Macchia discusses in this text?

Key Terms

Filioque: Latin phrase that means "and from the Son," which is inserted in some versions of the Nicene-Constantinopolitan Creed.

Pneumatomachoi: Greek word that means "fighters against the Spirit"; it was used to describe some early Christians who denied the personhood of the Holy Spirit.

Montanism: second-century Christian movement with prophets and prophetesses who claimed to be the spokespersons of the Holy Spirit.

73. See Bruner, *Theology of the Holy Spirit*, 61ff.
74. *Machia*, Baptized in the Spirit, 113.

Review Questions

1. What is the role of the Holy Spirit in the Trinity?

2. What roles have the Pentecostal, Charismatic, and Healing Movements played in rediscovering the significance of the person and work of the Holy Spirit?

3. What were the contributions of the Councils of Nicaea and Constantinople to the doctrine of Trinity?

4. How did the New Testament and the Old Testament authors understand God's Spirit and the Holy Spirit?

Suggestions for Further Reading

Congar, Yves. *I Believe in the Holy Spirit*. Translated by David Smith. New York: Crossroad, 1997.

Fergusson, Sinclair B. *The Holy Spirit*. Downers Grove, IL: InterVarsity, 1996.

Macchia, Frank D. *Baptized in the Spirit: A Global Pentecostal Theology*. Grand Rapids: Zondervan, 2006.

Pinnock, Clark H. *Flame of Love: A Theology of the Holy Spirit*. Downers Grove, IL: InterVarsity, 1996.

7

Divine Providence

This chapter discusses Christian understandings of God's relationship to the world. It explores the ideas and the major theological issues that are associated with God's providence.

Whenever a tragedy happens, people often ask questions such as the following: Why do things happen the way they do? Does the world have any meaning beyond the survival of the fittest and death? These are some of the deepest questions that haunt human beings. For Christian theologians, God ought to be at the center of reflection on these questions. Following Genesis' creation narratives, Christian theologians postulate that the world and everything in it (in its original state) exist because God brought them into existence (Gen 1 and 2).

The majority of Christian theologians also claim that God did not abandon the world after creating it. God upholds and directs the affairs of the world. Theologians differ, however, on the nature and extent of God's involvement in the affairs of the world. Some theologians address this issue in a manner that drives a wedge between God and creation. Others discuss God's relation to creation in a way that emphasizes God's presence *in* creation without reducing God to part of the creation. Some believe that God directly causes *all* things to happen; others believe that God does not

directly cause all things to happen. These issues are central to Christian theologies of divine providence.

Ideas of Divine Providence

Christianity is a religion that emphasizes divine providence—that is, God's
acts of creating and sustaining God's creation. Christian doctrines such as
creation, Scripture, salvation,
sin, Christian life, and hope are
intrinsically connected to God's
providence. For Christians, God
creates, redeems, forgives, enables moral rectitude, and shapes the future
outcomes of creation. The clues the Bible provides for the theologian are
dialectical: God created a good creation but evil and sin are present in God's
creation; God is sovereign over God's creation but human beings are responsible for their actions (Gen 1:31; Jer 10:23; 12:1–1; Rom 14:12; 2 Cor
5:10). The Bible also indicates "that the work of God is not exhausted by an
initial act of creation; that the rhythms of nature and life are well ordered;
and that struggle and an overriding of sin, suffering, and death are necessary for the fulfillment of the divine purpose."[1]

FOCUS QUESTION:
What is divine providence?

Broadly, two major views of divine providence are prominent in theological discussions: meticulous providence and general providence. Within
these two major categories, there are diverse opinions that stand in tension
with one another. Sometimes the differences in these opinions depend on
the theologians' view of God's sovereignty and human freedom. Also, the
differences may depend on a theologian's view of the nature of divine agency
in creation—whether God's involvement in creation should be understood
as *supernatural intervention* or as action that is consistent with the law of
nature.

Meticulous or Specific Providence

Meticulous providence (also known as *specific providence*) is the view that
sees God's providential act as involving complete control of human affairs.
For this view, God has a purpose for every human action and experience.
Nothing happens without God's prior knowledge of it and God's decision
to *cause* it or *allow* it to happen. This implies that things that happen in the
world are causally determined by God.

1. Fergusson, "Divine Providence and Action," 154.

Meticulous providence is explained in various ways. To highlight these differences, it will be helpful to propose a scenario. In 2011, a healthy Nigerian pregnant woman who had carried her baby for nine months lost the baby during childbirth. The medical explanation for the tragedy was that the baby was too big to be born without a Caesarean section, but her (incompetent) doctor wanted her do deliver the baby naturally. After about six hours of painful labor, the baby died. Does God have a role in this tragedy? Below is the summary of two theological positions within the meticulous providence view.

The Strict Determinist Position

For some theologians who adopt the meticulous providence model, God created a world in which God determines whatever happens. God knows everything that will happen in the present and future because God has foreordained events. This is the position of *strict determinism*. According to this theological position, "all that happens is causally determined" by God and "there is no human free will of any sort."[2] Theologians who hold to strict determinism will respond to the experience of the woman who lost her baby during childbirth by saying that it could not have happened without God *causing* or *decreeing* it to happen. Many strict determinists will go so far as to say that God predetermined the tragedy and experience of the woman in order to bring glory to God's self. In this sense, God was the remote cause of the tragedy; the incompetent doctor was the immediate cause. In other words, God only used the doctor to accomplish what God had already planned would happen. According to John Calvin, "Carnal reason ascribes all such happenings, whether prosperous or adverse, to fortune. But anyone who has been taught by Christ's lips that all the hairs of his head are numbered . . . will look farther afield for a cause, and will consider that all events are governed by God's secret plan."[3]

Strict determinists are charged with *fatalism*—the belief that "there is an inherent necessity in the way things are so that they could not be any other way."[4] For example, was the doctor whose bad decision led to the death of the baby legally and morally responsible for his action? A major criticism of strict determinism is how to account for God's and humans' moral responsibility for what happens in the world. Most strict determinists usually respond to this criticism by citing a biblical passage such as Romans

2. Feinberg, *No One Like Him*, 635.

3. Calvin, *Institutes*, 1.16.2.

4. Feinberg, "God Ordains All Things," 23.

9:16–21, which recounts God's dealing with the Pharaoh of Egypt: "It does not, therefore, depend on man's desire, but on God's mercy. For the Scripture says to Pharaoh: 'I raised you up for this very purpose, that I might display my power in you and that my name might be proclaimed in all the earth.' Therefore, God has mercy on whom he wants to have mercy, and he hardens whom he wants to harden" (NIV).[5] As with Pharaoh, God caused the doctor to make the decision that led to the death of the baby, a tragedy that will bring glory to God or will display God's power, even if that power may not be apparent to human beings. God, it seems, is culpable for Pharaoh's decision not to free the Israelites. Yet God holds Pharaoh responsible for his maltreatment of the Israelites and also his refusal to free the Israelites. There seems to be contradiction and unfairness in God's action in the strict determinism position. Soft determinists seek to avoid the contradiction and the charge of unfairness in God's action.

The Soft Deterministic and Compatibilistic Free Will Position

Some theologians adopt the meticulous providence model but reject the notion that God's sovereignty totally obliterates human freedom. They contend that free will (in the compatibilistic sense) and determinism are not contradictory. Like strict determinists, soft determinists believe that everything that happens in the world is causally determined by God. Unlike strict determinists, however, soft determinists argue that some human actions arise from genuine human free will, which is "compatible with causal conditions that decisively incline the will without constraining it."[6] For soft determinists, the issue is not "whether someone's acts are causally determined or not, but rather *how* they are determined."[7] The "causes" of an action can be either *constraining* (on human will) or *non-constraining*. As John Feinberg explains, "The causal conditions are sufficient to move the agent to choose one option over another, but the choice and resultant action are free as long as the person acts without constraint."[8] God in some cases does not decree every human action; rather, God *authorizes* or *allows* human actions that originate from human free will. A soft determinist, therefore, might say it was possible that God caused the woman to lose her baby during childbirth and that it was equally possible God did not constrain the doctor to make the poor decision that led to the death of the baby.

---

5. See also Exod 9:16.
6. Feinberg, *No One Like Him*, 637.
7. Feinberg, "God Ordains All Things," 37.
8. Feinberg, *No One Like Him*, 637.

One of the criticisms of this view is how to determine when an action is compatible with a person's free will and when an action is constrained by an external agent or force. Also, how is it possible that God can guarantee the outcomes of human choices without coercing or forcing human beings to make specific choices? If human beings "can decide contrary to" God-given desires, it follows that God cannot always guarantee the outcomes of human choices.[9] If a soft determinist argues that "the God-given desire is coercive," then he or she has fallen into strict determinism, which he or she rejects.[10] It seems that the freedom that soft determinists ascribe to human beings is an illusion, "for there are *no* events where there are no sufficient causes present."[11]

General Providence

General providence (also known as *general sovereignty*) is the view that seeks to preserve God's sovereignty and human (libertarian) freedom. It argues that God has not ordained or decreed all human actions. It also argues that human freedom places limitations on God's sovereignty. Since God has given human beings free will, it follows that God does not control all human actions. God does not have a preordained purpose for every human action; God does not micromanage all things; God has limited what God can do in God's dealings with humanity. John Sanders describes general providence in this way:

> God has sovereignly established a type of world in which God sets up general structures or an overall framework for meaning and allows the creatures significant input into exactly how things will turn out. God desires a relationship of love with his creation and so elects to grant it the freedom to enter into a give-and-take relationship with himself. Since God macromanages the overall project (while remaining free to micromanage some things), God takes risks in governing the world. In contrast to specific sovereignty, this model does not claim that God has a specific purpose for each and every event which happens. Instead, God has general purposes in connection with the achievement of the divine project. Within these general structures God permits things to happen, both good and bad, that he does not

9. Geisler, "Norman Geisler's Response," 47.

10. Ibid.

11. Reichenbach, "Bruce Reichenbach's Response," 51.

specifically intend. Yet God may act to bring about a specific event in order to bring the divine project to fruition.[12]

How would those theologians who adopt the general providence model explain the tragedy of the woman who lost her baby during childbirth? There are varying opinions within the general providence model. While some theologians tend to overemphasize human free will and freedom of choice over God's sovereignty, others aim to hold both God's sovereignty and human free will in paradoxical tension.

The Libertarian Free Will/Soft Divine Sovereignty Position

Libertarian free will and soft divine sovereignty are two of the popular views within the general providence category. For some theologians, those Scriptures that present God as accomplishing whatever God wishes to accomplish (Ps 135:6; Dan 4:35) do not imply that God is "pleased to control everything."[13] God does not always have God's way (Gen 6:6; Jer 18:9–10; 2 Pet 3:9). On the basis of a genuine desire to have relationship with human beings, God has created a world in which God does not decree and foreordain *all* human actions and circumstances. To achieve this, God has given humanity a *libertarian free will* or *contra-causal freedom*—the ability to act in a way that may not be in compliance with God's intent or desired choice. At the moment of decision-making, a person may ignore God's persuasion: "No matter how strong the forces upon the will, the agent could choose another option, even if he doesn't."[14] God has limited God's exercise of power in God's governance of the world. As Bruce Reichenbach argues, "God is sovereign in authority and power. Yet at the same time he willingly limited his power and created us with the freedom to choose between good and evil, between God and ourselves."[15]

For theologians holding the libertarian free will/soft divine sovereignty position, human beings are morally responsible for their actions because God has given them free will. The occurrence of a tragedy does not show the absence of God's providential care. For example, a tragedy could have been worse had God not intervened. Reichenbach writes, "The Christian might well contend that were not God directly active in the creation, the world would be a much worse place to live than it presently is. But since many of

---

12. Sanders, *God Who Risks*, 213–14.

13. Boyd, *Is God to Blame?*, 178.

14. Feinberg, *No One Like Him*, 629.

15. Reichenbach, "God Limits His Power," 118–19.

God's more important purposes have to do with our moral and spiritual development and restitution, God works through natural laws and us to achieve his intentions."[16] Therefore, "God's sovereignty does not necessitate that every human or non-human action is predetermined, a part of his plan, or even desired."[17]

The major criticism of the libertarian free will/soft divine sovereignty positions is its failure to account properly for the biblical texts that present God as having control over human actions. A lack of scriptural texts that *explicitly* state God has limited God's power in order to accommodate human free will and free action is a problem for this view.

The Strict Indeterminism Position

Theologians who adopt the *strict indeterminism* position agree that human beings have libertarian free will but deny that God has decreed any human action or circumstance. They argue that no human actions are causally determined by God. For strict indeterminists, free will equals free action. A strict indeterminist will argue that human beings are able to choose whatever they wish and to do whatever they choose without *external* constraints or forces (God, person, government, etc.).[18]

Some theologians who follow the strict indeterminism position are influenced by the quantum indeterminacy (uncertainty) principle developed by the Copenhagen school in the 1920s. For these theologians, quantum mechanics "has shown that the microworld is essentially indeterministic and so this provides the means whereby God, by acting within the limits of quantum uncertainty, can affect the world without violating the laws of physics."[19] The casual indeterminacy suggested by quantum mechanics, for these theologians, is a fertile theological ground in which God's involvement in the world can be explained without suggesting supernatural intervention.

Some critics of strict indeterminism argue that the uncertainty principle of quantum mechanics may not be theologically helpful. Timothy Sansbury has argued that given "the minuscule nature of quantum-level interactions, in order to produce macroscopic effects either God would have to determine all or most quantum events over an extended period of time or a smaller number of determinations would require amplification

16. Ibid., 119.
17. Ibid.
18. Ibid., 102.
19. Hodgson, "God's Action in the World," 506.

through some deterministic natural process such as highly sensitive chaotic systems."[20] Sansbury goes on to argue that

> The first option on its own is severely limited by the actual range of quantum indeterminacy, so that divine action would be either incredibly slight or possible only over extremely long periods of time. The latter is more promising, although there are significant theoretical concerns about whether the structures necessary for amplification are common enough to be useful. Even if conditions turn out to be optimal for the proposed theories, quantum mechanics cannot resolve the underlying theological issues. There are two central questions in the dialogue on divine action. The first is whether God acts in the universe apart from the original creation—that is, whether God continues to act in creation other than by preserving it. The second is whether divine action occurs within the boundaries of the regular order of causal laws or by intervention into that order with the breakdown of those laws."[21]

Concluding Reflections

Our views of God's sovereignty and human freedom will shape our views of divine providence. If God predetermined all human actions and determined all things in advance, can we speak of God's continual active involvement in creation? If God depends entirely on the laws of nature and unpredictable human free action to act in the world, can we be sure that God is lord of God's creation and will bring it to God's intended fulfillment? In working out our theology of divine providence, we must account for the scriptural teaching on God's sovereignty (God's rule over God's creation) and God's free will—God's ability to create beings with free will and with the capacity to use it (Isa 45:9). We should also account for the scriptural teaching on God's ability not to allow the actions of God's creatures to thwart God's eschatological purpose (Gen 50:20; Rom 8:28–39). Finally, we should account for God's ability to hold human beings accountable for their free actions and choices (Rom 14:12).

20. Sansbury, "False Promise of Quantum Mechanics," 111.

21. Ibid., 111–12.

Creation as God's Providential Act

The Bible teaches that God "created the heavens and the earth" (Gen 1:1). It also teaches that God is worthy "to receive glory and honor and power" because God "created all things," and it is because of God's will that all things "existed and were created" (Rev 4: 11). One of the things theists (those who believe in God's existence) share in common is the belief that the world exists because God brought it into existence. Theists, however, disagree on the manner in which God brought the world into being. A similar disagreement exists within Christianity. Christian theologians have proposed several models of creation. Each of these models aims to explain the relationship between God and God's creation. While some present a radical distinction between God and creation, others propose a more intimately connected relationship between God and creation.

Creatio ex nihilo

The model *of creatio ex nihilo* (a Latin expression that means "creation out of nothing") is popular in Christianity. Theologians who adopt this model have understood it in slightly different ways. For the majority of them, *creatio ex nihilo* does not imply that God created the world "out of nothing from something that is nothing,"[22] such as an independent eternal matter. Rather, God created the world through God's creative word. Therefore, there is an ontological difference between God and creation. God did not organize a chaotic, eternally existing matter—a view that is taught in some ancient Near East cosmologies, such as the Babylonian *Enuma Elish*.

Some theologians who hold *creatio ex nihilo* argue that the writer of Genesis 1 intentionally used two different Hebrew verbs—*bārā'* ("to create") and *'āśāh* ("to make") to distinguish two acts of God in bringing the world into existence. For them, *bārā'* is used for the creation as a whole (Gen 1:1), indicating that God created the world *ex nihilo* and without any precondition.[23] The verb *'āśāh* is used by the author to describe God's "manufacturing" work—indicating God's act of giving the creation specific forms and aptitudes.[24]

There is no consensus on what "creation out of nothing" means exactly. For John Feinberg, *creatio ex nihilo* means that "God's creative activity

---

22. Torrance, *Christian Doctrine of God*, 207.

23. Moltmann, *God in Creation*, 74.

24. Ibid., 73.

involved a miracle."[25] For Stanley Grenz, *creatio ex nihilo* does not mean that God fashioned "the world with no real material at his disposal. Rather, the assertion declares that we need no additional principles beyond the triune God in order to explain the existence of the universe."[26] Vladimir Lossky uses *creatio ex nihilo* to express the idea that creation is a free act of God, which must be distinguished from God. He writes, "To create is not to reflect oneself in a mirror, even that of prime matter, it is not vainly to divide oneself in order to take everything unto oneself. It is a calling forth of *newness*. One might almost say: a risk of newness. When God raises, outside of Himself, a new subject, a free subject, that is the peak of His creative act."[27] *Creatio ex nihilo* implies, as Colin Gunton notes, God "had no need to rely on anything outside himself, so that creation is an act of divine sovereignty and freedom, an act of personal willing. It further implies that the universe, unlike God who is alone eternal and infinite, had a beginning in time and is limited in space."[28]

Exponents of the *creatio ex nihilo* model appeal to both the Bible and philosophy to explain their views. For most of these theologians, although creation out of nothing is not explicitly stated in the Bible, the idea is strongly present in some biblical passages. Some understand Genesis 1:1 in the absolute sense ("In the beginning God created")—even though in the Hebrew text the definite article does not precede the word *beginning*—rather than in the construct or temporal sense ("When God created").[29] If understood in the absolute sense, the expression "In the beginning God created" implies that God's initial creation "marks the beginning of time and earthly history."[30] Some also cite New Testament passages in support of *creatio ex nihilo*, such as John 1:3; Rom 4:17; Col 1:15–16; Heb 11:3.

> "I beseech thee, my son, look upon the heaven and the earth, and all that is therein, and consider that God made them of things that were not; and so was mankind made likewise" (2 Macc 7:28).

Three major criticisms of the *creatio ex nihilo* model are noteworthy. First, a philosophical challenge to the *creatio ex nihilo* model is the Platonist claim about the existence of "infinite realms of being that are metaphysically necessary and uncreated by God," a claim that suggests the possibility

25. Feinberg, *No One Like Him*, 552.

26. Grenz, *Theology for the Community of God*, 99.

27. Lossky, *Orthodox Theology*, 54.

28. Gunton, "Doctrine of Creation," 141–142.

29. Copan and Craig, *Creation Out of Nothing*, 30.

30. Ibid.

of "endless infinities of infinities of beings," reducing God to one being among many.[31] Some holders of the *creatio ex nihilo* model respond to the Platonic challenge by appealing to *conceptualism* (a philosophical view that construes Plato's realm of Forms or Ideals as existing in the mind of God).[32]

Second, *creatio ex nihilo* seems to be a foreign metaphysical concept that is imposed on the biblical teaching on creation. The Bible does not say in precise terms how God brought the world into existence. The Hebrew words *bārā'* ("to fashion," "to create," or "to divide") and *'āśāh* ("to do" or "to make,"), which are used interchangeably in the Genesis creation narratives, do not indicate that God created the world *out of nothing*. Some biblical texts portray God as a craftsman who formed human beings from what was already in existence (Gen 2:7; Ps 139:13–14). These texts seem to present a synergistic model of creation: "Creation is the result of divine initiative, but the process involves a working together of the divine with earthly and human powers."[33]

Third, some critics of *creatio ex nihilo* have pointed out that it drives an unwarranted wedge between an all-powerful God and God's weak creatures. For John Caputo, in the *creatio ex nihilo* model, God's omnipotence does not merely entail God's transcendence but also God's domination. This God, for Caputo, is like a Hellenistic god whose style of relationship with the world is "cause causing"—this God causes all things to be and controls every human action. Caputo proposes a counter model, which he claims is more faithful to the Hebraic creation accounts. He writes, "The name of God is to be thought in terms of the Hebraic model of the call calling rather than the Hellenistic model of cause causing, of covenant rather than of causality, of underlying loyalty to his word rather than of eternal being, of primordial promise rather than a prime mover—or if a mover, then one who moves by a motivating call or a provocation or a promise rather than by the strong force of an efficient cause."[34]

Emanation

Some Christian theologians adopt the concept of generation or emanation in their explanation of God's relationship with the world. This theory may be traced to the metaphysics of Plotinus (c. 205–270 CE), an Egyptian-born philosopher, who proposed a hierarchal (top-down) explanation of

31. Copan and Craig, *Creation Out of Nothing*, 173.
32. Ibid., 189.
33. Tate, *Psalms 51–100*, 440.
34. Caputo, *Weakness of God*, 94.

the world in terms of emanation. For him, the self-caused "First Principle" (the *One*) is the non-emanate and unknowable reality.[35] The *One* (which is transcendent and without property) directly and indirectly generates other ontologically lower-ranking realities. The *Intellect* (eternal "forms" that make intelligent predictions possible) is the first level of reality that emanates from the *One*. The *Soul*, which gives form to the bodily cosmos, emanates or flows from the *Intellect*.

The emanation model construes creation as "something that is in God, part of God, or created out of God."[36] Creation derives from or flows from God. Advocates of the emanation model disagree on whether creation, which is a metaphysical necessity of God, is an *automatic generation* from God or a *free act* of God (an act of God's self-fulfillment).[37] They are unanimous, however, in rejecting *creatio ex nihilo*. If creation necessarily generated from God, it follows that creation could not but flow from God, and therefore it was not subject to God's act of will (i.e., God did not *will* it into existence). In this sense, creation must continue to exist as long as God exists. Creation, then, is the essence of God, the result of an involuntary cause, as in the case of a body's shadow. If creation generated from God, as God's act of will, then creation is temporal and its existence is contingent upon God's act of choice.

Theologians who hold the emanation model believe it addresses what they consider to be a dualistic understanding of the God-world relationship inherent in the *creatio ex nihilo* model. Some emanation theorists hold *pantheism*—the view that "everything is God, and that primordial energy, atoms, stones, mountains, stars, and human beings form part of the deity."[38] If the creation inherently derived from God, creation shares in the essence of God. Some Christian theologians reject the emanation theory because it rids God of the capacity of choice. As Alister McGrath argues, "The Christian tradition has consistently emphasized that the act of creation rests upon a prior decision on the part of God to create, which the [emanation] model cannot adequately express."[39]

---

35. See Plotinus, *Enneads*.

36. Copan and Craig, *Creation Out of Nothing*, 15.

37. Gilkey, "Creation, Being, and Nonbeing," 228.

38. Boff, *Ecology and Liberation*, 50–51.

39. McGrath, *Christian Theology*, 300–301.

Theistic Evolution

For some theologians, proposing a scientific basis for theology is "anti-theological," just as for some scientists proposing a theological or biblical basis for science is "anti-scientific." The usefulness and adequacy of such proposals have been called into question. Since the publication of Charles Darwin's *Origin of Species* (1859) and *The Descent of Man* (1871), however, many Christian theologians have explored the relationship between theology and the natural sciences.

Evolution is an umbrella term used by natural scientists and theologians to describe changes in genetic code and the process of changes and development in biotic life on earth. Evolution involves a natural process, which includes competition and survival, cooperation and symbiosis. Some theories of evolution have remained attractive to Christian theologians who are committed to the creative activity of God and who value the information about the world that natural sciences supplies. But does "evolution" merely *describe* (through the war of nature or survival of the fittest and mutation) how biotic life dies or survives?

"In an evolving universe, if its history is truly to be understood as a continuous creation, God must be presently active not only in the gift of fruitful potentiality expressed in the form of lawful Necessity, but also in the contingent happenings of exploratory Chance. Only thus could we see cosmic process as involving the full participation of both Creator and creatures."

—Polkinghorne, "Scripture and an Evolving Creation"

Or does "evolution" also *explain the origins* of biotic life? Although theistic theologians might respond to these questions differently, they have an interest in developing a mutually dependent view of theology and the natural sciences. Some theologians remain very cautious about the encroachment of the natural sciences into the territory of theology.[40]

Theistic evolutionists distinguish *naturalistic evolution* (which aims to eliminate God from the explanation of the world) from *biological evolution* (which aims to explain how life develops on Earth through the mechanism of natural selection or a "chance association of biomonomers").[41] Some scholars who applauded the intelligent design movement have done so because of its attack on naturalism.[42] They also distinguish *macroevolution* (which proposes changes from one species to another or changes from non-

40. Donald, "Evolution and the Church," 19–23; Migliore, *Faith Seeking Understanding*, 113–16.

41. Walton, "Origin of Life," 205.

42. See Dembski, *Intelligent Design*.

living matter to living cells) from *microevolution* (which proposes changes within species).

Many theistic evolutionists reject both naturalistic evolution and macroevolution because these concepts of evolution exclude the belief in God's existence and creative act in the explanation of the world. They also reject the idea that evolution is an unguided process. On the contrary, theistic evolutionists posit that evolution is the mechanism God uses to create and sustain life in the universe. The contention is that "natural process" and God's creative action are not in opposition. John Polkinghorne makes this point: "The God who is Love did not bring into being a puppet theatre in which the divine Puppet Master would pull every string, but the gift of the divine agape was a world in which creatures are granted a due independence to be themselves and to make themselves."[43] The theistic evolution model of creation presents both God and the creation as active "actors" or participants in the ongoing creation and subsistence of life in the universe.

Theistic evolutionists disagree on the exact role of God in the evolutionary process. For some, "God's direct intervention occurred at several distinct points where naturalistic processes alone would not suffice."[44] For others, God's intervention is restricted to the moments of change "from non-living things to the first living organisms or the change from ape-like creatures to man."[45]

The dilemma the advocates of theistic evolution face is how to address the claim the natural evolutionists make about the *non-purposefulness* of nature (apart from surviving and reproducing, of course) and the claim Christianity makes about God's purposeful intentions in creating and directing creation.[46] Ted Peters has argued that "to think of the natural world as the creation of a loving God eschews nihilism and pessimism. The very idea of creation implies purpose; and we mean purpose in its grand and overarching scope. The nonteleological view of nature in science cannot be allowed to have the last word."[47] Some critics of theistic evolution argue that evolution essentially eliminates the traditional Christian belief about the historicity of Adam and Eve and the fall (the disobedience of Adam and Eve and God's judgment of humanity as a result of their mistrust). The theistic evolutionists, who admit God's rare intervention in the mechanism of the natural process of evolution, might argue that God intervened to bring

43. Polkinghorne, "Scripture and an Evolving Creation," 169.

44. Feinberg, *No One Like Him*, 546.

45. Ibid., 546.

46. See Blackmore and Page, *Evolution*.

47. Peters, "Constructing a Theology of Evolution," 926.

about the existence of Adam and Eve, making Adam or Eve (or both) the product of God's "special act."

God and God's Relation to Time

Reflections on creation and providence usually lead to reflections on God's relation to time. This has a precedent in the Old Testament. Psalm 90:2 is an example: "Before the mountains were brought forth, or ever you had formed the earth and the world, from everlasting to everlasting you are God" (ESV). The psalmist extols Yahweh as the God who antedates both human generations and the world. The claim of the psalmist invites the following questions: Does time come into existence with God's act of creation? Does God exist *in* time (God is eternal but *temporal*), or exist *outside* of time (God as *atemporal*)? Does God experience temporal succession (past, present, and future), or does God experience an eternal present? While some theologians define eternity as *timelessness*—that which exists "outside" of time—others define eternity as *everlasting*—that which exists "in" time but as "never-ending existence within time."[48] I will now highlight two major ways in which theologians have responded to the issue of God's eternity in relation to creation.

Divine Temporality: God as Everlasting but Temporal

The *divine temporality* view posits that as a bodiless being, God is not spatially bound (not confined to space). As a being who acts, God has a history because God acts in time. Exponents of divine temporality disagree on whether God is "in" time (in the sense that time is part of God's being) or "outside" of time (in the sense that time is finite and not part of God's being).[49]

Nicholas Wolterstorff has presented three arguments in support of the

> "In spite of appeals by defenders of the doctrine [of divine timelessness] to texts such as Exod 3:14; John 8:58; and 2 Pet 3:8, there simply is no trace in the Scripture of the elaborate metaphysical and conceptual apparatus that is required to make sense of divine timelessness. On the positive side, the biblical writers undeniably do present God as living, acting, and reacting in time. . . ."
>
> —Hasker, "A Philosophical Perspective"

48. Feinberg, *No One Like Him*, 375.

49. See Padgett, "Response to Nicholas Wolterstorff," 219–21.

divine temporality view. First, Wolterstorff highlights two theories of the nature of time: the *tenseless* theory and the *tense* theory. The tenseless theory argues that "time" is not objectively real; it has no ontological or real existence. The tense theory of time argues that "time" has an ontological status. Wolterstorff accepts the tense theory view of time but rejects the notion that the tense theory treats the "past," "present," and "future" as properties of an event and that these properties are equal in status. Conversely, he argues, in the tense theory, "The distinction between present, past and future marks a difference in the ontological status of event; and of these, the status of the present is basic."[50]

Second, Wolterstorff argues that the Bible presents God as a being-in-history: "The God of Scripture is One of whom a narrative can be told; we know that not because Scripture tells us that but because it offers such a narrative."[51] Wolterstorff also argues that the biblical representation of God as one who "has a history" implies that "God is in time."[52] We know God only as the being who acts and relates to God's creation in temporality (that is, God acts and responds successively), and thus God is temporal. According to Wolterstorff, Psalm 90:1–4 does not support the view of "divine timelessness" or eternality. Rather, what it says is that God exists *before* creation, implying that to "God's experience there is a felt temporality."[53] For Wolterstorff, although God is "everlasting [and] necessarily so," God is not "timeless."[54]

Third, Wolterstorff argues that a being who is not spatially located can act in time. He distinguishes "space" and "time." For him, whereas tensed facts are ineliminable, spatially bound facts are eliminable. Something that is *outside* of time is timeless or eternal. That "something" does not have a history. For example, "numbers" are timeless because they have no history: "They neither come into existence nor go out; nor do they change."[55] For him, because "numbers" do not act, they do not have a history. Like numbers, God's ontology does not change, but unlike numbers, God acts. Wolterstorff makes a distinction between God's *ontology* and God's *actions*. According to him, "There is nothing to be narrated about God coming into or going out of existence."[56] In other words, God does not have a *spatial loca-*

50. Wolterstorff, "Unqualified Divine Temporality," 196.

51. Ibid., 188.

52. Ibid.

53. Ibid., 190.

54. Ibid., 193.

55. Ibid., 202.

56. Ibid., 203.

tion. Wolterstorff argues that there is a story to be told about God's actions, about God's responses to what transpires in God's creation.[57] Wolterstorff uses Moses' encounter with Yahweh at Horeb (Exod 3:1–22) to buttress his claims.

Divine Eternality: God as Timelessly Eternal

The divine eternality position asserts that "God exists as timelessly eternal" and as such "exists 'outside' time."[58] Jürgen Moltmann has argued that "before the creation of the world, God resolved to be its Creator in order to be glorified in his kingdom."[59] This implies that the relationship between eternity and time should be understood in relation to God's self-determination and God's decision to create the world.[60] For Moltmann, "time" has a beginning: "God created the world with *its* time—in *his* time."[61]

> "O Lord, since you are outside of time in eternity, are you unaware of the things that I tell you? Or do you see in time the things that occur in it? If you see them, why do I lay this lengthy record before you? Certainly it is not through me that you first hear of things."
>
> —Augustine, *Confessions*

Paul Helm is one the most articulate exponents of the divine eternality position. On the grounds of the assumption of "divine self-sufficiency" (the claim that God "possesses the whole of his life together"), Helm contends that God does not have a history—past, present, and future.[62] To Helm, the "temporalist view may be intelligible, but it does not do justice to the nature of God's being."[63]

In response to the question about the biblical warrants for God's self-sufficiency, Helm concedes the ambiguous biblical teaching on God's relation to time (see Isa 57:15; Heb 1:10–12; Ps 90:2; 1 Cor 2:7; 2 Tim 1:19). For him, "The language of Scripture about God and time is not sufficiently precise so as to provide a definitive resolution of the issues one way or the other."[64] However, he contends that the biblical teachings on God's

---

57. Ibid.
58. Helm, "Divine Timeless Eternity," 28.
59. Moltmann, *God in Creation*, 114.
60. Ibid.
61. Ibid., 115.
62. Helm, "Divine Timeless Eternity," 30.
63. Ibid., 31.
64. Ibid.

relationship to time are "compatible with eternalism but do not require it."[65] This ambiguity of scriptural teaching on God and time, Helm argues, should not bother contemporary inquirers because "the issues of temporalism and eternalism . . . were not before the minds of the [biblical] writers as they wrote—or at least there is no real evidence that they were."[66] Helm also argues that Christians need not be agnostics on the issue of God's relationship to time simply because it did not preoccupy the minds of the writers of the Bible. On the contrary, Christians should be ready to tackle the important theological questions that their contexts raise, for "once important questions have been raised it is extremely difficult, if not impossible, to live as if they had never been raised."[67]

If God is eternally timeless, how could God's timeless life be simultaneous with the things that happen in time, such as the attack on the World Trade Center on September 11, 2001? Some critics of the divine eternality position deem it internally incoherent.[68] Helm believes that the best response to this criticism, which he admits may be intellectually less satisfying, is embedded in the word *timelessness*. He highlights the "less" in "timelessness," and argues that it suggests or implies a negative thinking about God. In other words, we can only successfully say what timeless eternity *is not*, but not what *it is*.[69]

Some critics of the divine eternality view also argue that a timelessly eternal God cannot genuinely have a *personal* relationship with human beings because such a God is by definition impassible.[70] To be impassible (*apatheia* in Greek) is to be incapable of having emotions. An impassible God is incapable of having genuine emotions. An impassible God cannot *change* because change takes time and occurs in time. If God is "outside of time," as construed in the divine eternality view, then God cannot genuinely grieve or rejoice in response to human actions.

The Bible, however, consistently presents God as a being who genuinely shows feelings in response to human actions (Gen 6:5–6; 18:16–33; 2 Pet 3:9). Helm responds to this criticism by distinguishing human affective actions (or emotions) from deep-seated attitudes, dispositions, or states of mind. He argues that human deep-seated attitudes and dispositions are analogous to God's form of emotion. Helm writes, "Joy, care, pleasure and

65. Ibid., 32.

66. Ibid., 31–32.

67. Ibid., 32.

68. Swinburne, *Coherence of Theism*, 220–21.

69. Helm, "Divine Timeless Eternity," 37–38.

70. For an extensive discussion on God's impassibility, see Gavrilyuk, *The Suffering of the Impassible God*.

love in a timelessly eternal God are much more like deep-seated attitudes or dispositions in us."[71] Adherents to the divine eternality view need to demonstrate how God can genuinely experience human responses to God's actions. For example, does God the Father accept and experience human praise and prayer?

Reflections on the Age of Creation

The earliest theological reflections on the age of the world arose in the context of the theology-philosophy dialogue. Some of the earliest theologians responded to atomistic theories of the world in the writings of ancient philosophers such as Epicurus and Hippolytus.[72] However, it is in the context of the theology-natural science dialogue since the appearance of Charles Darwin's theory of evolution that more robust and extensive theological reflections on the age of the world have occurred.

> "If then the beginning of time is called 'one day' rather than 'the first day,' it is because Scripture wishes to establish its relationship with eternity. . . . Thus whether you call it day, or whether you call it eternity, you express the same idea."
> —Basil the Great, "Hexaemeron"

Four major theological views on the age of the world have emerged. The four views may be subsumed under two broad categories: the *literalist theory* and the *nonliteralist theory*. The literalist theory includes two views that require a literal reading of the Genesis creation stories—the *twenty-four-day view* and *gap view*. The nonliteral theory includes two views that argue the Genesis creation stories need not be understood literally—the *literary artistic view* and the *day-age view*.

The Literalist Theory

The twenty-four-day view argues that "day" (*yôm* in Hebrew) must be understood in its literal usage. Some theologians and biblical exegetes who hold this view, such as James Ussher and John Lightfoot, have argued that the world was created in 4004 BCE. Lightfoot pinpointed the time and date of creation as 9 A.M. on October 23, 4004 BCE.[73] Basing their calculations on the genealogical accounts in Genesis, these theologians trace the human

71. Helm, "Divine Timeless Eternity," 39.

72. Allison, *Historical Theology*, 255.

73. See Blackmore and Page, *Evolution*, 27.

generations from Adam to Jesus Christ. They contend that the context of the Genesis 1 creation narrative requires that *yôm* be taken literally. They point out that the expression "there was evening and there was morning" (Gen 1:5, 8, 13, 19, 23, and 31) indicate that the solar day was intended by the author of Genesis. For them, theology, and not natural science, should determine how Genesis should be read. Advocates of the twenty-four-day view contend that the earth is "young" (several thousand years old) and reject geological estimates, which depict the earth as "old" (several billion years old).

B. B. Warfield challenged the attempt to estimate the age of the earth on the basis of the genealogical accounts in the Bible, particularly the accounts in Genesis 5 and 11. According to him, "The genealogies of Scripture were not constructed for a chronological purpose, and any appearance they present of affording materials for chronological inferences is accidental and illusory. While they must be esteemed absolutely trustworthy for the purpose for which they were given, these genealogies are not to be pressed into use for other purposes for which they were not intended and for which they are not adapted."[74]

The strongest argument for the twenty-four-day view is the appeal to the Genesis author's choice of the expression "there was evening and there was morning" at the end of each "day." The author of Exodus seemed to have understood the usage of *yôm* in Genesis literally (Exod 20:8–11). However, it can be argued that "there was evening and there was morning" does not necessarily refer to the solar day since the expression was used for days 1 through 3 (Gen 1:5–13), and yet it was only on day 4 that the sun, moon, and stars were made (Gen 1:14–19).

The gap or reconstructionist view (*a*) maintains a literal understanding of the Genesis creation stories and (*b*) adopts some of the scientific findings on the age of the earth. The gap view proposes that Genesis 1 speaks about two distinct conditions of creation. Genesis 1:1 refers to the perfect (or non-fallen) creation, and Genesis 1:2 refers to a re-creation or reconstruction of the fallen condition of creation. Thus "the six days are not . . . days of creation, but days of reconstruction."[75] The Bible, however, does not tell us how the original or non-fallen creation *became* a fallen creation. Exponents of the gap view argue that it is reasonable to assume there was a lengthy "gap" that separated the perfect condition of God's creation (Gen 1:1) and the re-created condition of the fallen creation (Gen 1:2). Some assume that

74. Warfield, "Manner and Time of Man's Origin," 217–18.
75. Blocher, *In the Beginning*, 41.

the original and perfect creation of Genesis 1:1 was inhabited and implied the existence of a pre-Adamic humanity.[76]

For the majority of the advocates of the gap view, the Hebrew verb *hayetah* in Genesis 1:2 should be translated as "became" or "had become" rather than "was." If it is translated as "became," Genesis 1:2 signals a shift in condition—the creation became what it was not originally. Also, they argue that *tōhû wābōhû* ("formless and void") should be understood as God's judgment upon the original creation, which became corrupt by the rebellion of Satan and pre-Adamic humanity. God used the flood (Gen 6–8) as a judgment upon the angelic beings (such as Satan) and pre-Adamic humanity. Therefore, the fossils scientists use in dating the earth came from the flood, which destroyed human beings, animals, and plants.

Nonliteralist Theory

The *literary artistic* (or framework) view argues that Genesis creation stories ought not to be taken literally because the author or redactor of Genesis does not present a scientific explanation of the origin of the world. On the contrary, in the creation stories, the author of Genesis freely employs a literary framework or device to teach a *theological truth* about the world, namely, that God brought it into existence. As Henri Blocher argues, "The theological treasures of the framework of the Genesis days come most clearly to light by means of the 'literary' interpretation. The writer has given us a masterly elaboration of fitting, restrained anthropomorphic vision, in order to convey a whole complex of deeply mediated ideas."[77]

The goal of the author of Genesis, in the literary artistic view, is neither to present a chronological account nor a historical account of how God created the world. In the literary artistic theory, Adam and Eve need not be understood as historical figures or the first creatures of God. Advocates of the literary artistic view also argue that *yôm* does not mean the literal twenty-four-hour solar day.[78] Sometimes *yôm* is used metaphorically to indicate an unspecified long period of time (Gen 2:4; Job 20:28; Ps 20:1; 2 Pet 3:8). These claims make the literary artistic theory more attractive to theologians who hold the theistic evolution model.[79] The critics of the literary artistic view have focused on the criteria for determining "historical" and "nonhistorical" events in the Genesis creation stories.

76. Ryrie, *Basic Theology*, 209.

77. Blocher, *In the Beginning*, 59.

78. Ibid., 50.

79. Polkinghorne, "Scripture and an Evolving Creation," 166–69.

The day-age view argues that *yôm* should be understood as a lengthy period or "ages" of time. Advocates of the day-age view argue that theology and science need not be in opposing camps on the matter of the age of the earth. They highlight the absence of the expression "there was evening and there was morning" on the seventh day (Gen 2:1–3). For many, the omission of this expression indicates that God's work of creation has not ended. If "the seventh day extends across thousands of years of history," it can be argued that the other six days "can cover millions of centuries of cosmogony."[80] By construing *yôm* as a lengthy period of ages, the advocates of the day-age view can easily accommodate the scientific estimations of the age of the earth. This "accommodation" does not entail relieving the Bible of the "right" to speak about the earth, but rather rediscovering the theological purpose and limitation of the Bible.

Therefore, in the day-age view, *yôm* can be understood (*a*) *holistically*— as a lengthy age covering the entire time in which the creation of the world occurred, or (*b*) *periodically*—as a lengthy age covering the time in which each category of the inhabitants of the world was created. If understood holistically, the "day" in which the sun, moon, and stars were made (day 4) need not be understood as lasting millions of years *prior* to the making of plants and animals (Gen 1:3–13). This could mean that the sun, moon, and stars were part of what God created on day 1, and Gen 1:16 could be understood in the perfect tense, "indicating something that God had done before: 'And God had made the two great lights, the greater light to rule the day, and the lesser light to rule the night; he had made the stars also.'"[81] If "day" is understood periodically and sequentially, the creation story in Genesis 1 and 2 stands in direct opposition to the scientific understanding of the development of life on the earth.[82]

God's Foreknowledge and Human Freedom

The words *foreknowledge* (*prognōsis* in Greek) and *foreknow* (*proginōskō* in Greek) are key to understanding the theological discussions of God's providence. The verb *proginōskō* is used five times in the New Testament (Acts 26:5; Rom 8:29; 11:2; 1 Pet 1:20; 2 Pet 3:17). In two instances, it is used in reference to human beings (Acts 26:5; 2 Pet 3:17). The noun *prognōsis* is used two times in the New Testament (Acts 2:23; 1 Pet 1:2) and in both instances is used in reference to God. *Prognōsis* connotes the idea of an

---

80. Blocher, *In the Beginning*, 44.

81. Grudem, *Systematic Theology*, 300.

82. Ibid., 299.

intimate knowledge of something or a person. Some theologians argue that *prognōsis* can convey a similar idea as the Hebrew word *yāda* and may carry something of the idea of God's act of choosing or electing.[83]

The eight prominent views on God's knowledge in relation to human freedom are *determinate foreknowledge, Molinism* (middle knowledge), *compatibilism, simple foreknowledge, presentism, process theology, classical theism,* and *open theism.* Some theologians combine key components of two or more of these views in developing their theology of God's knowledge and providence. For example, Bruce Ware combines some elements from compatibilism and middle knowledge to develop the view he calls "compatibilist middle knowledge."[84]

Deterministic Foreknowledge

The deterministic view of divine foreknowledge argues that God's decrees to create, plan, control, and order the world are logically prior to human actions and choices. In this view, God foreknows the future exhaustively (including humans' future choices). But how is it possible that God knows exhaustively future contingencies? The proponents of deterministic foreknowledge respond to this question by invoking the doctrine of foreordination. For them, God's exhaustive knowledge of the world is based on God's foreordination and decrees. God did not consider human free choice before creating the world. God foreknows because God has foreordained.[85]

In the deterministic foreknowledge view, God's "will" is efficacious because whatever God wills to happen does in fact happen. For example, in Acts 4:27–28, Jesus' death is presented as the result of God's will and plan: "Indeed Herod and Pontius Pilate met together with the Gentiles and the people of Israel in this city to conspire against your holy servant Jesus, whom you appointed. They did what your power and will had decided beforehand should happen" (NIV).

Some theologians who adopt the deterministic foreknowledge view argue that there are "two wills" in God: what God *would like to see happen* and what God does *will to happen.*[86] The proposal of God's "two wills" is an attempt to explain passages in the Bible that teach human freedom of choice and moral responsibility. Some proponents of the deterministic view

---

83. Erickson, *What Does God Know?*, 48.

84. Ware, *God's Greater Glory*, 110.

85. Helseth, "God Causes All Things," 25–52.

86. Piper, "Are There Two Willis in God?," 110.

of divine foreknowledge argue that the scriptural teaching on human free will and God's sovereignty is a paradox.

Criticism: If everything that happens in the world is determined by God in accordance with God's eternal decrees, then human beings have no freedom of choice. This clearly contradicts the biblical teaching on human free will, moral responsibility, and God's desire for personal relationships with human beings.

Molinism (Middle Knowledge)

Molinism was developed by the Jesuit theologian Luis de Molina (1535–1600) in part IV of his *Concordia*, which was first published in 1588.[87] Molina argued that prior to creating the world God had access to three logical moments of knowledge. Molina named the three logical moments (*a*) "natural or necessary knowledge"—the knowledge of what *could* happen in all possible worlds; (*b*) "free knowledge"—the knowledge of what *will* happen, that is, the knowledge of all future actualities, which are contingent upon the *actual* world (among many possible worlds) that God creates or actualizes; and (*c*) "middle knowledge"—the knowledge of counterfactuals or the knowledge of what *would* happen in all possible worlds in all circumstances.[88]

The word *middle* is used here because God's *middle knowledge* logically comes between God's *natural knowledge* and God's *free knowledge*. For the Molinists, the knowledge of what God's creatures *would* do is different from what they *could* do and prior to what they *will* do.[89] On the grounds that God is "eternal," and therefore the past, present, and future are always *present* to God in eternity, Molina argues that God knows all future contingencies with certainty.[90] Since God is omniscient, God knows all *counterfactuals*—hypothetical events that could happen under certain circumstances (see John 18:36).

The middle knowledge view upholds both God's sovereignty and human libertarian free will. For the Molinists, human freedom is incompatible with a deterministic view of God's foreknowledge. They insist that God's ability to know with certainty all future contingencies is compatible with human libertarian freedom. They argue that God is able to know all future

87. Molina, *On Divine Knowledge*.
88. Craig, *Only Wise God*, 129–131.
89. Tiessen, "Why Calvinists Should Believe in Divine Middle Knowledge," 347.
90. Molina, *On Divine Knowledge*, 101.

contingencies because of God's "middle knowledge" or God's knowledge of *true counterfactuals*.[91] As an omniscient being, "God must know every truth there is and so can never exist in a state of ignorance."[92]

Since God's "middle knowledge" is logically *prior* to God's "free knowledge" and creative decrees, God directs God's creation without violating human libertarian free will: "God can plan a world down to the last detail and yet do so without annihilating creaturely freedom, since God has already factored into the equation what people would do freely under various circumstances."[93] Thus, in Molinist theology, before decreeing this actual (present) world, God knew and freely considered all the choices human beings will freely make in all circumstances and in all possible worlds. Molinism's view of God's foreknowledge is *conceptual*—an "innate" knowledge—and not *perceptual*—a knowledge acquired by "foresight," by "looking ahead," or by an act of "foreseeing."[94]

Criticism: If human beings have libertarian freedom, it follows that God cannot have knowledge of what human beings will *actually* do until they do it even in all possible worlds. In the end, God cannot have a prior exhaustive knowledge of human potential actions as actual actions.

Compatibilism

This view seeks to uphold (*a*) God's meticulous sovereignty, which includes God's foreknowledge and foreordination, and (*b*) human (compatibilistic) freedom. As a sovereign creator, God decrees all things, including what human beings will do and the factors that will *cause* them to act.[95] For the proponents of compatibilism, human freedom ought to be defined in a manner that fits into God's meticulous or specific providence.[96] The primary way compatibilists define human freedom in order to make room for God's meticulous sovereignty is by locating human free choice within human inclinations or desires.[97] In this view, human beings do not have libertarian freedom or free will. God created human beings with the capacity for free

91. Craig, "God Directs All Things," 79.
92. Ibid., 80.
93. Ibid., 82.
94. Ibid., 85.
95. Feinberg, *No One Like Him*, 741.
96. Ware, *God's Greater Glory*, 78.
97. Ibid.

will but not with the power of contrary choice.[98] Human freedom consists in what human beings are most inclined to do.[99] Human beings, however, do not have control over the circumstances (hereditary, environment, divine decree, etc.) that may or may not constrain their inclinations.[100]

For some compatibilists, God knows exhaustively what human beings will freely do at the moment of decision without constraining them to make such decisions. Also, God knows exhaustively what human beings will do if God creates constraints that will inform and influence their decisions.[101] God determines what will eventually occur either by *permitting* God's creatures to what they will naturally do (without divine constraints) or by *persuasively* constraining them (through the activity of the Holy Spirit) from doing what they desire.[102]

Human freedom is ultimately a freedom within the boundary of God's meticulous sovereignty and control. God's decree—what will happen—is based entirely on God's desires. This means that whatever God desires and decrees to occur must occur.[103] This does not mean that God eliminates human freedom or free will. Theologians whot hold a compatiblisitc model of divine foreknowledge and human free will reject the notion that God's decree rules out human freedom. They argue that God decrees human actions in a way that is in accordance with human wishes and desires. God has decreed what we will do and also the circumstances that will constrain our choices on the basis of our wishes.[104] According to Feinberg, "Human actions, though causally determined, are still free if they are done in accordance with the agent's wishes."[105] God's decree is logically *subsequent* to human wishes. God decrees that human wishes come to fulfillment by decreeing the circumstances that sometimes constrain human actions. Human free choices do not alter God's plans because they fall within God's sovereignty. God has sovereignly incorporated human free choice and action into God's decision to create the present world out of other possible worlds that God could have created. By decreeing the constraints that shape our freedom, God can influence us in direct but noncoercive ways.[106]

98. Ibid., 79.

99. Ibid.

100. Ibid., 80.

101. Tiessen, "Why Calvinists Should Believe in Divine Middle Knowledge," 352.

102. Ibid.

103. Feinberg, *No One Like Him*, 741.

104. Ibid.

105. Ibid.

106. Ware, *God's Greater Glory*, 81–82.

Criticism: If God has decreed the constraints (external or internal conditions) that influence human inclinations, and if such constraints actually inhibit human beings from making contrary choices in the moment of decision, then they do not have genuine freedom.

Simple Foreknowledge

Simple foreknowledge teaches that God simply knows exhaustively all that will happen in the world because God created it. This knowledge of God is not based on God's foreordination or mere knowledge of hypothetical future events but rather on direct apprehension. God does not guess; God simply knows. God has prevision or direct vision of all events that will actually occur in the world.[107] In the simple foreknowledge view, God does not consider possible human choices before choosing to create a certain world. Also, God does not create the present world on the basis of God's exhaustive knowledge of all human actions under all circumstances in all possible worlds. In reference to God's knowledge, therefore, simple foreknowledge implies that God knows only what *will* happen in the created world, and not what *could* happen in an uncreated (possible) world. God only had to make a decision to create a world, and by actualizing the decision (that is, by creating the world), God knew every event that would actually occur. Like Molinism, the simple foreknowledge view argues that human beings have libertarian free will.[108] Unlike Molinism, the simple foreknowledge view rejects the notion that God has "middle knowledge" or knowledge of counterfactuals.[109]

Criticism: The simple foreknowledge view presupposes that God did not know the type of world God could create until God actually created it. If this is the case, God seems to be a *gambler*, for God did not know what the world might turn out to be *before* God created it. What then are the practical values of God's foreknowledge? If God possesses simple foreknowledge, how could God act on it to provide sovereign care for the world? Since God already knows or sees "that he will perform a given action, it is impossible for him to do anything other than what he foresees."[110] But if God, upon reflection, can genuinely make a choice contrary to what God foreknows, then God does not have simple foreknowledge.[111]

107. Hunt, "Divine Providence and Simple Foreknowledge."
108. Hasker, "Philosophical Perspective," 147.
109. Ibid.
110. Feinberg, *No One Like Him*, 744–45.
111. Ibid., 745. See also Hasker, "Why Simple Foreknowledge Is Still Useless."

Presentism

In presentism, God's knowledge of the future is partial and nonexhaustive. While presentism accepts that God knows past events and present events exhaustively, it argues that God does not have unlimited knowledge of the future. Given that God is sovereign—the one who has general control of the world—God foreordains and decrees some future events. God alone has an exhaustive knowledge of such events. Since God has created human beings with the capacity for libertarian freedom, God can only predict or guess what future contingents, such as the future choices and actions of free agents, will be.[112]

God's predictions and informed guesses about the future are based on (*a*) what God intends to do regardless of human responses, (*b*) conditional promises that are dependent on human free responses, or (*c*) what God hopes, on the grounds of God's vast knowledge of the past and present, may happen.[113] Therefore, God can experience genuine surprise and disappointment whenever human beings freely choose what God does not intend for them.

Criticism: If God only predicts and guesses, how can God truly accomplish God's purposes for God's creation? It seems that in the end it is human libertarian freedom, and not God's sovereignty, that determines the future of the world. Human beings might have just subtly replaced God in ruling the affairs of the world.

Process Theology

Process theology developed around the metaphysics of the English mathematician Alfred North Whitehead (1861–1947). Whitehead construes "reality" as what is *becoming* rather than as *static*. For Whitehead, there are four notions that constitute and govern the philosophy of organism. These are "actual entity," "prehension," "nexus," and "ontological principles."[114] Since his concept of "actual entity" is what is most relevant to this chapter, I will discuss it alone.

To Whitehead, actual entities "are the final real things of which the world is made up. There is no going behind actual entities to find anything more real."[115] The world is composed of "a vast number of microcosmic

---

112. Sanders, *God Who Risks*, 129.

113. Ibid., 136.

114. Whitehead, *Process and Reality*, 18.

115. Ibid.

entities."[116] Although actual entities differ in function and importance, they are by definition of the same level—each one is an organism that "grows, matures, and perishes."[117]

For Whitehead, God is an actual entity and "the most trivial puff of existence in far-off empty space."[118] Whitehead construes God as a *dipolar* actual entity: God has both a *primordial nature* and a *consequent nature*. He writes, "Thus, analogously to all actual entities, the nature of God is dipolar. He has a primordial nature and a consequent nature. The consequent nature of God is conscious; and it is the realization of the actual world in the unity of his nature, and through the transformation of his wisdom. The primordial nature is conceptual, the consequent nature is the weaving of God's physical feelings upon his primordial concepts."[119] For Whitehead, the primordial nature of God is "free, complete, eternal, actually deficient, and unconscious."[120] Conversely, although God's consequent nature derives from God's primordial nature, it is "determined, incomplete, consequent, 'everlasting,' fully actual, and conscious."[121]

So what is God's relation to the world, according to Whitehead? God is not its "creator" but rather its "savior." Whitehead writes, "God's role is not the combat of productive force with productive force, of destructive force with destructive force; it lies in the patient operation of the over-empowering rationality of his conceptual harmonization. He does not create the world, he saves it: or more accurately, he is the poet of the world, with tender patience leading it by his vision of truth, beauty, and goodness."[122] Some process theologians reject the notion that God is not the creator of the world. Charles Hartshorne, for example, argues that as an eminently social being God created and predated the world. He writes, "There is no presupposed 'stuff' alien to God's creative work; but rather everything that influences God has already been influenced by him, whereas we are influenced by events of the past with which we had nothing to do."[123]

---

116. Sherburne, *Key to Whitehead's Process and Reality*, 6.

117. Ibid.

118. Whitehead, *Process and Reality*, 18.

119. Ibid., 345.

120. Ibid.

121. Ibid.

122. Ibid., 346.

123. Hartshorne, *Divine Relativity*, 30.

Major Claims and Arguments of Process Theology

God is an "actual" entity but need not be a "physical" entity. One of the major criticisms of process theology is its definition of God as "energy-event." John Cobb describes two ways in which human beings can imagine an energy-event. According to Cobb, an energy-event can be imagined as an "electronic event" or as a "moment of human experience."[124] In the "electronic event" sense, we "try to conceive visually or otherwise how such a burst of energy might appear to an observer, even though we know it cannot be observed."[125] When understood in the "moment of human experience" sense, we think of an energy-event "from the inside as it feels to itself, for we are thinking of those events which constitute our own existence."[126] Cobb contends that God is an "energy-event" in the sense of the "moment of human experience," that is, in the sense of thinking, willing, feeling, and loving.[127]

As an energy-event, God could be "nowhere" or "everywhere" but cannot be "bound to any limited standpoint within the whole of space-time."[128] For Cobb, a panentheistic view of God is the most useful way of imagining the answer to the question, "Where can God, an energy-event, be?" He writes, "God's standpoint is all-inclusive, and so, in a sense, we are parts of God. But we are not parts of God in the sense that God is simply the sum total of the parts or that the parts are lacking in independence and self-determination. God and creatures interact as separate entities, while God includes the standpoints of all of them in his omnispatial standpoint. In this sense, God is everywhere, but he is not everything."[129]

God is complete and perfect in some respects, and incomplete and imperfect in some respects. For process theologians, if God is complete and perfect in all respects, it means that there is nothing the world, or human beings in particular, can do that can "bring any additional values to God."[130] This implies that God cannot grow in knowledge or change in any way. Process theologians frown at this conception of God because such a God "could not love in a real sense, for to love is to find joy in the joy of others and sorrow in their sorrows, and thus to gain through their gains and lose . . . through

---

124. Cobb, *God and the World*, 70–71.

125. Ibid., 72.

126. Ibid.

127. Ibid., 73.

128. Ibid., 78.

129. Ibid., 79–80.

130. Hartshorne, *Reality as Social Process*, 155.

their losses, and the wholly perfect could neither gain nor lose."[131] On the opposite spectrum, the God who is incomplete and imperfect in all respects by definition cannot be God, for no one can "place ultimate reliance upon a deity in every way subject to imperfection and alternation."[132] In process theology, God spontaneously responds to ever-changing human actions and circumstances. God has not willed or determined every human action or choice.

God's knowledge is additive. Process theologians argue that God's knowledge is temporal and additive. As the being that is becoming, God grows in knowledge about God's self and the world. Although some process theologians use the word *omniscience* (all-knowing) to describe God's knowledge, they define it as "God's complete awareness of all things, the actual as actual, and the possible as possible. Perfect knowledge is temporal as well as spatial in nature."[133] God's knowledge increases and God learns from human actions and choices, which are in constant flux. To say that God's knowledge is additive implies that God's omniscience is an "infinite class of relationships, not all of which are actual."[134] This means that God can only know things according to their state of affairs: God knows things that are *actual as actual* and things that are *potential as potential.*[135]

God's power is to be understood in terms of "persuasion." The word *persuasion* in this context does not refer to a "trick of rhetoric" but rather to the *power of thought over thought* or "the agency whereby ideas are transmitted by reasonable presentation to reasonable reception."[136] God's power of persuasion ensures and protects the human freedom of choice and action. In the context of divine providence, process theology rejects the idea of an all-controlling God and the idea of a world that is determined by divine decrees. As Shaw argues, "What sort of picture emerges if we apply the notion of God's power as the power of 'persuasion' here? Clearly, it would mean abandoning for good the notion of a divine super-plan governing every detail of life and existence. 'Persuasion' leaves too much room for creaturely freedom and spontaneity for that."[137]

131. Ibid., 156.
132. Ibid., 155.
133. Epperly, "Process Theology and Lived Omnipresence," 22.
134. Hartshorne, *Divine Relativity*, 121.
135. Ibid.
136. Shaw, "Providence and Persuasion," 17.
137. Ibid., 21.

Critique of Process Theology

Some theologians are critical of process theology's conception of God as a dipolar entity, an entity with two natures, namely, a *primordial* (atemporal) nature and a *consequent* (temporal and relative) nature. John Feinberg, for example, argues that the idea of a primordial nature reduces God to mere abstract generalities like Plato's doctrine of forms.[138] Feinberg also argues that the consequent nature of God, as construed in process theology, does not successfully avoid pantheism, the belief that God is everything. To Feinberg, if "God is really there, the only thing verifiably present in the physical world, then the view lapses into pantheism, where God and world are identical."[139]

Other critics of process theology have pointed out that its view of omniscience deprives God of the ability to predetermine or foreknow the future. Gregory Boyd makes this claim. For Boyd, biblical passages such as Isa 46:9–10 and Isa 48:3–5 "demonstrate that the future is settled to whatever extent the sovereign Creator decides to settle it. God is not at the mercy of chance or free will."[140] Process theology also poses threats to the "not-yet" aspect of Christianity's eschatology. A God who is *becoming*, and who can only simultaneously respond to ever-changing human actions and circumstances, cannot have a definite purpose or goal to which God is bringing God's creation. Since God does not coerce but persuades, God cannot guarantee any definite outcome of God's creation. Feinberg argues that process theology, therefore, gives us a God who is impotent.[141]

Classical Theism

Classical theism (also known as the "traditional view") construes God as a being who is ontologically distinct from the world. God is an immutable, impassible, transcendent, simple (without division), atemporal, and all-powerful being who controls everything in the world. God is complete and perfect in all respects. While God is immanent (God interacts with the world), God is also transcendent (God is above or not bound by God's interaction with the world). The classical theistic God is the God who governs all human actions. As Bruce Ware argues, "What comfort, joy, and strength believers receive from the truths of divine providence. Nowhere else are we

138. Feinberg, *No One Like Him*, 172–73.

139. Ibid., 173.

140. Boyd, *God of the Possible*, 31.

141. Feinberg, *No One Like Him*, 174.

given such assurance that the One who perfectly knows the past, present, and future, the One whose wisdom can never be challenged or excelled, the One whose power reigns and accomplishes all that he wills, governs all the affairs of creation, fulfilling in all respects what he alone knows is good, wise , and best. What may seem to us as 'accidents' are no such things in the universe governed by the providence of the true living God."[142]

Major Claims and Arguments of Classical Theism

Scriptural warrants: For classical theists, the Bible presents overwhelming evidence in support of God's exhaustive knowledge of the past, present, and future. For example, of the all-knowing God, the psalmist says, "Even before a word is on my tongue, behold, O LORD, you know it altogether. . . . Your eyes saw my unformed substance; in your book were written, every one of them, the days that were formed for me, when as yet there were none of them" (Ps 139:4, 16, ESV). Classical theists claim that a text such as Ps 139:4 teaches God's foreknowledge and not God's informed guessing about what could happen.[143] Many classical theists also cite Isaiah 41–48 as biblical texts that clearly teach and bear witness to God's foreknowledge.[144] In these chapters, God seems to be grounding God's distinctiveness vis-à-vis idols on God's exhaustive knowledge of the past, present, and future. For example, Isa 41:21–23 reads, "'Present your case,' says the LORD. 'Set forth your arguments,' says Jacob's King. 'Bring in your idols, to tell us what is going to happen. Tell us what the former things were, so that we may consider them and know their final outcome. Or declare to us the things to come, tell us what the future holds, so we may know that you are gods'" (NIV).

God's knowledge of the future is intuitive and exhaustive. This means that God does not *learn* about the future through observation. God's knowledge of the future is innate—God simply knows. God does not discover something in the future; God's knowledge is not contingent upon unpredictable future circumstances; and God's knowledge of the future is simultaneous and not successive.

Classical theists disagree on the nature and meaning of God's foreknowledge. Broadly, there are two different ways classical theists answer the question, how is it possible for God to foreknow a future event? The first view can be described as *determinate foreknowledge* (see above). This view teaches that God has a complete knowledge of all future events because God

142. Ware, *God's Greater Glory*, 15.

143. Ware, *God's Lesser Glory*, 123.

144. Erickson, *What Does God Know?*, 42–49.

has foreordained and decreed them to happen. In this view, foreknowledge equals or entails foreordination.[145] God knows every human action as an "actual" state of affairs because God has already determined or ordained all human actions. God's knowledge of future events is not affected by human free will or circumstances. In other words, human beings *will* their choices because God has already *willed* that they make such choices.

The second view may be described as *compatibilist foreknowledge*. This view claims that God knows the *actual* future not because God has already predetermined it. Classical theists who hold a compatibilist view of God's foreknowledge, on the contrary, argue that God only *wills* human actions on the basis of what God has foreknown human beings will choose to do with their freedom. In this view, God's foreknowledge can be described as a "foreseen" knowledge: God knows human actions without predetermining them.

Critique of Classical Theism

Classical theism correctly points out that God's foreknowledge of the future is consistently taught in the Bible. However, does foreknowledge necessarily entail foreordination? If we accept the biblical teaching on human free will and freedom of choice, the answer must be in the negative. Classical theists present God as "a solitary, domineering monarch who has little to do with his subjects."[146] Classical theism fails to take seriously biblical texts that teach God's desire to have a relationship with human beings. The character of God seems to be at stake. For example, why would God genuinely want all people to be saved and to come to the knowledge of the truth (see 1 Tim 2:3–4) if God has already predetermined that not all will be saved?

Open Theism

The prominence of open theism is due to North American evangelical theologians who aimed to preserve the openness of future free human choices. If human beings are genuinely created with free will, it follows that the exact choices they will make in the future are unknown to God.

Open theism has been articulated in different ways. All open theists, however, hold that God has given human beings a libertarian free will. Therefore, God does exhibit elements of surprise concerning human

145. Ibid., 48.
146. Feinberg, *No One Like Him*, 504.

choices. Deuteronomy 13:3 presents God as genuinely testing people in order to know if they truly love God.[147] Jeremiah 26:3 indicates that God can change God's mind in response to human repentance: "It may be they will listen, and every one turn from his evil way, that I may relent of the disaster that I intend to do them because of their evil deeds" (ESV).

Major Claims and Arguments of Open Theism

Scriptural warrants: Like classical theists, open theists contend that the Bible plays an important role in constructing a theology of God's knowledge. Unlike classical theists, open theists deny that the Bible teaches exhaustive divine foreknowledge. Open theists claim that the Bible teaches divine *presentism*—God knows the past and present exhaustively, but has only a partial knowledge of the future.[148] Some open theists argue that Psalm 139:1–6, Job 28:23–24, and Isaiah 46:10 may be compatible with divine foreknowledge but do not require it.[149] According to John Sanders, Psalm 139:4 could be "explained by divine foreknowledge or by God knowing the psalmist so well that he can 'predict' what [the psalmist] will say and do."[150]

> "The open view is rooted in the conviction that the [biblical] passages that constitute the motif of future openness should be taken just as literally as the passages that constitute the motif of future determinism. For this reason, the open view concludes that the future is literally settled to whatever degree God wants to settle it, and literally open to the extent that God desires to leave it open to be resolved by the decisions of his actions. This view, open theists argue, is truer to the whole counsel of Scripture, truer to our experience, and offers a number of theological and practical advantages as well."
>
> —Boyd, *God of the Possible*

God's knowledge of the future is partial and successive. Open theists contend that God's knowledge of the future is partial and contingent upon several unpredictable future circumstances. This does not mean that there is nothing in the future that God knows exhaustively. Many open theists claim that God has chosen to foreknow some things (such as the Incarnation) and also chosen not to foreknow other things.[151] While God's knowledge of the future is far-reaching, it is not limitless. Even God's pre-

---

147. See also Gen 22:12.
148. Sanders, *God Who Risks*, 129.
149. Ibid., 130.
150. Ibid.
151. Ibid.

dictions and prophecies, open theists argue, are "generally open-ended and dependent in some way on the human responses to them."[152]

The future is not exhaustively *settled*, open theists contend. God has chosen to surrender some of God's power in order to make room for human freedom. This is a necessary consequence of bringing creatures with free will into existence. In response to Isaiah 41–48, the key Old Testament texts cited by the classical theists in their criticism of open theism, Gregory Boyd argues that the Isaiah texts *do not* teach (a) that all future events will occur because God has foreordained them, or (b) that God possesses exhaustive knowledge of future contingencies and human free actions.[153] On the contrary, they teach (c) that God will accomplish God's intentions for creation.[154]

Love is a "controlling metaphor" for understanding God's relationship with God's creation. According to 1 John 4:8, "Whoever does not love does not know God, because God is love" (NIV). Open theists, while recognizing that there are other metaphors in the Bible that describe God's character and nature, argue that "love" ought to be given a place of pride among other theological metaphors.[155] God's genuine offer of a loving relationship can only be grounded on libertarian freedom. Open theists argue that the triune God, whose nature is love, seeks to enjoy a loving relationship with humanity. To achieve this, God has given human beings the freedom to choose or to reject God. As Richard Rice argues, "God interacts with his creatures. Not only does he influence them, but they also exert an influence on him. God's will is not the ultimate explanation for everything that happens; human decisions and actions make an important contribution too."[156]

God has taken a risk by opting to not control every human action. For open theists, God's repentance (Gen 6:6; 1 Sam 15:35; Jonah 3:9–10) is one of the important controlling metaphors for God-talk. That God genuinely experiences regret, surprise, or repentance signifies that God alters God's plans in order to accommodate future human free choices and actions.[157] The cost of seeking a genuine and non-coercive relationship with the world is the risk of human rejection of God. As Clark Pinnock has noted, "God freely decided to be, in some respects, affected and conditioned by creatures and he established things in such a way that some things he desires may

152. Pinnock, "Systematic Theology," 122.

153. Boyd, *God of the Possible*, 30–31.

154. Ibid., 30.

155. Rice, "Biblical Support for a New Perspective," 18.

156. Ibid., 15.

157. Sanders, *God Who Risks*, 72.

not happen. For example, God may want everyone to receive his love but apparently not all do so."[158] However, God sometimes does not allow human evil actions to have the final say in the course of life. Gregory Boyd's comment on Genesis 50:20 highlights this claim: "The fact that Joseph's brothers did not have to choose to sell him into slavery, according to the open view, does not at all compromise the effectiveness with which God is able to weave their evil decision into his good sovereign plan."[159]

Critique of Open Theism

Open theists seek to account for God's genuine offer of relationship with humanity. God does not coerce human beings into relationship. Open theism here addresses the issue of human freedom, which is denied in classical theism. One of the greatest criticisms of open theism's view of God's limited knowledge of some future contingencies and human free actions is that God might not successfully accomplish God's intentions without violating human libertarian free will. The God that open theism presents us is like a Grand Chess Master who anticipates and also predicts the moves of an opponent. But in the end, like the Grand Chess Master, God does not know with certainty that God's plans will succeed.[160]

Providence and the Problem of Evil

The world is replete with suffering, pain, and agony, the result of what theologians call "evil." Theologians, as well as philosophers, make a distinction between two kinds of evil. *Moral evil* is the wrongdoing (such as murder) of moral agents and the consequences of that wrongdoing on the victim or victims. Alvin Plantinga describes evil as "a matter of free creatures' doing what is wrong, including particularly the way we human beings mistreat and savage each other. Often pain and suffering result from evil, as in some of the events for which our century will be remembered . . ."[161] Christian theologians call moral evil "sin." *Natural evil* refers to the pain and suffering that result from natural disasters (such as earthquakes, tornadoes, famines, etc.) and some diseases (such as a cancer).

---

158. Pinnock, *Most Moved Mover*, 5.

159. Boyd, "Response to William Lane Craig," 125.

160. Craig, "God Directs All Things," 87.

161. Plantinga, *Warranted Christian Belief*, 458. Among the events Plantinga mentions are the Holocaust and the genocide in Bosnia and Africa.

The presence of both moral and natural evils poses serious intellectual and practical problems to people who believe that an omnibenevolent, omnipotent, and omniscient God created the world. Theologians and philosophers refer to these problems as the "problem of evil." Critics of the theistic God and the Christian God argue that it is irrational and contrary to sound morality to believe that an all-good, all-powerful, and all-knowing God created and is sustaining a world that continually experiences immense suffering and loss of life through genocide, murder, disease, natural disaster, oppression, and poverty. Since most people do not deny the existence of evil, the problem of evil entails either that the Christian God, who is all-powerful, all-good, and all-knowing, can prevent and eradicate evil but chooses not to do so, or that such a God does not exist.. As David Hume argues, "Is he willing to prevent evil but not able? Then he is impotent. Is he able but not willing? Then he is malevolent. Is he both willing and able? Whence then is evil?"[162]

Christian theologians have responded to the problem of evil by revisiting God's sovereignty, human freedom, and human sin. In what follows, I will discuss some theological defenses of God's goodness and righteousness in the presence of evil (*theodicies*). While some theologians aim to justify God's goodness and righteousness in the presence of evil, others question God's righteousness and use of power in permitting and allowing evil to happen in the world.

The Augustinian Position: *Evil as Privation*

Augustine remains one of the most influential theologians in Christian history. Augustine's childhood experiences, especially his struggle with sexual appetite or desire, informed his theological reflection on the origin, sources, and consequences of evil. His introduction to Cicero's *Hortensius* inspired him to explore the power of the philosophical quest for wisdom as the medium through which human beings can curb and overcome carnal desires—to pursue "the wisdom of eternal truth."[163]

In book 4 of his *Confessions*, Augustine describes his intellectual disappointment with the Manicheans' dualistic solution to the problem of evil, which he had previously admired.[164] The Manicheans proposed that there were two forces that eternally engaged in conflict, namely, "Darkness" (that which is responsible for evil and carnal desires) and "Light." Evil ex-

162. Hume, *Dialogues Concerning Natural Religion*, 198.
163. Augustine, *Confessions*, 3.4: 58–59.
164. Ibid., 7.2: 135.

ists because the good God (Light) is powerless to eradicate the activities of the bad God (Darkness). Augustine was particularly disappointed with the Manichaean theory of evil because of the impotence of Light to overpower Darkness. His contact with the Christian teaching about one true and all-powerful God contributed to his rejection of Manichean dualism.

After several years of reflection, Augustine concluded that evil is the absence or privation of good (*privatio boni* in Latin). His contact with Ambrose, the bishop of Milan, helped him see that evil was not an eternal force but rather bad choices or the consequences of those choices. But it was Augustine's contact with Neo-Platonism through the writing of Plotinus that enabled him to see evil as the absence of perfection or of the fullness of goodness in changeable beings. Augustine concluded that evil is the absence of perfection or fullness of goodness that God demands from God's creatures, particularly the angels and human beings.[165] This privation of goodness is the result of self-love, pride, and the misuse of free will. For Augustine, however, God permits evils and uses them both to expose and correct the hidden sin of pride (self-love). Human beings can only overcome evil through union with God on account of Jesus' obedience and through the activity of the Holy Spirit, who is the bond of divine love.

Critics of Augustine's view of evil contend that his description of evil as *privatio boni* does not successfully explain how a good angel (Lucifer, to whom Augustine traces the origin of evil), created by a good God, could become the source of evil. John Roth is also critical of the *free will defense* (the theodicy that justifies God's permission of evil in the world with God's wise decision to endow human beings with free will). As creatures endowed with freedom of choice, human beings can maximize goodness or evil. For Roth, human beings most often maximize evil. Roth insists that the existence of evil far exceeds the benefits of freedom.[166]

The two excerpts below are taken from Augustine's *Confessions* and *On Grace and Free Will*, respectively. The texts highlight some of the key contributions made by Augustine to the issue of the problem of evil.

> So, once I had seen that the incorruptible is superior to the corruptible, I had to search for you in the light of this truth and make it the starting point of my inquiry into the origin of evil, that is, the origin of corruption, by which your substance cannot possibly be violated. For there is no means whatsoever by which corruption can injure our God, whether by an act of will, by necessity,

165. Ibid., 7.20:154–55.
166. Roth, "Theodicy of Protest," 14.

or by chance. This is because he is God and what he wills is good and he is himself that same Good: whereas to be corrupted is not good. And you are never compelled, my God, to do or suffer anything against your will, because your will is not greater than your power. It would be greater only if you were greater than yourself, for the will and power of God are God himself. Neither can anything unforeseen happen to you, because you know all things and nothing, whatever its nature, exists except by reason of the very fact that you know it. Need I say more to prove that the substance which is God cannot be corruptible since, if it were, it would not be God?

Where then does evil come from, if God made all things and, because he is good, made them good too? It is true that he is the supreme Good, that he is himself a greater Good than these lesser goods which he created. But the Creator and all his creation are both good. Where then does evil come from? . . .

So we must conclude that if things are deprived of all good, they cease altogether to be; and this means that as long as they are, they are good. Therefore, whatever is, is good; evil, the origin of which I was trying to find, is not a substance, because if it were a substance, it would be good. For either it would be an incorruptible substance of the supreme order of goodness, or it would be a corruptible substance which would not be corruptible unless it were good. So it became obvious to me that all that you have made is good, and that there are not substances whatsoever that were not made by you. And because you did not make them equal, each single thing is good and collectively they are very good, for our God made his whole creation *very good*.

For you evil does not exist, and not only for you but for the whole of your creation as well, because there is nothing outside it which could invade it and break down the order which you have imposed on it.[167]

There are, however, persons who attempt to find excuse for themselves even from God. The Apostle James says to such: "Let no man say when he is tempted, I am tempted of God; for God cannot be tempted with evil, neither tempteth He any man. But every man is tempted when he is drawn away of his own lust, and enticed. Then, when lust hath conceived, it bringeth forth sin: and sin, when it finished, bringeth forth death." Observe how very plainly is set before our view the free choice of the human will.[168]

Question: How does Augustine come to the conclusion that evil has no ontological existence?

167. Augustine, *Confessions* 7.4, 5, 12, 13: 137–49.
168. Augustine, *On Grace and Free Will* (NPNF[2] 2:444).

John Hick's Position: Evil as Remedy for Humanity's Immaturity

The British theologian John Hick developed a theory of evil that he claims is grounded on Irenaeus of Lyons' concept of creaturely growth and movement toward maturity. Unlike Augustine, Hick argues that evil is not a loss of perfection. Hick argues that perfection does not lie in the distant past but rather in the future. For Hick, humans are born spiritually and morally immature; God's desires them to grow and to reach spiritual maturity. In order to achieve this goal, God created the world as a vale of soul-making in which evil is designed to help human beings cultivate virtue and character. For Hick, God does not shield human beings from evil. Rather, God facilitates their progress toward perfection and maturity.

The major criticism of Hick's theory of evil is that there seem to be needless evils, evils that serve no purpose. Since not everyone has the opportunity to run the track of moral virtue—in such cases, for example, when evil leads to the death of the victims—there seem to be evils that do not bring the victims to spiritual and moral maturity.

As the excerpt below demonstrates, John Hick argues that Augustine's free will defense theory is flawed because it is built on the idea of the fall. Hick proposes a "soul-making" theodicy that does not depend on the idea of the fall.

Christian thought has always included a certain range of variety, and in the area of theodicy it offers two broad types of approach. The Augustinian approach, representing until fairly recently the majority report of the Christian mind, hinges upon the idea of the fall, which has in turn brought about the disharmony of nature. This type of theodicy is developed today as "the free will defense." The Irenaean approach, representing in the past a minority report, hinges upon the creation of humankind through the evolutionary process as an immature creature living in a challenging and therefore person-making world....

Most educated inhabitants of the modern world regard the biblical story of Adam and Eve, and their temptation by the devil, as myth rather than as history; they believe further that far from having been created finitely perfect and then falling, humanity evolved out of lower forms of life, emerging in a morally, spiritually, and culturally primitive state. Further, they reject as incredible the idea that earthquake and flood, disease, decay, and death are consequences either of the human fall or of a prior fall of angelic beings who are now exerting an evil influence upon the earth....

I believe that we find the light that we need in the main alternative strand of Christian thinking, which goes back to important constructive suggestions by the early Hellenistic Fathers of the church, particularly St. Irenaeus (A.D. 120–202). Irenaeus himself did not develop a theodicy, but he did . . . build a framework of thought within which a theodicy became possible that does not depend upon the idea of the fall, and which is consonant with modern knowledge concerning the origins of the human race. . . .

Let us now try to formulate a contemporary version of the Irenaean type of theodicy, based on this suggestion of the initial creation of humankind, not as finitely perfect, but as an immature creature at the beginning of a long process of further growth and development. . . . In order to be a person, exercising some measure of genuine freedom, the creature must be brought into existence, not in the immediate divine presence, but at a "distance" from God. This "distance" cannot of course be spatial, for God is omnipresent. It must be epistemic distance, a distance in the cognitive dimension. And the Irenaean hypothesis is that this "distance" consists, in the case of humans, in their existence within and as part of a world that functions as an autonomous system and from within which God is not overwhelmingly evident. . . . We are free to acknowledge and worship God, and free—particularly since the emergence of human individuality and the beginnings of critical consciousness during the first millennium B.C.—to doubt the reality of God.

Within such as situation the possibility enters of human beings coming freely to know and love their Maker. Indeed, if the end-state that God is seeking to bring about is one in which finite persons have come in their own freedom to know and love him, this requires creating them initially in a state which is not that of their already knowing and loving him. For it is logically impossible to create beings already in a state of having come into the state by their own free choices.

A world in which there can be no pain or suffering would also be one without moral choices and hence no possibility of moral growth and development.[169]

Question: How does Hick justify the existence of both moral and natural evils in a world created by a perfect God?

---

169 Hick, "Irenaean Theodicy," 40–42, 47.

John Roth's Position: Evil as Divine and Human Responsibility

John Roth's theory of evil is heavily influenced by the painful experience of the Jews, particularly the Holocaust, in which approximately six million Jews lost their lives in Nazi concentration camps. He has written several works on the Holocaust. Roth's theory of evil is technically a *non-theodicy*, for he does not aim to defend God's righteousness or justice in the presence of evil. On the contrary, Roth questions God's use of power or God's failure to stop heinous evil (such as genocide) in the world. We should not defend God's complicity in evil, Roth contends, but rather put God on trial. When an all-powerful and sovereign God refuses to intervene to stop evil, we should hold God, like the perpetrators themselves, responsible. For Roth, justifying God's permission of evil entails legitimizing evil. Yet, in the presence of a gross waste of life, Roth insists that it is still meaningful to trust in God's ability to prevent evil. Both God and human beings are to fight against and undo evil.

Some critics of Roth have pointed out that his pessimism about God's ability to completely redeem or justify the pain and suffering that evil brings upon God's creatures contradicts his belief in God's omnipotence. Since God is all-powerful, "God can redeem all evil in the eschaton."[170]

The following text summarizes the main arguments of John Roth's protest theodicy. Roth argues that both God and human beings are to be held responsible for the presence of evil in the world.

> Usually "theodicy" refers to human vindications of God's justice in permitting evil to exist. Most theodicies of the Protestant Christian variety belong in that tradition. The outlook developed here is related to it, too, but the breaks with classical Christian Protestantism are no less important than the lines of continuity. My approach underscores God's sovereignty. It allows for his disappointment with human life gone wrong. It also holds out for the possibility of grace experienced through faith and for the hope of God's salvation. The Jewish voices belong to a dissenting spirit that quarrels with God over *his* use of power. That confrontation is rooted not so much in rejection of God but rather in recognition that such defiance is crucial in struggles against despair. Jewish insight, ancient and contemporary, calls for men and women—particularly Christians—to consider a theodicy of protest.
>
> What does "evil" mean? That question itself is a crucial element in the problem of evil. The word often functions as a noun, suggesting that evil is an entity. In fact, evil is *activity*, sometimes *inactivity*, and thus it is a manifestation

170. Davis, "Problem of Evil in Recent Philosophy," 539.

of power. Evil power displays are those that *waste*. That is, evil happens when-ever power ruins or squanders, or whenever it fails to forestall those results. Evil comes in many shapes and sizes. The kind that concerns us here ignores and violates the sanctity of individual persons. Everyone inflicts that sort of pain, and yet some individuals and societies are far more perverse than others. The measure is taken by the degree to which one's actions waste human life....

The slaughter-bench makes God's luxury wasteful. And one point more: No matter what horn of the dilemma is seized, any ways in which God could rationally justify his economy as purely cost-effective in pursing goodness that we can appreciate ... well, those ways are beyond imagining. This result testi-fies that such a wasteful God cannot be totally benevolent. History itself is God's indictment. It is irresponsible to assign responsibility inequitably. God must bear his share, and it's not small unless he could never be described as one for whom all things are possible. God's responsibility is located in the fact the he is the one who ultimately sets the boundaries in which we live and move and have our being.

If God raised Jesus from the dead, he had the might to thwart the Ho-locaust long before it ended. Coupled with the view that resurrection is not merely the release of an immortal spirit from a lifeless physical body, but rather the re-creation of a person for whom all life has ceased, that premise governs a theodicy of protest. In doing so, it makes God harder to excuse. But that fact, in turn, leaves us to ask: Why should anybody bother with a God like this one, who seems so infrequently to do the best that is within God's power? A theodicy of protest *acknowledges* and *yearns* for the love of God. It does the former because life is a created gift, one that is basically good and able to become even better.

This God is no bumbler. He knows what he is doing, and that reality is the problem. Our protests do him no harm. Indeed, his license gives us a mandate to say what we feel, and we must ... so long as we speak for the sake of human well-being. When dissent is raised in that spirit, its rebellious care may grip God's heart.[171]

Question: What theological and existential arguments does Roth raise in defense of a protest theodicy?

---

171. Roth, "Theology of Protest," 7, 11, 14, 18.

John Pobee's Position: Evil as the Work of Spiritual Forces and Human Beings

The Ghanaian John Pobee is one of the leading African theologians who aim to contextualize Christianity in Africa. Although in *Toward an African Theology* Pobee focuses on the cultural context of the Akan of Ghana, he intentionally highlights some similarities between Akan culture and the cultures of other sub-Saharan African societies. Like his contemporaries who followed the *inculturation* model of contextualization, Pobee insists that "African theology has to be rooted in the Bible."[172]

Pobee construes evil as the work of human beings and evil spirit-beings. He locates his theologies of evil and providence in the indigenous African concept of the interrelationship between the spiritual world and the human world. He dissociates God from evil by holding human beings and malevolent spirit-beings responsible for the presence of evil in the world. God, however, does not sit idly by and watch to see how evil plays out in the world; God holds the perpetrators of evil responsible. Pobee, however, does not explain how an all-powerful and all-good God can allow evil to continue to destroy God's creation.

Christian scholarship has been dominated by the problem of evil—the existence, for example, of natural disasters such as earthquakes, typhoons, and volcanic eruptions which take a heavy toll on human lives, in the world which a good God created and of which he said: "Behold, it was very good" (Gen 1:31). But broadly speaking, evil is a privation, "the absence of some good which should be present."

In Christian theology the issue of privation appears to be a challenge to the goodness of God and has been debated by every theologian since the advent of the Judaic and Christian faiths. Such a problem does not really exist in traditional African society. For that society, starting with a spiritual ontology (that the world of man is surrounded by hosts of spirit-beings), attributes evil to personal forces of evil, which are able to affect and influence a man's life for good or evil. Thus earthquake or flood is explained as the anger of some spirit-being at some wrongdoing, hidden or not, in the society. An unsuccessful or difficult delivery is attributed to the violation of family taboo or to infidelity by the expectant mother. In other words, evil is the confluence of anger from the spirit-world and man's waywardness. The two are not contradictory. The situation is no different from Christians praying to God for success in war against

172. Pobee, *Toward an African Theology*, 20.

Hitler and at the same time saying the gallant soldiers have won the victory. God is the primary cause and the soldiers the secondary cause. So too the primary cause of evil in traditional [African] society is the sprit-beings, notably the witches; and the secondary cause is the man who has done something wrong.

This analysis of traditional society is not without its problems. For example, the suspicion of waywardness on the part of the victim of evil is often not matched by the facts. It is not always that infidelity causes a difficult delivery, and so forth. For all its weaknesses it makes, perhaps, an important point which should not be lost sight of in a discussion of evil: there is, at one point or other, human responsibility or input into the occurrence of evil. And that human responsibility is either by action or inaction.

Again, the spiritual ontology has its own set of problems. Some aspects of the religious ontology are still not accepted, at least in their entirety. Principally, evil is attributed to witches. But modern African man doubts witchcraft until he is in a crisis. For all the question marks raised against the notion of witchcraft, it appears to be a world-taken-for-granted which surfaces in crises; it is a psychological reality in African societies.

The solidarity of men in sin and the attribution of evil to personal forces of evil do not absolve man of individual and personal responsibility (James 1:13–15). On this, also, both the biblical and traditional African worldviews agree. Two Akan maxims should suffice to make the point. First, *Onyame mmpe bone nti na omaa dine biako biako*—because God hates evil, he gave each one a name so as to identify the perpetrator of evil. In other words, each individual is responsible for his sin and accountable to God for it. The second saying is *oketee nnkowe mako ma fire nnfi opankyerene*—it is the lizard that eats hot pepper that will get the burning sensation and not the frog which has not tasted it. Both sayings affirm individual and personal responsibility for sin, in spite of the ideas of corporate solidarity and demonic forces.[173]

Question: How does Pobee's view of evil reflect African traditional religious thought and Christian thought?

---

173. Pobee, *Toward an African Theology*, 99–100, 116.

Christine Smith: The Church's Response to "Radical Evil"

Christine Smith, an American theologian and expert in homiletics (preaching), in her *Preaching as Weeping, Confession, and Resistance*, discusses the pain and suffering that derive from dehumanizing ideologies such as racism and classism. Smith's visit to Guatemala in 1989 had a profound impact on her decision to describe the interlocking web of oppression she sensed as "radical evil." Writing specifically from the context of the United States, Smith contends that "hadicappism, ageism, sexism, heterosexism, racism, and classism" are strands of the web of oppression. Her goal is to expose the silence and inaction of some people in the face of the dehumanization and exploitation of people with disabilities, women, gays and lesbians, and African Americans. For Smith, publicly naming (through preaching) the web of oppressive structures "radical evil" will bring to light the extent of the pain and suffering they bring to humanity. Smith highlights the force of preaching in exposing, resisting, and undoing evil. She writes, "Naming this web of oppression as the expression of radical evil has everything to do with preaching."[174] Preaching is an act of naming: "It is an act of disclosing and articulating the truths about our present human existence. It is also an act of redeeming and transforming reality, an act of shattering illusions and cracking open limited perspectives. It is nothing less than the interpretation of our present world and an invitation to build a profoundly different world."[175]

Smith ignores the issue of God's complicity and willingness to allow evil to ruin God's creation. Although her interest is to expose and confront evil, the question about the involvement and responsibility of God in dealing with evil remains one of the theological issues that haunt Christians.

In the excerpt below, Smith writes of the "reality of oppression" and the importance of preaching, which she equates with "weeping."

> During the past fifteen years a primary focus of my personal and professional life has been exploration and analysis of a web of "isms" that structures a foundation of oppression worldwide. As a woman, my first and primary experience of this web was through the painful and systematic oppression of sexism. My entry into an understanding of these oppressive structures and systems was through feminism. As my own critique has expanded, so have my exploration and transformation. As I have come to acknowledge and understand the breadth and depth of oppression in the human community, I have come to see the interlocking partners of oppression more clearly as handicappism,

174. Smith, *Preaching as Weeping, Confession, and Resistance*, 3.
175. Ibid., 2.

ageism, sexism, heterosexism, racism, and classism. There are other systems and ideologies that form part of this reality of oppression....

My world reality, my theology, my faith, and my preaching have shifted over these years in direct relationship to my deepening analysis and experience of these expressions of oppression. Because of my experience in Guatemala, I now must name this interlocking mass of oppression "radical evil." Yet even as I write these words, I am confronted by the depth of my own denial for so long. Why has it taken me this many years to give the name "radical evil" to this web of oppressive structures and systems?...

Naming this web of oppression as the expression of radical evil has everything to do with preaching. I find myself asking how any person can preach a word of hope, a word of faith, in a day such as this. And yet, a voice just as strongly imbedded in my spirit says, "How can we not preach a word of hope and faith in a day such as this?" As the breadth of evil becomes clearer to me I experience both despair about the focus of present preaching and renewed commitment to the possibility that preaching can be an expression of faith that enlightens and unleashes the compassion and convictions of religious communities....

As my understanding of preaching deepens, I have found myself saying over and over again, "Preaching is weeping." Often when people weep, they are most in touch with the deepest passions, strongest yearnings, and greatest desires of their lives. These are some of the most difficult and richest moments in life. People weep when they are alive to those things they cherish and value the most and are touched by something they can hardly name or utter....

But weeping is not enough. A world infected and diseased by radical evil also needs truth just as radical. Much of the Christian community has come to understand confession as speaking about the sinfulness of our lives and receiving God's forgiveness and grace.

Even confession is not enough. In the face of radical evil, preaching must be weeping, it must be confession, but it also must be resistance. Resistance is not just our reaction to the evil we experience and participate in, but it is our stand against it. It is not an act of standing still and defending ourselves against the evil that surrounds us, but it is a movement into it, and through it, with speech and presence and action. The church's resistance to evil needs to be strong and compelling. If preaching is to be a transforming act, then the power and integrity of our proclamations will surely be measured by their ability to mobilize communities to resist the reality that confronts us.[176]

Question: In what ways can Smith's understanding of "preaching" help Christian communities deal with evil?

---

176. Smith, *Preaching as Weeping, Confession, and Resistance*, 2–4.

Some Concluding Reflections on Theodicy

In dealing with God's providence and the presence of evil, asking an appropriate question is crucially important. For example, if a theologian aims to answer only the question, "How could an all-good, all-powerful, and all-knowing God have created a world that experience immense evil?" the theologian may discover or construct theodicies that excuse God of complicity but that have no practical relevance in terms of how to undo or deal with evil. If a theologian aims to answer only the question, "What is God doing in and about the presence of evil in the world?" the theologian may develop a theology of providence that does not aim to defend God's permission of evil in the world but rather one that articulates God's act of dealing with evil.

When developing a theodicy, theologians need to respond to these questions: Does God need a defense in the face of evil? In light of the Bible, what kind of God needs a human defense? Does the Bible require us to defend God or rather to defend our perceptions of God? Some Old Testament writers wondered what God was doing about evil. In the presence of misery and the posterity of the wicked, Habakkuk asked, "How long, O LORD, must I call for help, but you do not listen? Or cry out to you, 'Violence,' but you do not save? Why do you make me look at injustice? Why do you tolerate wrongdoing?" (Hab 1:2–3, NIV). Yet in the midst of this honest conversation with God, one is constantly reminded that God is not to be accused of evil (Jas 1:13), that God can discipline sinners in a manner that brings suffering and pain on those sinners (Gen 3:14–19; Isa 10:5; 2 Sam 12:11–12, Amos 3:6), and that God will ultimately overcome evil (Gen 50:20; Job 19:19–27; Rom 8:28–39; Rev 21:3–4).

A Christian theology of divine providence and evil cannot be reduced to "theodicy"—defending or justifying God's goodness and righteousness in the presence of evil. To do so is theologically irresponsible. On the contrary, a Christian theology of divine providence and evil should explain what God is doing about evil (especially in the event of Jesus Christ, who embodies God's kingdom) and what God expects human beings to do about evil.

Key Terms

Ex nihilo: Latin phrase that means "out of nothing" and that has been used by some theologians to express the belief that God created the world without using an externally existing material or matter.

Emanation: term that is used by some theologians to express the idea that creation flowed or derived (necessarily or non-necessarily) from God.

Immensity: term used to describe the idea that God is not confined to space and located in space. This does not mean that God does not act in space.

Pantheism: the view of the God-world relation that teaches "everything is God" (from the Greek *pan*, "every," and *theos*, "God.")

Panentheism: the view of the God-world relation that teaches that God is in everything or God flows in everything (from the Greek *pan*, "every," *en*, "in," and *theos*, "God").

Theodicy: the defense of God's goodness and righteousness in the presence of evil.

Review Questions

1. What are the theological implications of the theories of creation discussed in this chapter?

2. What are the theological implications of the views of God's foreknowledge and human freedom discussed in the chapter?

3. What is theodicy? In answering this question, (*a*) articulate how the presence of evil in the world constitutes a theological problem, and (*b*) describe and critique the responses of Augustine, Hick, Roth, Smith, and Pobee to the problem of evil.

Suggestion for Further Reading

Gundry, Stanley N., and Dennis W. Jowers, editors. *Four Views on Divine Providence.* Grand Rapids: Zondervan, 2011.

Keating, James F., and Thomas Joseph White, editors. *Divine Impassibility and the Mystery of Human Suffering.* Grand Rapids: Eerdmans, 2009.

Leibniz, Gottfried Wihelm. *Theodicy: Essays on the Goodness of God, the Freedom of Man, and the Origin of Evil.* Edited by Freiherr Gott. London: Routledge & Kegan Paul, 1951.

Moreau, Scott A., et al., editors. *Deliver Us from Evil: An Uneasy Frontier in Christian Mission.* Monrovia, CA: World Vision International, 2002.

Sands, Kathleen M. *Escape from Paradise: Evil and Tragedy in Feminist Theology.* Minneapolis: Fortress, 1994.

Bibliography

Allison, Gregg R. *Historical Theology: An Introduction to Christian Doctrine*. Grand Rapids: Zondervan, 2011.

Anatolios, Khaled. *Athanasius*. London: Routledge, 2004.

Anderson, Allan. *Introduction to Pentecostalism*. Cambridge: Cambridge University Press, 2004.

Anderson, David. "Introduction." In *On the Holy Spirit*, by Saint Basil the Great, 7–13. Translated by David Anderson. Crestwood, NY: St. Vladimir's Seminary Press, 1980.

Anselm. "An Address (*Proslogion*)." In *A Scholastic Miscellany: Anselm to Ockham*, edited by Eugene R. Fairweather, 69–93. Philadelphia: Westminster, 1956.

———. *Cur Deus Homo*. In *A Scholastic Miscellany: Anselm to Ockham*, edited by Eugene R. Fairweather, 100–183. Philadelphia: Westminster, 1956.

Aquinas, Thomas. "Theology, Faith and Reason. On Boethius *On the Trinity*, 1–2." In *Thomas Aquinas: Selected Writings*, edited and translated by Ralph McInerny, 109–41. New York: Penguin, 1998.

Athanasius. *Life of Anthony of Egypt*. In *Readings in World Christian History: Earliest Christianity to 1453*, edited by John W. Coakley and Andrea Sterk, 131–44. Maryknoll, NY: Orbis, 2004.

———. *Orations Against the Arians*. In Khaled Anatolios, *Athanasius*, 178–211. London: Routledge, 2004.

Augustine. *Confessions*. Translated by R. S. Pine-Coffin. London: Penguin, 1961.

———. *On the Trinity*. In vol. 3 of *A Select Library of the Nicene and Post-Nicene Fathers*, Series 1. Edited by Philip Schaff. 1886–1889. 14 vols. Reprint, Grand Rapids: Eerdmans, 1956.

Ayres, Lewis. "(Mis)Adventures in Trinitarian Ontology." In *The Trinity and an Entangled World: Relationality in Physical Science and Theology*, edited by John Polkinghorne, 130–45. Grand Rapids: Eerdmans, 2010.

———. *Nicaea and Its Legacy: An Approach to Fourth-Century Trinitarian Theology*. Oxford: Oxford University Press, 2004.

Baker, William R. "The Chalcedonian Definition, Pauline Christology, and the Postmodern Challenge of 'From Below' Christology." *Stone-Campbell Journal* 9 (2006) 77–97.

Baillie, D. M. *God Was in Christ*. London: Faber & Faber 1948.

Barr, William R. "Christian Hope: Introducing the Issue." In *Constructive Christian Theology in the Worldwide Church*, edited by William R. Barr, 475–77. Grand Rapids: Eerdmans, 1997.

Barry, Carol. "Trinity." In *Exploring Theology*, edited by Anne Hession and Patricia Kieran, 110–27. Dublin: Veritas, 2007.

Barth, Karl. *Church Dogmatics* 1/1. *The Doctrine of the Word of God*. Translated by G. W. Bromiley. 2nd ed. 1975. Reprint, Peabody, MA: Hendrickson, 2010.

———. "No." In *Natural Theology: Comprising "Nature and Grace" by Professor Dr. Emil Brunner and the Reply "No!" by Dr. Karl Barth*, translated by Peter Fraenkel, 65–128. 1946. Reprint, Eugene, OR: Wipf & Stock, 2002.

———. *The Word of God and the Word of Man*. Translated by Douglas Horton. New York: Harper & Row, 1956.

Basil. *De Spiritu Sancto*. In vol. 8 of *A Select Library of the Nicene and Post-Nicene Fathers*, Series 2. Edited by Philip Schaff and Henry Wace. 14 vols. 1890–1900. Reprint, Grand Rapids: Eerdmans, 1978.

———. *On the Holy Spirit*. Translated by David Anderson. Crestwood, NY: St. Vladimir's Seminary Press, 1980.

Bauckham, Richard J. *Jude, 2 Peter*. Word Biblical Commentary. Waco, TX: Word, 1983.

———. "Monotheism and Christology in the Gospel of John." In *Contours of Christology in the New Testament*, edited by Richard N. Longenecker, 148–66. Grand Rapids: Eerdmans, 2005.

Beatrice, Pier Franco. "The Word 'Homoousios' from Hellenism to Christianity." *Church History* 71(2002) 243–72.

Bediako, Kwame. *Jesus and the Gospel in Africa: History and Experience*. Maryknoll, NY: Orbis, 2004.

Beeley, Christopher A. "The Holy Spirit in the Cappadocians: Past and Present." *Modern Theology* 26 (2010) 90–119.

Bekye, Paul. *Divine Revelation and Traditional Religions: With Particular Reference to the Dagaaba of West Africa*. Rome: Leberit, 1991.

Bevans, Stephen B. *Models of Contextual Theology*. Rev. ed. Maryknoll, NY: Orbis, 2002.

Blackmore, Vernon, and Andrew Page, editors. *Evolution: The Great Debate*. Oxford: Lion, 1989.

Blocher, Henri. *In the Beginning: The Opening Chapter of Genesis*. Translated by David G. Preston. Downers Grove, IL: InterVarsity, 1984.

Boff, Clodovis, and Leonardo Boff. *Introducing Liberation Theology*. Translated by Paul Burns. Maryknoll, NY: Orbis, 1987.

Boff, Leonardo. *Church: Charism and Power: Liberation Theology and the Institutional Church*. Translated by John W. Diercksmeier. New York: Crossroad, 1985.

———. *Ecology and Liberation: A New Paradigm*. Maryknoll, NY: Orbis, 1995.

———. *Jesus Christ Liberator: A Critical Christology for Our Time*. Translated by Patrick Hughes. Maryknoll, NY: Orbis, 1978.

———. *Trinity and Society*. Translated by Paul Burns. Maryknoll, NY: Orbis, 1988.

Boyd, Gregory A. *God of the Possible: A Biblical Introduction to the Open View of God*. Grand Rapids: Baker, 2000.

———. *Is God to Blame? Beyond Pat Answers to the Problem of Suffering*. Downers Grove, IL: InterVarsity, 2003.

———. "Response to William Lane Craig." In *Four Views on Divine Providence*, edited by Stanley N. Gundry and Dennis W. Jowers, 123–39. Grand Rapids: Zondervan, 2011.

Boyd, Gregory A., and Paul R. Eddy. *Across the Spectrum: Understanding Issues in Evangelical Theology*. 2nd ed. Grand Rapids: Baker, 2009.

Braaten, Carl E. "A Shared Dilemma: Catholics and Lutherans on the Authority and Interpretation of Scripture." *Pro Ecclesia* 10 (2001) 63–75.

———. "Scripture, Church, and Dogma: An Essay on Theological Method." *Interpretation* 50 (1996) 142–55.

Brown, David. *Divine Humanity: Kenosis and the Construction of a Christian Theology.* Waco, TX: Baylor University Press, 2011.

———. "Trinitarian Personhood and Individuality." In *Trinity, Incarnation and Atonement: Philosophical and Theological Essays*, edited by Ronald J. Feenstra and Cornelius Plantinga Jr., 48–78. Notre Dame: University of Notre Dame Press, 1989.

Bruce, F. F. *The Gospel of John.* Grand Rapids: Eerdmans, 1983.

Bruner, Dale. *A Theology of the Holy Spirit: The Pentecostal Experience and the New Testament Witness.* Grand Rapids: Eerdmans, 1970.

Brunner, Emil. *The Mediator: A Study of the Central Doctrine of the Christian Faith.* Translated by Olive Wyon. London: Lutterworth, 1934.

———. "Nature and Grace." In *Natural Theology: Comprising "Nature and Grace" by Professor Dr. Emil Brunner and the Reply "No!" by Dr. Karl Barth*, translated by Peter Fraenkel, 15–64. 1946. Reprint, Eugene, OR: Wipf and Stock, 2002.

Bultmann, Rudolf, and Karl Kundsin. *Form Criticism: Two Essays on New Testament Research.* Translated by Frederick C. Grant. New York: Willet, Clark, 1934.

Burgess, Stanley M. *The Holy Spirit: Ancient Christian Traditions.* Peabody, MA: Hendrickson, 1984.

Burns, Peter. "The Problem of Socialism in Liberation Theology." *Theological Studies* 53 (1992) 493–516.

Calian, Carnegie Samuel. *Theology Without Boundaries: Encounters of Eastern Orthodoxy and Western Tradition.* Louisville: Westminster John Knox, 1992.

Calvin, John. *Commentaries.* Vol. 19. Edited by Henry Beveridge. Reprint, Grand Rapids: Baker, 2009.

———. *Institutes of the Christian Religion.* Vol. 1. Edited by John T. Neill. Translated by Ford Lewis Battles. Philadelphia: Westminster, 1960.

Campbell, Ted A. "The Interpretive Role of Tradition." In *Wesley and the Quadrilateral: Renewing the Conversation*, 65–75. Nashville: Abingdon, 1997.

Caputo, John D. *The Weakness of God: A Theology of the Event.* Indianapolis: Indiana University Press, 2006.

Carlton, Clark C. "The Temple that Held God: Byzantine Marian Hymnography and the Christ of Nestorius." *St. Vladimir's Theological Quarterly* 50 (2006) 99–125.

Carr, Anne E. "Providence, Power, and the Holy Spirit." *Horizons* 29 (2002) 80–93.

Clark, Kelly James. *Return to Reason: A Critique of Enlightenment Evidentialism and a Defense of Reason and Belief in God.* Grand Rapids: Eerdmans, 1990.

Cobb, John B., Jr. *God and the World.* Philadelphia: Westminster, 1969.

Congar, Yves. *I Believe in the Holy Spirit.* Translated by David Smith. New York: Crossroad, 1997.

Copan, Paul, and William Lane Craig. *Creation Out of Nothing: A Biblical, Philosophical and Scientific Exploration.* Grand Rapids: Baker, 2004.

Craig, William Lane. "God Directs All Things: On Behalf of a Molinist View of Providence." In *Four Views on Divine Providence*, edited by Stanley N. Gundry and Dennis W. Jowers, 79–100. Grand Rapids: Zondervan, 2011.

———. *The Only Wise God: The Compatibility of Divine Foreknowledge and Human Freedom.* Grand Rapids: Baker, 1987.

Cranfield, C. E. B. *The Gospel According to St. Mark.* Cambridge: Cambridge University Press, 1963.

Crawford, A. Elaine. "Womanist Christology and Wesleyan Tradition." *Black Theology* 2 (2004) 213–20.

Crisp, Oliver D. *Divinity and Humanity: The Incarnation Revisited.* Cambridge: Cambridge University Press, 2007.

Criswell, W. A. *Why I Preach that the Bible Is Literally True.* Nashville: Broadman, 1969.

Darwin, Charles. *On the Origin of Species by Means of Natural Selection, or the Preservation of Favoured Races in the Struggle for Life.* London: John Murray, 1859.

Davis, Stephen T. *The Debate about the Bible: Inerrancy versus Infallibility.* Philadelphia: Westminster, 1977.

———. *Disputed Issues: Contending for Christian Faith in Today's Academic Setting.* Waco, TX: Baylor University Press, 2009.

———. "The Problem of Evil in Recent Philosophy." *Review and Expositor* 82 (1985) 535–48.

Del Colle, Ralph. "The Triune God." In *The Cambridge Companion to Christian Doctrine*, edited by Colin E. Gunton, 121–40. Cambridge: Cambridge University Press, 1997.

Dembski, William A. *Intelligent Design: The Bridge between Science and Theology.* Downers Grove, IL: InterVarsity, 1999.

Donald, Alistair. "Evolution and the Church." In *Should Christians Embrace Evolution? Biblical and Scientific Responses*, edited by Norman C. Nevin, 15–26. Phillipsburg, NJ: P. & R., 2011.

Dulles, Avery. *Models of Revelation.* New York: Doubleday, 1983.

———. "Scripture: Recent Protestant and Catholic Views." *Theology Today* 37 (1980) 7–26.

Dunn, James D. G. *Christology in the Making: A New Testament Inquiry into the Doctrines of the Incarnation.* 2nd ed. Grand Rapids: Eerdmans, 1989.

Dunzl, Franz. *A Brief History of the Doctrine of the Trinity in the Early Church.* Translated by John Bowden. New York: T. & T. Clark, 2007.

Ellens, Harold J. "The Jesus Quest." *Pastoral Psychology* 51(2003) 435–40.

Epperly, Bruce G. "Process Theology and Lived Omnipresence: An Essay in Practical Theology." *Encounter* 68 (2007) 19–31.

Erickson, Millard J. *Christian Theology.* 2nd ed. Grand Rapids: Baker, 1998.

Eusebius. *Life of Constantine.* Translated by Averil Cameron and Stuart G. Hall. New York: Oxford University Press, 1999.

Ezigbo, Victor I. *Re-imagining African Christologies: Conversing with the Interpretations and Appropriations of Jesus in Contemporary African Christianity.* Eugene, OR: Pickwick, 2010.

Fairweather, Eugene, editor. *A Scholastic Miscellany: Anselm to Ockham.* Philadelphia: Westminster, 1956.

Fee, Gordon D. *God's Empowering Presence: The Holy Spirit in the Letters of Paul.* Peabody, MA: Hendrickson, 1994.

———. "The New Testament and Kenosis Christology." In *Exploring Kenotic Christology: The Self-Emptying of God*, edited by C. Stephen Evans, 25–36. New York: Oxford University Press, 2006.

———. *Pauline Christology: An Exegetical-Theological Study.* Peabody, MA: Hendrickson, 2007.

Feinberg, John S. "God Ordains All Things." In *Predestination and Free Will: Four Views of Divine Sovereignty and Human Freedom*, edited by David Basinger and Randall Basinger, 19–43. Downers Grove, IL: InterVarsity, 1986.

———. *No One Like Him: The Doctrine of God*. Wheaton, IL: Crossway, 2001.

Ferguson, Sinclair B., David F. Wright, and J. I. Packer, editors. *New Dictionary of Theology*. Downers Grove, IL: InterVarsity, 1988.

Fergusson, David. "Divine Providence and Action." In *God's Life in Trinity*, edited by Miroslav Volf and Michael Welker, 153–65. Minneapolis: Fortress, 2006.

———. "Eschatology." In *The Cambridge Companion to Christian Doctrine*, edited by Colin E. Gunton, 226–44. Cambridge: Cambridge University Press, 1997.

Ford, David F., and Daniel W. Hardy. *Living in Praise: Worshipping and Knowing God*. Grand Rapids: Baker, 2005.

Ford, Lewis S. "The Eternity of God and the Temporality of the World." *Encounter* 36 (1975) 115–22.

Fowl, Stephen E. "Scripture." In *The Oxford Handbook of Systematic Theology*, edited by John Webster et al., 345–61. Oxford: Oxford University Press, 2007.

Funk, Robert W., and Roy W. Hoover. *The Five Gospels: The Search for the Authentic Words of Jesus*. New York: Macmillan, 1993.

Ganssle, Gregory E. "Introduction." *God and Time: Essays on the Divine Nature*, edited by Gregory E. Ganssle and David M. Woodruff, 3–18. Oxford: Oxford University Press, 2002.

Gaussen, Louis. *The Divine Inspiration of the Bible*. Translated by David D. Scott. 1841. Reprint, Grand Rapids: Kregel, 1971.

Gavrilyuk, Paul. *The Suffering of the Impassible God: The Dialectics of Patristic Thought*. New York: Oxford University Press, 2004

Geisler, Norman. "God Knows All Things." In *Predestination and Free Will: Four Views of Divine Sovereignty and Human Freedom*, edited by David Basinger and Randall Basinger, 65–84. Downers Grove, IL: InterVarsity, 1986.

———. "Norman Geisler's Response." In *Predestination and Free Will: Four Views of Divine Sovereignty and Human Freedom*, edited by David Basinger and Randall Basinger, 45–48. Downers Grove, IL: InterVarsity, 1986.

———. *Systematic Theology*. Vol. 1. Minneapolis: Bethany House, 2002.

Gilkey, Langdon. "Creation, Being, and Nonbeing." In *God and Creation: An Ecumenical Symposium*, edited by David B. Burrell and Bernard McGinn, 226–41. Notre Dame: University of Notre Dame Press, 1990.

———. "God." In *Christian Theology: An Introduction to Its Traditions and Tasks*, edited by Peter Hodgson and Robert King, 88–113. 3rd ed. Minneapolis: Augsburg, 1994.

González, Justo L. *The Story of Christianity: The Early Church to the Dawn of the Reformation*. Vol. 1. New York: Harper & Row, 1984.

Grant, Jacquelyn. *White Women's Christ and Black Women's Jesus: Feminist Christology and Womanist Response*. Atlanta: Scholars, 1989.

———. "Womanist Theology: Black Women's Experience as a Source for Doing Theology with Special Reference to Christology." In *Constructive Christian Theology in the Worldwide Church*, edited by William R. Barr, 337–54. Grand Rapids: Eerdmans, 1997.

Grenz, Stanley J. "An Agenda for Evangelical Theology in the Postmodern Context." *Didaskalia* 9 (1998) 1–16.

―――. "Articulating the Christian Belief-Mosaic: Theological Method after the Demise of Foundationalism." In *Evangelical Futures: A Conversation on Theological Method*, edited by John G. Stackhouse, 107–36. Grand Rapids: Baker, 2000.

―――. *Rediscovering the Triune God: The Trinity in Contemporary Theology*. Minneapolis: Fortress, 2004.

―――. *Theology for the Community of God*. Grand Rapids: Eerdmans, 2000.

Grillmeier, Alloy. *Christ in Christian Tradition: From the Apostolic Age to Chalcedon (451)*. Vol. 1. Atlanta: John Knox, 1965.

Groppe, Elizabeth Teresa. "The Contribution of Yves Congar's Theology of the Holy Spirit." *Theological Studies* 62 (2001) 451–78.

Grudem, Wayne. *Systematic Theology: An Introduction to Biblical Doctrine*. Grand Rapids: Zondervan, 1994.

Gunter, W. Stephen, et al. *Wesley and the Quadrilateral: Renewing the Conversation*. Nashville: Abingdon, 1997.

Gunton, Colin E. *The Christian Faith: An Introduction to Christian Doctrine*. Oxford: Blackwell, 2002.

―――. "The Doctrine of Creation." In *The Cambridge Companion to Christian Doctrine*, edited by Colin E. Gunton 141–57. Cambridge: Cambridge University Press, 1997.

―――. "Historical and Systematic Theology." In *The Cambridge Companion to Christian Doctrine*, edited by Colin E. Gunton, 3–20. Cambridge: Cambridge University Press, 1997.

Gutiérrez, Gustavo. *The Power of the Poor in History*. Maryknoll, NY: Orbis, 1983.

―――. "The Task and Content of Liberation Theology." Translated by Judith Condor. In *The Cambridge Companion to Liberation Theology*, edited by Christopher Rowland, 19–38. Cambridge: Cambridge University Press, 1999.

―――. *A Theology of Liberation: History, Politics, and Salvation*. Translated and edited by Caridad Inda and John Eagleson. Rev ed. Maryknoll, NY: Orbis, 1998.

Haight, Roger. *Jesus, Symbol of God*. Maryknoll, NY: Orbis, 1999.

Hart, Trevor. "Revelation." In *The Cambridge Companion to Karl Barth*, edited by John Webster, 37–56. Cambridge: Cambridge University Press, 2000.

Hartshorne, Charles. *The Divine Relativity: A Social Conception of God*. New Haven: Yale University Press, 1948.

―――. *Reality as Social Process: Studies in Metaphysics and Religion*. Boston: Free Press, 1953.

Hasker, William. "A Philosophical Perspective." In *The Openness of God: A Biblical Challenge to the Traditional Understanding of God*, edited by Clark Pinnock et al., 126–54. Downers Grove, IL: InterVarsity, 1994.

―――. "Why Simple Foreknowledge Is Still Useless (in Spite of David Hunt and Alex Pruss)." *Journal of the Evangelical Theological Society* 59 (2009) 537–44.

Helm, Paul. "Divine Timeless Eternity." In *God and Time: Four Views*, edited by Gregory E. Ganssle, 28–60. Downers Grove, IL: InterVarsity, 2001.

Helseth, Paul Kjoss. "God Causes All Things." In *Four Views on Divine Providence*, edited by Stanley N. Gundry and Dennis W. Jowers, 25–52. Grand Rapids: Zondervan, 2011.

Henry, Carl F. H. *God, Revelation and Authority*. Vol. 1, *God Who Speaks and Shows: Preliminary Considerations*. Waco, TX: Word, 1976.

————. "The Priority of Divine Revelation: A Review Article." *Journal of the Evangelical Theological Society* 27 (1984) 77–92.

Heron, Alasdair. "The Filioque Clause." In *One God in Trinity: An Analysis of the Primary Dogma of Christianity*, edited by Peter Toon and James D. Spiceland. Westchester, IL: Cornerstone, 1980.

Hick, John. "An Irenaean Theodicy." In *Encountering Evil: Live Options in Theodicy*, edited by Stephen T. Davis, 39–52. Atlanta: John Knox, 1981.

————. "Jesus and the World Religions." In *The Myth of God Incarnate*, edited by John Hick, 167–85. London: SCM, 1977.

————. *The Metaphor of God Incarnate: Christologies in a Pluralistic Age.* 2nd ed. Louisville: Westminster John Knox, 2005.

Hodgson, Peter E. "God's Action in the World: The Relevance of Quantum Mechanics." *Zygon* 35 (2000) 505–16.

Hoffmeier, James F. "'The Heavens Declare the Glory of God': The Limits of General Revelation." *Trinity Journal* 21 (2002) 17–24.

Holmes, Michael W. "The Biblical Canon." In *The Oxford Handbook of Early Christian Studies*, edited by Susan Ashbrook Harvey and David C. Hunter, 409–26. New York: Oxford University Press, 2008.

Horton, Michael. *The Christian Faith: A Systematic Theology for Pilgrims on the Way.* Grand Rapids: Zondervan, 2011.

Hui, Archie. "The Spirit of Prophecy and Pauline Pneumatology." *Tyndale Bulletin* 50 (1999) 93–115.

Hume, David. *Dialogues Concerning Natural Religion.* Edited by Norman Kemp Smith. New York: Social Sciences, 1948.

Hunt, David P. "Divine Providence and Simple Foreknowledge." *Faith and Philosophy* 10 (1993) 394–414.

Hurtado, Larry W. *Lord Jesus Christ: Devotion to Jesus in Earliest Christianity.* Grand Rapids: Eerdmans, 2003.

Idowu, E. Bọlaji. *African Traditional Religion: A Definition.* Maryknoll, NY: Orbis, 1973.

Irenaeus. *Against Heresies.* In vol. 1 of *The Ante-Nicene Fathers.* Edited by Alexander Roberts and James Donaldson. 1885–1887. 10 vols. Reprint, Grand Rapids: Eerdmans, 1969.

Jacobsen, Douglas, editor. *A Reader in Pentecostal Theology: Voices from the First Generation.* Bloomington: Indiana University Press, 2006.

Jenson, Robert W. *The Triune God.* Philadelphia: Fortress, 1982.

Johnson, Elizabeth. *She Who Is: The Mystery of God in Feminist Theological Discourse.* New York: Crossroad, 1993.

Jones, Scott J. "The Rule of Scripture." In *Wesley and the Quadrilateral: Renewing the Conversation*, 39–61. Nashville: Abingdon, 1997.

Justin. *Apologia I.* In *The Early Christian Fathers: A Selection from the Writings of the Fathers from St. Clement of Rome to St. Athanasius*, edited and translated by Henry Bettenson, 58–64. New York: Oxford University Press, 1956.

————. *Dialogue with Trypho.* In *The Fathers of the Church: A New Translation*, edited by Thomas B. Falls, 6:141–366. Washington, DC: Catholic University of America Press, 1948.

Kärkkäinen, Veli-Matti. *Christology: A Global Introduction.* Grand Rapids: Baker, 2003.

————. *Pneumatology: The Holy Spirit in Ecumenical, International, and Contextual Perspective.* Grand Rapids: Baker, 2002.

————. *The Trinity: Global Perspectives.* Louisville: Westminster John Knox, 2007.

Kawashima, Robert S. "A Revisionist Reading Revisited: On the Creation of Adam and then Eve." *Vetus Testamentum* 56 (2006) 46–57.

Kelly, J. N. D. *Early Christian Doctrines.* London: Black, 1958.

Kelsey, David H. *The Uses of Scripture in Recent Theology.* Philadelphia: Fortress, 1975.

Kenner, Craig S. *The Gospel of John: A Commentary.* Vol. 1. Peabody, MA: Hendrickson, 2003.

Kitamori, Kazō. *Theology and the Pain of God.* Richmond, VA: John Knox, 1965.

Kleinknecht, Hermann. "Πνεῦμα, Πνευματικός." In *Theological Dictionary of the New Testament,* edited by Gerhard Friedrich and translated by Geoffrey Bromiley, 6:332–59. Grand Rapids: Eerdmans, 1968.

Knight, George W. *The Pastoral Epistles: A Commentary on the Greek Text.* Grand Rapids: Eerdmans, 1992.

LaCugna, Catherine Mowry. *God for Us: The Trinity and Christian Life.* San Francisco: HarperSanFrancisco, 1991.

———. "Philosophers and Theologians on the Trinity." *Modern Theology* 2 (1986) 169–81.

———. "The Practical Trinity." *The Christian Century* 109 (1992) 678–82.

Ladd, George Eldon. *A Theology of the New Testament.* Rev ed. Grand Rapids: Eerdmans, 1993.

Lampe, G. W. H. *God as Spirit.* Oxford: Clarendon, 1977.

Leibniz, Gottfried Wihelm. *Theodicy: Essays on the Goodness of God, the Freedom of Man, and the Origin of Evil.* Edited by Freiherr Gott. London: Routledge & Kegan Paul, 1951.

Leslie, Ben. "Does God Have a Life? Barth and LaCugna on the Immanent Trinity." *Perspectives in Religious Studies* 24 (1997) 377–98.

Lindsell, Harold. *The Battle for the Bible.* Grand Rapids: Zondervan, 1976.

Longenecker, Richard N. "Christological Materials in the Early Christian Communities." In *Contours of Christology in the New Testament,* edited by Richard N. Longenecker, 47–76. Grand Rapids: Eerdmans, 2005.

Lossky, Vladimir. *Orthodox Theology: An Introduction.* Translated by Ian and Ihita Kesarcodi-Watson. Crestwood, NY: St. Vladmiir's Seminary Press, 1978.

Lull, Timothy F. *Martin Luther's Basic Theological Writings.* Minneapolis: Fortress, 1989.

Luther, Martin. *Luther's Works.* Vol. 35. Edited by E. T. Bachmann. Philadelphia: Muhlenberg, 1960.

———. "Preface to the New Testament (1522, Revised 1546)." In *Martin Luther's Basic Theological Writings,* edited by Timothy F. Lull., 112–17. Minneapolis: Fortress, 1989.

———. "Preface to the Old Testament (1523, Revised 1545)." In *Martin Luther's Basic Theological Writings,* edited by Timothy F. Lull., 118–34. Minneapolis: Fortress, 1989.

MacCulloch, Diarmaid. *Christianity: The First Three Thousand Years.* New York: Viking, 2009.

Macquarrie, John. *Jesus Christ in Modern Thought.* London: SCM, 1990.

Marshall, Howard I. *Biblical Inspiration.* Grand Rapids: Eerdmans, 1982.

Mbiti, John S. "The Role of the Jewish Bible in African Independent Churches." *International Review of Mission* 93 (2004) 219–37.

———. "Some African Concepts of Christology." In *Christ and the Younger Churches,* edited by G. F. Vicedom, 51–62. London: SPCK, 1972.

———. *Theology: The Basics*. 3rd ed. West Sussex, UK: Wiley-Blackwell, 2012.

McCormack, Bruce L. "Karl Barth's Christology as a Resource for a Reformed Version of Kenoticism." *International Journal of Systematic Theology* 8 (2006) 243–51.

———. *Karl Barth's Critically Realistic Dialectical Theology: Its Genesis and Development, 1909–1936*. New York: Clarendon, 1995.

———. *Orthodox and Modern: Studies in the Theology of Karl Barth*. Grand Rapids: Baker, 2008.

McDonald, Lee Martin. *The Biblical Canon: Its Origin, Transmission, and Authority*. Peabody, MA: Hendrickson, 2007.

McGrath, Alister E. *Christian Theology: An Introduction*. 3rd ed. Oxford: Blackwell, 2001.

———. "The Doctrine of the Trinity: An Evangelical Reflection." In *God the Holy Trinity: Reflections on Christian Faith and Practice*, edited by Timothy George, 17–35. Grand Rapids: Baker Academic, 2006.

———. *Knowing Christ*. London: Hodder & Stoughton, 2001.

———. *Theology: The Basics*. 3rd ed. Oxford: Wiley-Blackwell, 2011.

McKenzie, Ross H., and Benjamin Myers. "Dialectical Critical Realism in Science and Theology: Quantum Physics and Karl Barth." *Science and Christian Belief* 20 (2008) 49–66.

Menzies, Robert P. *Empowered for Witness: The Spirit in Luke-Acts*. Sheffield: Sheffield Academic, 1994.

Metzger, Paul Louis. "Introduction: What Difference Does the Trinity Make?" In *Trinitarian Soundings in Systematic Theology*, edited by Paul Louis Metzger, 5–8. London: T. & T. Clark, 2005.

Migliore, Daniel L. *Faith Seeking Understanding: An Introduction to Christian Theology*. 2nd ed. Grand Rapids: Eerdmans, 2004.

Milbank, John. *The Word Made Strange: Theology, Language, Culture*. Cambridge, MA: Blackwell, 1997.

Mitchem, Stephanie Y. "Finding Questions and Answers in Womanist Theology and Ethics." In *Feminist Theologies: Legacy and Prospect*, edited by Rosemary Radford Ruether, 66–78. Minneapolis: Fortress, 2007.

Molina, Luis de. *On Divine Foreknowledge: Part IV of the Concordia*. Translated by Alfred J. Freddoso. Ithaca: Cornell University Press, 1988.

Moltmann, Jürgen. *Experiences in Theology: Ways and Forms of Christian Theology*. London: SCM, 2000.

———. *God in Creation: A New Theology of Creation and the Spirit of God*. San Francisco: HarperCollins, 1985.

Morris, Thomas V. *The Logic of God Incarnate*. Ithaca: Cornell University Press, 1986.

———. *Our Idea of God: An Introduction to Philosophical Theology*. Vancouver, BC: Regent College Publishing, 2002.

Mouw, Richard J. "The *Imago Dei* and Philosophical Anthropology." *Christian Scholar's Review* 41 (2012) 253–66.

Nash, Ronald H. *Faith and Reason: Searching for a Rational Faith*. Grand Rapids: Zondervan, 1988.

Nestorius. *The Bazaar of Heracleides*. Translated and edited by G. R. Driver and L. Hodgson. 1925. Reprint, Eugene, OR: Wipf & Stock, 2002.

Newman, Robert C., and Herman J. Eckelmann. *Genesis One and the Origin of the Earth*. Downers Grove, IL: InterVarsity, 1977.

Ogbonnaya, A. Okechukwu. *On Communitarian Divinity: An African Interpretation of the Trinity*. New York: Paragon House, 1994.

Oladipo, Caleb Oluremi. *The Development of the Doctrine of the Holy Spirit in the Yoruba (African) Indigenous Christian Movement*. New York: Peter Lang, 1996.

Olson, Roger E. *The Story of Christian Theology: Twenty Centuries of Tradition and Reform*. Downers Grove: InterVarsity, 1999.

Orobator, Agbonkhianmeghe E. *Theology Brewed in an African Pot*. Maryknoll, NY: Orbis, 2008.

Osborn, Robert T. "Some Problems of Liberation Theology: A Polanyian Perspective." *Journal of the American Academy of Religion* 51 (1983) 79–95.

Outler, Albert C., editor. *John Wesley*. New York: Oxford University Press, 1964.

Padgett, Allan G. "Response to Nicholas Wolterstorff." In *God and Time: Four Views*, edited by Gregory E. Ganssle, 219–21. Downers Grove, IL: InterVarsity, 2001.

Pannenberg, Wolfhart. "Introduction." In *Revelation as History*, edited by Wolfhart Pannenberg and translated by David Granskou, 3–21. New York: Macmillan, 1968.

———. *Jesus—God and Man*. Philadelphia: Westminster, 1968.

———. *Systematic Theology*. Vol. 1. Translated by Geoffrey W. Bromiley. Grand Rapids: Eerdmans, 1988.

Papadakis, Aristeides. "Beyond the Filioque Divide: The Late Thirteenth Century Revisited." *St. Vladimir's Theological Quarterly* 55 (2011) 141–63.

Pedraja, Luis G. *Jesus Is My Uncle: Christology from a Hispanic Perspective*. Nashville: Abingdon, 1999.

Pelikan, Jaroslav. *The Christian Tradition: A History of the Development of Doctrine*. Vol. 1, *The Emergence of the Catholic Tradition (100–600)*. Chicago: University of Chicago Press, 1971.

———. *Mary Through the Centuries: Her Place in the History of Culture*. New Haven: Yale University Press, 1991.

———. "Montanism and Its Trinitarian Significance." *Church History* 25 (1956) 99–109.

Pelt, M. V. Van, W. C. Kaiser, and D. I. Block. "Rûaḥ." In *NIDOTE* 3:1073–78, edited by Willem A. VanGemeren. Grand Rapids: Zondervan, 1997.

Peters, Ted. "Constructing a Theology of Evolution: Building on John Haught." *Zygon: Journal of Science and Religion* 45 (2010) 921–37.

Phillips, Timothy R., and Dennis L. Okholm. *A Family of Faith: An Introduction to Evangelical Christianity*. Grand Rapids: Baker, 1996.

Pierson, Arthur Tappan, editor. *The Inspired Word: A Series of Papers and Addresses Delivered at the Bible-Inspiration Conference in Philadelphia, 1887*. New York: Randolph, 1888.

Pinnock, Clark H. *Biblical Revelation: The Foundation of Christian Theology*. Chicago: Moody, 1971.

———. *Flame of Love: A Theology of the Holy Spirit*. Downers Grove, IL: InterVarsity, 1996.

———. *Most Moved Mover: A Theology of God's Openness*. Grand Rapids: Baker, 2001.

———. *The Scripture Principle*. San Francisco: Harper & Row, 1984.

———. "Systematic Theology." In *The Openness of God: A Biblical Challenge to the Traditional Understanding of God*, edited by Clark Pinnock et al., 101–25. Downers Grove, IL: InterVarsity, 1994.

Piper, John. "Are There Two Wills in God?" In *Still Sovereign: Contemporary Perspectives on Election, Foreknowledge, and Grace*, edited by Thomas R. Schreiner and Bruce Ware, 107–31. Grand Rapids: Baker, 2000.

Plantinga, Alvin. *Warranted Christian Belief*. New York: Oxford University Press, 2000.

Plotinus. *Enneads*. Translated by Stephen MacKenna. Boston: C. T. Branford, 1950.

Pobee, John S. *Toward an African Theology*. Nashville: Abingdon, 1979.

Polkinghorne, John. "Scripture and an Evolving Creation." *Science and Christian Belief* 21 (2009) 163–73.

Porter, Lawrence B. "On Keeping 'Persons' in the Trinity: A Linguistic Approach to Trinitarian Thought." *Theological Studies* 41 (1980) 530–48.

Rahner, Karl. *Inspiration in the Bible*. Translated by Charles H. Henkey. Rev ed. New York: Herder & Herder, 1964.

———. *The Trinity*. Translated by Joseph Donceel. New York: Crossroad, 1997.

Ratzinger, Joseph. *Credo for Today: What Christians Believe*. San Francisco: Ignatius, 2009.

Reichenbach, Bruce. "Bruce Reichenbach's Response." In *Predestination and Free Will: Four Views of Divine Sovereignty and Human Freedom*, edited by David Basinger and Randall Basinger, 49–55. Downers Grove, IL: InterVarsity, 1986.

———. "God Limits His Power." In *Predestination and Free Will: Four Views of Divine Sovereignty and Human Freedom*, edited by David Basinger and Randall Basinger, 101–24. Downers Grove, IL: InterVarsity, 1986.

Rice, Richard. "Biblical Support for a New Perspective." In *The Openness of God: A Biblical Challenge to the Traditional Understanding of God*, edited by Clark Pinnock et al., 11–58. Downers Grove, IL: InterVarsity, 1994.

Robeck, Cecil M. "Montanism and Present-Day 'Prophets.'" *Pneuma* 32 (2010) 413–29.

Robinson, Paul W. *Martin Luther: A Life Reformed*. New York: Longman, 2010.

Roth, John K. "A Theodicy of Protest." In *Encountering Evil: Live Options in Theodicy*, edited by Stephen T. Davis, 7–22. Atlanta: John Knox, 1981.

Ruether, Rosemary Radford. *Sexism and God-Talk: Toward a Feminist Theology*. London: SCM, 1983.

Ryrie, Charles. *Basic Theology*. Chicago: Moody, 1986.

Sanders, James A., and Lee Martin McDonald, editors. *The Canon Debate*. Peabody, MA: Hendrickson, 2002.

Sanders, John. *The God Who Risks: A Theology of Providence*. Downers Grove, IL: InterVarsity, 1998.

Sands, Paul Francis. "The *Imago Dei* as Vocation." *Evangelical Quarterly* 82 (2010) 28–41.

Sansbury, Timothy. "The False Promise of Quantum Mechanics." *Zygon: Journal of Religion and Science* 42 (2007) 111–21.

Satyavrata, Ivan. *The Holy Spirit: Lord and Life-Giver*. Downers Grove, IL: InterVarsity, 2009.

Schleiermacher, Friedrich. *The Christian Faith*. Vol. 1. Edited by H. R. Mackintosh and J. S. Stewart. New York: Harper & Row, 1963.

Schottroff, Luise, Silvia Schroer, and Marie-Theres Wacker, editors. *Feminist Interpretation: The Bible in Women's Perspective*. Translated by Martin and Barbara Rumscheidt. Minneapolis: Fortress, 1998.

Schreiner, Thomas R. *1, 2 Peter, Jude*. New American Commentary 37. Nashville: Broadman & Holman, 2002.

Schweitzer, Albert. *The Quest of the Historical Jesus.* Edited by John Bowden. Minneapolis: Fortress, 2001.

Schweizer, Eduard. "Πνεῦμα." In *Theological Dictionary of the New Testament,* edited by Gerhard Friedrich and translated by Geoffrey W. Bromiley, 6:389–455. Grand Rapids: Eerdmans, 1968.

Second Vatican Council. *Dogmatic Constitution on Divine Revelation.* Edited by Ronald E. Murphy. Washington, DC: National Catholic Welfare Conference, 1965.

Shaw, Douglas W. D. "Providence and Persuasion." *Duke Divinity School Review* 45 (1980) 11–22.

Sherburne, Donald W., editor. *A Key to Whitehead's Process and Reality.* Bloomington: Indiana University Press, 1975.

Smith, Christine M. *Preaching as Weeping, Confession, and Resistance: Radical Responses to Radical Evil.* Louisville: Westminster John Knox, 1992.

Spoerl, Kelly McCarthy. "Liturgical Argument in Apollinarius: Help and Hindrance on the Way to Orthodoxy." *Harvard Theological Review* 91 (1998) 127–52.

Sweet, John. "Docetism: Is Jesus Really Human or Did He Appear to Be So?" In *Heresies and How to Avoid Them: Why It Matters What Christians Believe,* edited by Ben Quash and Michael Ward, 24–31. London: SPCK, 2007

Swinburne, Richard. *The Coherence of Theism.* Rev. ed. New York: Oxford University Press, 1993.

Tabbernee, William. *Prophets and Gravestones: An Imaginative History of Montanists and Other Early Christians.* Peabody, MA: Hendrickson, 2009.

Tanner, Kathryn. "Jesus Christ." In *The Cambridge Companion to Christian Doctrine,* edited by Colin E. Gunton, 245–72. Cambridge: Cambridge University Press, 1997.

Tate, Marvin E. *Psalms 51–100.* Word Biblical Commentary 20. Dallas: Word, 1990.

Tertullain. *Against Praxeas.* Translated by A. Souter. New York: Macmillan, 1919.

Thomasius, Gottfried. "Christ's Person and Work." In *God and Incarnation in Mid-Nineteenth Century Theology,* edited by Claude Welch, 31–114. New York: Oxford University Press, 1965.

Thompson, William E. Review of *Models of Revelation,* by Avery Dulles. *Theological Studies* (1984) 357–59.

Tiessen, Terrance L. *Who Can Be Saved? Reassessing Salvation in Christ.* Downers Grove, IL: InterVarsity, 2004.

———. "Why Calvinists Should Believe in Divine Middle Knowledge, although They Reject Molinism." *Westminster Theological Journal* 69 (2007) 345–66.

Tillich, Paul. *The Shaking of the Foundations.* London: SCM, 1949.

———. *Systematic Theology.* Vol. 1. Chicago: University of Chicago Press, 1951.

Toon, Peter. *Our Triune God: A Biblical Portrayal of the Trinity.* Wheaton, IL: Victor, 1996.

Torrance, Thomas F. *The Christian Doctrine of God: One Being, Three Persons.* Edinburgh: T. & T. Clark, 1996.

———. *Incarnation: The Person and Life of Jesus Christ.* Edited by Robert T. Walker. Grand Rapids: InterVarsity, 2008.

———. *Reality and Evangelical Theology: A Fresh and Challenging Approach to Christian Revelation.* Philadelphia: Westminster, 1982.

Tracy, David. *The Analogical Imagination: Christian Theology and the Culture of Pluralism.* New York: Crossroad, 1981.

———. "Theological Method." In *Christian Theology: An Introduction to Its Traditions and Tasks*, edited by Peter Hodgson and Robert King, 35–60. Minneapolis: Augsburg, 1994.

Trau, Jane Mar. "Modalism Revisited: Persons and Symbols." In *Negation and Theology*, edited by Robert P. Scharlemann, 56–71. Charlottesville: University Press of Virginia, 1992.

Trible, Phyllis. "Eve and Miriam: From the Margins to the Center." In *Feminist Approaches to the Bible*, edited by Hershell Shanks, 5–24. Washington, DC: Biblical Archeology Society, 1995.

———. *God and the Rhetoric of Sexuality*. Philadelphia: Fortress, 1978.

———. *Texts of Terror: Literary-Feminist Readings of Biblical Narratives*. Philadelphia: Fortress, 1984.

Turner, Max. *The Holy Spirit and Spiritual Gifts: Then and Now*. Carlisle: Paternoster, 1996.

———. *Power from on High: The Spirit in Israel's Restoration and Witness in Luke-Acts*. Sheffield: Sheffield Academic, 1996.

Vanhoozer, Kevin J. *First Theology: God, Scripture and Hermeneutics*. Downers Grove, IL: InterVarsity, 2002.

———. *Is There a Meaning in This Text? The Bible, the Reader, and the Morality of Literary Knowledge*. Leicester, UK: Apollos, 1998.

Visser, Hans, with Gillian Bediako. "Introduction." In *Jesus and the Gospel in Africa: History and Experience*, xi–xvii. Maryknoll, NY: Orbis, 2004.

Volf, Miroslav. "Being as God: Trinity and Generosity." In *God's Life in Trinity*, edited by Miroslav Volf and Michael Welker, 3–12. Minneapolis: Fortress, 2006.

Wainwright, Geoffrey. "The Holy Spirit." In *The Cambridge Companion to Christian Doctrine*, edited by Colin E. Gunton, 273–96. Cambridge: Cambridge University Press, 1997.

Walton, John C. "The Origin of Life: Scientists Play Dice." In *Should Christians Embrace Evolution? Biblical and Scientific Responses*, edited by Norman C. Nevin, 187–209. Phillipsburg, NJ: P. & R., 2011.

Ware, Bruce A. *God's Greater Glory: The Exalted God of Scripture and the Christian Faith*. Wheaton, IL: Crossway, 2004.

———. *God's Lesser Glory: The Diminished God of Open Theism*. Wheaton, IL: Crossway, 2000.

Ware, Kallistos. "The Holy Trinity: Model for Personhood-in-Relation." In *The Trinity and an Entangled World: Relationality in Physical Science and Theology*, edited by John Polkinghorne, 107–29. Grand Rapids: Eerdmans, 2010.

———. *The Orthodox Way*. Rev ed. Crestwood, NY: St. Vladimir's Seminary Press, 1995.

Warfield, Benjamin B. "The Divine and Human in the Bible." In *The Princeton Theology, 1812–1921*, edited by Mark A. Noll, 275–79. Grand Rapids: Baker, 1983.

———. *Evolution, Science, and Scripture: Selected Writings*. Edited by Mark A. Noll and David N. Livingstone. Grand Rapids: Baker, 2000.

———. "The Inerrancy of the Original Autographs." In *The Princeton Theology, 1812–1921*, edited by Mark A. Noll, 268–74. Grand Rapids: Baker, 1983.

———. "Inspiration." In *The Princeton Theology, 1812–1921*, edited by Mark A. Noll, 280–88. Grand Rapids: Baker, 1983.

————. *The Inspiration and Authority of the Bible.* Edited by Samuel G. Craig. Philadelphia: Presbyterian & Reformed, 1964.

————. "The Manner and Time of Man's Origin." In *Evolution, Science, and Scripture: Selected Writings,* edited by Mark A. Noll and David N. Livingstone, 211–99. Grand Rapids: Baker, 2000.

————. *Revelation and Inspiration.* New York: Oxford University Press, 1927.

Webster, John. "One Who Is Son: Theological Reflections on the Exordium to the Epistle to the Hebrews." In *Epistle to the Hebrews and Christian Theology,* edited by Richard Bauckham et al., 69–94. Grand Rapids: Eerdmans, 2009.

Wegner, Paul D. *The Journey from Texts to Translations: The Origin and Development of the Bible.* Grand Rapids: Baker, 1999.

Whitehead, Alfred North. *Process and Reality: An Essay in Cosmology.* Edited by David Ray Griffin and Donald W. Sherburne. New York: Free Press, 1978.

Williams, Rowan. *Arius: Heresy and Tradition.* Rev. ed. Grand Rapids: Eerdmans, 2002.

————. *On Christian Theology.* Oxford: Blackwell, 2000.

————. *Tokens of Trust: An Introduction to Christian Belief.* Louisville: Westminster John Knox, 2007.

Wolterstorff, Nicholas. "Unqualified Divine Temporality." In *God and Time: Four Views,* edited by Gregory E. Ganssle, 187–213. Downers Grove, IL: InterVarsity, 2001.

Wright, Christopher J. H. *Arius: Heresy and Tradition.* Rev ed. Grand Rapids: Eerdmans, 2001.

————. *Knowing the Holy Spirit through the Old Testament.* Downers Grove, IL: InterVarsity, 2006.

Young, Frances M. *From Nicaea to Chalcedon: A Guide to the Literature and Its Background.* 2nd ed. Grand Rapids: Baker Academic, 2010.

Zizioulas, John D. *Being as Communion: Studies in Personhood and the Church.* Crestwood, NY: St. Vladimir's Seminary Press, 1985.

————. *Lectures in Christian Dogmatics.* Edited by Douglas H. Knight. London: T. & T. Clark, 2008.

————. "Relational Ontology: Insights from Patristic Thought." In *The Trinity and an Entangled World: Relationality in Physical Science and Theology,* edited by John Polkinghorne, 147–56. Grand Rapids: Eerdmans, 2010.

Index

CPSIA information can be obtained
at www.ICGtesting.com
Printed in the USA
LVHW090905240723
753027LV00079B/40